Israel L. Gaither
Man With A Mission

By Henry Gariepy

CREST BOOKS

The Salvation Army National Publications

Alexandria, Virginia

Copyright © 2006 by The Salvation Army

Published by Crest Books
The Salvation Army National Headquarters, 615 Slaters Lane, Alexandria, VA 22314
Major Ed Forster, National Editor in Chief and Literary Secretary

Sponsored by and in partnership with The Salvation Army, USA Eastern Territory
Commissioner Lawrence R. Moretz, Territorial Commander

Available from Supplies and Purchasing Departments

Printed in the United States of America

Cover design by Karen Yee Lim
[Salvation Army's flag as backdrop with its text "Blood and Fire" that symbolizes the atoning
work of Christ and the cleansing work of the Holy Spirit]

Book design and layout by ATLIS Graphics

Unless otherwise indicated, Scripture is taken from the New International Version. Used by
permission of Zondervan. All rights reserved.

Library of Congress Control Number: 2006932815
    Israel L. Gaither: Man With A Mission, by Henry Gariepy
    1. The Salvation Army
    2. Christian biography
    3. Interracial issues and leadership in the church
    4. Interracial issues within an ordained ministry
    5. Black church leaders
    6. Social services

ISBN–13: 978-0-9740940-8-3
ISBN–10: 0-9740940-8-0

Israel L. Gaither

Man With A Mission

By Henry Gariepy

Crest Books

The Salvation Army National Publications
&
The Salvation Army USA Eastern Territory

Also by Henry Gariepy

Daily Meditations on Golden Texts of the Bible (Eerdmans, 2004)

When Life Gets Tough (Cook Communications, 2003)

The Write Way—A Christian Writer's Handbook (The Salvation Army, 2003)

The Salvation Army 101 (The Salvation Army USA Eastern Territory, 2003)

Treasures from the Psalms (Eerdmans, 2002)

Andy Miller—A Legend and a Legacy (Crest Books, 2002)

A Salvationist Treasury (Crest Books, 2000)

Mobilized For God: International History of The Salvation Army (The Salvation Army IHQ, 2000)

A Century of Service in Alaska (The Salvation Army Alaska Division, 1996)

Songs in the Night (Eerdmans, 1996)

Healing in the Heartland (The Salvation Army, Arkansas and Oklahoma Division, 1996)

Guidebook for Salvation Army Writers and Editors (The Salvation Army IHQ, 1995)

Light in a Dark Place—From the Prophets (Victor Books, 1995)

40 Days With the Savior (Thomas Nelson Publishers, 1995)

Challenge and Response—Documentary of Christianity in Action (The Salvation Army, 1994)

General of God's Army (Victor Books, 1993)

Wisdom to Live By (Victor Books, 1991)

Christianity in Action—The Salvation Army in the USA Today (Victor Books 1989)

Portraits of Perseverance—From the Book of Job (Victor Books, 1989)

100 Portraits of Christ (Victor Books, 1987)

Study Guide: Advent of Jesus Christ (The Salvation Army, USA Eastern Territory, 1979)

Advent of Jesus Christ (The Salvation Army, USA Eastern Territory, 1979)

Study Guide: Footsteps to Calvary (Fountain Press, 1977)

Footsteps to Calvary (Fountain Press, 1977)

Devotional Study of the Names of Jesus (Fleming Revell, 1972)

Henry Gariepy is also a contributor of chapters and content to over 40 books and anthologies by other authors and publishers, and has edited and prepared two full–length books for publication.

MISSION STATEMENT

The Salvation Army, an international movement,

is an evangelical part of the universal Christian Church.

Its message is based on the Bible.

Its ministry is motivated by the love of God.

Its mission is to preach the gospel of Jesus Christ

and to meet human needs

in His name without discrimination.

"Mission matters most."—*Israel L. Gaither*

To

The "blessing of gifts" in my life

Eva—
My partner in life and ministry.
The most treasured gift a missioner could ever desire!

Michele, Mark and Amy—
Priceless gift blessings! Thank you for standing with
Dad!

Isaiah and Matthew and Virginia—
Grandchildren—gifts of unspeakable joy!

Mother Gaither—
A source of never-ending support!

Dad Gaither—
My father and model missioner!

By God's grace—and your love—I'm blessed!

Israel L. Gaither

Eva and Israel Gaither with grandson Isaiah, daughter Michele, grandson Matthew, son Mark, daughter-in-law Amy, and granddaughter Virginia Marie [July 2006]

Contents

List of Illustrations and Sources

Black and white photos

1. Young Israel with his parents (Lillian Gaither, Jacqueline Respress)
2. Israel L. Gaither II (Lillian Gaither, Jacqueline Respress)
3. Israel with mother and sisters (Lillian Gaither, Jacqueline Respress)
4. Cadet Israel Gaither (The Salvation Army USA Eastern Territory Personnel Dept.)
5. Israel as basketball player (School for Officer Training 1963 Year Book)
6. Cadet Gaither renders a solo, accompanied by Cadet Nancy Burke (1963 Year Book)
7. The Shue family (Henry Gariepy)
8. Candidate Eva D. Shue (The Salvation Army USA Eastern Territory Personnel Department)
9. Rev. Israel Gaither II performs wedding ceremony
10. Ken Burton, OF
11. Captains Gaither with local officers (Brooklyn Bedford Corps)
12. Grandson Isaiah with Michele (Henry Gariepy)
13. Grandson Matthew with Amy and Mark (Henry Gariepy)
14. Grandfather Israel with Isaiah and Matthew (Henry Gariepy)
15. Star Lake camp staff, 1976 (Colonel Walter French)
16. Candidates and leaders, 1978 (Colonel Walter French)
17. Gaither prepares pig roast at Home League camp (Major Veronica Demeraski)
18. Gaither with Holy Land carving (Robin Bryant)
19. Gaithers in Mozambique (Warren Maye)
20. Opening new library at Bethany Children's Home (Major Darren Mudge)
21. Gaithers and Gowanses visit with Nelson Mandela (Major Darren Mudge)
22. Gaither's visit with President Thabo Mbeki (Major Darren Mudge)
23. 1999 High Council candidates (The Salvation Army IHQ)
24. General Gowans' installation of Gaithers (Jeffrey Schultz)
25. The Chief of Staff at his IHQ desk (Robin Bryant)
26. The Chief with his personal secretary, Major Garrad (Berni George, IHQ)
27. Gaither preaching "I hear mission calling" (Hilde Dagfinrud–Valen, editor, The Salvation Army, Norway)
28. Gaithers at the Berlin Wall (The Salvation Army in Germany)

Color photos (Section 1)

Color photos (Section 2)

Foreword

When we read the history of The Salvation Army and learn something of the giants who bestride its pages, and then look around us today, we are sometimes tempted to wonder whether the era of heroic figures has come to an end. But not at all. And this book is living proof of that fact. For here is the story of a contemporary giant who has become a legend in his own lifetime.

The giants of history were not, to adapt Isaac Watts' famous lines, "carried to the skies on flowery beds of ease, while others fought to win the prize, and sailed through stormy seas." They discovered early in life where they were going. They did not allow circumstances to hold them back. They overcame obstacles, weathered storms, and came through triumphantly.

Israel L. Gaither comes from a secure and loving family. His parents gave him, in the words of his biographer, both roots and wings. But as the journey through life unfolded he came to turning points. Was it to be a life of ease and comfort along predictable paths? Or was it to be a life of venturing out by faith wherever that road might lead? The story of Israel Gaither is the story of a man who at each turn of his life has taken the demanding decision. He has been an overcomer. And he has come through triumphantly.

When I was elected to be the next General of The Salvation Army at the High Council held in September 2002, there was no doubt in my mind as to who I wanted to be Chief of the Staff. It had to be Israel Gaither. There was no Plan B. The only problem was that Israel and Eva had commenced their ministry as territorial leaders of the USA Eastern territory just five weeks previously. With my term of office commencing on 13 November, they would only have three months as leaders of their home territory. I knew the territory loved them, and I knew that they loved being there. And they had just been reunited with their family after three and a half years' absence on service overseas. Was it fair to even ask them?

But the conviction that it should be Israel was strong. He had all the necessary qualities. I knew that our hearts beat as one. And it was right that Israel and Eva with their complementing gifts should be released for ministry to the global Army. I was convinced that that must be the over–riding consideration. So, after having consulted with the required number of commissioners, I approached them within a couple of hours of having become the General–elect, while we were still at the Sunbury conference centre.

I know something of the personal agony that my request caused them. But I was delighted when soon after their return to New York, Israel was in touch to say that they felt that their answer could only be yes, and that they must leave everything else in God's hands.

"Dare I show my face here with you tonight?" is how I began my video message to the congregation gathered at the Centennial Memorial Temple in New York City for the farewell meeting of the Gaithers before they set out for London. But the Eastern Territory's loss was the world's gain. And as I look back over my term of office as General I am more than ever convinced that one of my best decisions was the first that I took—to ask Israel L Gaither to be my Chief of the Staff.

In the pages of this book is recorded the story of a man who from his earliest years was destined to be a leader—a leader with a passion for the God–given mission of The Salvation Army. It is a multi–dimensional story, for the author takes us behind the scenes and reveals to us not only the official Israel L. Gaither but also the man himself in all the richness of his personality. And it is the story of a duo. For one cannot imagine Israel without Eva. They were meant for each other. And the story of the one is the story of them both.

Colonel Henry Gariepy, The Salvation Army's foremost writer today, has gathered a vast amount of information about his subject, has called on the services of seemingly hundreds of witnesses, and has then, with the amazing skill which is his hallmark as an historian and biographer, distilled this immense conglomeration of facts and insights into an outstanding biography of an outstanding man. We are all indebted to Henry Gariepy.

May God use this biography as an extension of the ministry of Commissioners Israel and Eva Gaither, and may God bless them as they lead The Salvation Army in the United States of America to achieve even greater things.

John Larsson
General (Rtd.)

Introduction

In an early letter concerning the biography, Israel Gaither wrote to me, "We're humbled by it, and after all, the life about which you will write is just a product of His grace. And the more I think about that in these days, the more I know it is true! So this is not about me, or Eva, or us—it is about His abounding work in us and through us." This volume goes forth with the prayer for the spirit and integrity of that statement to be conveyed within these pages.

Responses from around the world revealed the consensus for a man who has an anointing of the Spirit, and whose life and leadership make a powerful statement. Inspired input from contributors often turned a biographer's time of drafting into a sacramental moment.

To a friend who shared with Israel a copy of what he had submitted for the book, Gaither wrote back, "Eva and I laughed as we recalled some of the previously hidden memories you now are making public! This 'bio' thing is dangerous!" Indeed, to give consent for the writing of one's biography is courting a vulnerable experience.

All biographers who embark on the quest to portray a life become heavy debtors to a vast network of people who contribute to the mosaic that eventually emerges. This volume is peopled by a great company—some of whom have left their own indelible marks on Salvation Army history—who touched Israel Gaither's life or who were touched by him.

Two years were devoted to drafting and gleaning from interviews, correspondence, documents, archival records, publications and videotapes. An exchange, worldwide, of more than 1,000 emails, both facilitated and substantially contributed to the research. A cache of videos, from Jeffrey Schultz (Media Ministries Bureau) and Major Darren Mudge, of major programs with the Gaithers both in the USA and South Africa also provided a rich vein of quotations and descriptions of events.

Israel Gaither was magnanimous in his cooperation and contributions for the biography. Family members of Israel and Eva were gracious and helpful, along with numerous friends and colleagues. I owe an inexpressible debt of gratitude to my life partner, Marjorie, whose keen editing skills and countless hours of discussion and poring through successive drafts (25) has rendered this volume both more accurate and more readable. I am also a heavy debtor to Linda Johnson and Abigail Ray for their astute editing suggestions, and to then Colonel James Knaggs (now Commissioner) for his initiation and leadership of the book's production.

At the outset a writer feels overwhelmed by the material gathered and wonders how the wilderness of random facts can be tamed into the formal garden of a book. Early research tends to record data with an indiscriminate pen. The biographer monitors responses. Does a story or passage stir the spirit? What inner tug or emotive response likely contains a deeper truth? Finally there emerges a central theme, which becomes the unifying focus and determines criteria for selection. With this biography, the twin underscored concepts that emerged—"anointing" and "mission"—became anchor points for writing the book, including its subtitle.

Seven Salvation Army leaders from Israel's high school days to the present became the Lord's instruments for encouragement and the creation of opportunities for his progressive leadership. Each one, identified as they appear in Israel's story, played a pivotal role in his life and ministry. To them he attributes much of his development, and with each one, he formed a bond of friendship that has endured through the years.

In that span of time, Israel Gaither has gone where no African–American in The Salvation Army had gone before. He redefined and raised the bar for leadership opportunities and mobility in the ranks of Salvation Army officers. He became the first African–American to be appointed to the highest offices of divisional and territorial leadership and was three times a nominee for the office of General. What Jackie Robinson did for baseball, Israel Gaither did for leadership positions within The Salvation Army. He established a level playing field.

At the time this writing got underway (2004), he held the second highest office in the international Salvation Army, that of Chief of Staff at the Army's International Headquarters in London. As we enter the closing chapters of the book, Israel Gaither holds the appointment of National Commander of The Salvation Army in the USA, responsible as spokesman and for coordinating the largest complex of Salvation Army services in the world.

Israel Gaither's life story is one of courage and grace in a contentious world of subtle racism. Paul Rader (Retired Salvation Army General) commented that these achievements had the result of "putting fresh heart into persons of color within the Army across America and around the world."

A biography needs to be more than a collection of data about a person. It should make a statement of importance. The life story of Israel Gaither portrays what God can do through a life totally dedicated to Him, helping to surmount formidable obstacles, and making a difference in our world. From it we also glean insights on the phenomenon of the worldwide Salvation Army, its ethos and mission, as intertwined with the life journey of Israel Gaither.

Midway through work on the biography I found myself on a quest to capture and convey, "What makes Israel Gaither tick? What is the secret of his spiritual effectiveness?" Then in one of those rare incandescent moments for a writer, the answer came. Privileged to introduce the Gaithers at a 2005 New Jersey weekend camp meeting, I cited his attributes and achievements. Israel graciously acknowledged the introduction, and then confided to his listeners, "Let me tell you what I want. There is only one thing I want. I want to be God's man." In that moment I realized, "That's it. That's his secret—to be God's man." That is the secret of every life that is effective for God.

A superficial observation could consider this account of Israel Gaither to border on a hagiography. However, the truth is that Israel Gaither has achieved an iconic status among those who have come to know him, because of his authentic life of holiness. He is all, and more, that people in this text say of him. Retired General Eva Burrows observes, "There is so much of sheer goodness about the man and his character and style, that he could almost seem too good to be true." The limited portrayal of this volume can only give the contours of a life, which is as one once described by Jesus, "Here is a man in whom there is nothing false" (John 1:47).

A highly effective lifetime ministry, a resolute champion of the Army's mission, elevation to positions of top leadership, and a legacy of powerful preaching, secure Israel Gaither's niche in the annals of Salvation Army history. This life portrait is in large part presented by those who know him best—family and friends, colleagues who worked closely with him, and people who have felt the impact of his ministry. These primary sources best describe and define the man and his mission.

John Ruskin wrote that the greatest reward of our toil is what we become from it. The inspiration of Izzy's life story, the opportunity of relating to him and Eva and to the many persons who contributed to the book, has been an immeasurably enriching experience.

Henry Gariepy

PART ONE

Early Life and Family

1944–1955

chapter 1

Roots and Wings

Train a child in the way he should go,
and when he is old he will not turn from it.
Proverbs 22:6

Israel Gaither admits to an unabashed pride in his family background and upbringing. "I had the privilege of being born into a warm Christian environment to Israel L. Gaither II and Lillian Johnson Gaither. My dad and mother were wonderful parents. My siblings and I consider ourselves very fortunate to be born to such godly parents."

Young Israel with his parents

Israel was born during the dark days of a world engulfed in war, on Oct. 27, 1944, in the small town of New Castle, Pa., where he was raised. Some 50 miles north of Pittsburgh and on the western end of Pennsylvania near the Ohio border, the town was noted for coal mining, manufacturing and porcelain pottery.

A town of about 50,000, New Castle had clear racial distinctions. African–Americans lived on the west and south sides, and a white, middle- and upper–class population on the north side. The schools drew together young people of all races and socioeconomic levels. At night everyone retreated to their separate corners of the city. Still, an integrated working class allowed Israel to cross cultures even then; he had friends on both sides of the color line.

The eldest of five children, Israel became the third to carry the full name of his father and grandfather. Israel describes his childhood as "rooted in

God's Word." He recalls, "Our whole family was surrounded by a clear and positive environment of Christian faith. My childhood gave me a foundation on which to stand. I early learned basic values that were more a starting point for my Christian faith than for a specific religious system."

BAPTIST BACKGROUND

Israel's earliest years of church life were spent in the family's church, Union Baptist. He remembers the day his father became an ordained minister and began serving as the associate pastor of the church. From the pulpit, he always made a remarkable impression on his son. "He was a masterful preacher who had an enormous influence on my preaching style and pulpit presence," Israel says.

"My father baptized me and that was a bit of a frightening experience," he admits. "To be baptized as a young teenager was a major step—and to be baptized in front of your friends was even more challenging. Baptism was by immersion—backwards! My father might have been a little upset with me on that Sunday morning, because I think he kept me under just a little too long. I came up gasping for breath."

His early experience in church life was full and rich. There were weekday activities for young people and worship on Sunday mornings and evenings. In later years his father began evangelistic work, and the family would accompany him on his preaching engagements. "I have a strong love for my church heritage," Israel says, "and those experiences have helped shape my belief system. My Christian faith and my understanding of what it means to be a believer were modeled in a superb way by my father and mother.

" God's Word to me has been a steadying force."

Israel's parents were not his only mentors during his youth. "When we worked in South Africa people often said, 'You need a whole village to bring up a child.' That's how it was when I grew up. There were adults who were role models and good examples, who watched out for us and related to us with love."

Israel has a clear recall of the moment of his own conversion. "I can picture it now. I was 11 or 12 years old, standing near the altar in Union Baptist Church. Sister Synetta Brizendine stood next to me—this warm and loving lay leader counseled and led me into a personal relationship with Christ, and I declared I wanted Jesus to live in my life. Of course, Dad's influence through his life and preaching and family prayers prepared me for that moment of public commitment.

"What I am now as a Salvationist was strongly influenced by what I was then as a teenage member of Union Baptist. Naturally there have been times when my faith has been tried, and I have had moments of doubt. But God's Word to me has been a steadying force, and although I may be mobile, I'm not rootless, because the power of God's Word sustains me every day."

ROOTS AND WINGS

The parents of Israel L. Gaither III gave to him two great gifts—roots and wings. The roots his parents planted would nourish his life and ministry through the years, and the wings they endowed would carry him to unimaginably far–flung frontiers of mission for God.

chapter 2

A Father's Indelible Imprint

*Listen, my child, to what your father teaches
you. Don't neglect your mother's teaching.
What you learn from them will crown you with
grace and clothe you with honor.*
Proverbs 1:8–9 *(New Living Translation)*

Israel's young life was centered in his father, who imparted his strong faith
and Christian values. "My father," says Israel, "was a model pastor and an
exceptional preacher."

Israel L. Gaither II, born on May 18, 1913, was raised in the small town
of Mocksville, N.C., just outside Winston–Salem. He migrated to New
Castle, as did a brother, Benjamin ("Uncle Bennie") a frequent visitor in the
Gaither home, along with his wife, Grace ("Aunt Gracie").

During Israel's young years, his father worked as a laborer at the Crane
Manufacturing Company in New Castle. Then, when Israel was in his early
teens, his father accepted the call to ministry. His outreach began in the living room of their home with a small group of believers who met weekly for
prayer meetings. From this group came the key individuals who later supported Israel's father in founding the House of Prayer Ministries. The call of
Israel II was to evangelistic work involving traveling for campaigns, then to
serving as the associate pastor of the Union Baptist Church in New Castle.

A LOVER OF THE WORD

Israel's parents reflected and modeled for him the priority of the Word of God,
with its enduring impact upon his life. Israel remembers his dad as "a lover of
the Word of God. He didn't have the luxury of a study as I do. The dining
room table became the place of preparation for his messages, with reference material and the Bible spread out upon it. Often he would show me something in
Scripture he was going to preach on. I learned from him the necessity of giving

time for preparation and saw the result of that when he was behind the pulpit.

Jacqueline, Israel's sister, says of her father: "He quoted Scripture that could just flow from him. He had the Scripture in his heart. He would take several points and preach from them. He couldn't preach the same message again, for he did not have notes." She adds, "He always shed tears when he preached."

Israel Lee Gaither II came from a family of preachers. His father was called to the ministry, as were two uncles, one a pastor in the Baptist church and the other a bishop in the AME Zion denomination (African Methodist Episcopal Zion). Another aunt was mar-

Israel L. Gaither II

ried to a Baptist minister. This strong commitment within the close family circle wielded a strong influence upon the five siblings in the Gaither household.

In addition to being a powerful preacher, Israel II was a gifted singer. During his son's preteen years, he organized and was the lead singer of a gospel quartet. "I can still hear the sound of the sweet harmonies," recalls Israel. The group traveled extensively and even produced a recording. These two hallmarks of Israel Gaither II's ministry—powerful preaching and a soul–stirring vocal ministry—would also be important facets of his son's ministry.

Israel had four younger sisters. His parents kept a close eye on his activity and the friends he chose. "My dad was a strict disciplinarian who had high standards with respect to behavior," he recalls. "If I misbehaved, I suffered the consequences of not adhering to his standards of behavior." But no discipline his father meted out could compare to Israel's own disappointment with himself. He confesses, "If I didn't meet my father's expectation, I felt it internally, and that was the greatest punishment."

A SPECIAL RELATIONSHIP

Israel's father had many friends in the community; the children recall visitors filling their home with laughter and lively conversation. They were captivated as they sat and listened to their dad and his buddies exchange stories.

An avid outdoorsman, Israel's father loved to fish and hunt. Many days after school and on Saturdays, on a riverbank or in the woods, father and son would enjoy each other's company. Sometimes the excursions would include one or two of his father's friends. These times forged a special relationship between them. Israel says, "I learned a lot about my father and what he believed as a result of those very special times with him."

Mornings often found Israel with his dad at a special spot near the causeway of Pennsylvania's Pymatuning Lake, where they would line up along the bank with other fishermen. He remembers, "It was great excitement to see carp, fish that were three feet in length, scrambling for bread thrown by tourists from the causeway. My dad would jokingly say, 'If you ever fall in there, you'll never come out alive.'" On occasion father and son would rent a boat and spend the day together on the lake. "Those are great memories," Israel says.

He and his dad also enjoyed hunting together. They would use hunting dogs, typically two, for small game such as rabbits, squirrels and pheasants. On one occasion Israel III ran off to chase one of the dogs in the woods, became confused and had no idea where his father was. he began to shout, "Dad! Dad! Where are you?" In the distance he heard his father's voice saying, "I'm over here, son. I'm over here." Israel vividly remembers shouting back, "I can't see you, Dad. I can't see you!" He remembers his father's voice as he called out, "It's all right that you can't see me; just follow the sound of my voice. Keep following the sound of my voice." Israel recalls, "And so he kept talking to me, and I followed the sound of his voice and within a few minutes, I was able to see him through the brush. That was a powerful image that sometimes I have used in sermon illustrations. I thank God for the voice of my heavenly Father as well as my earthly father, who prodded me to keep following the sound of his voice. Even though I couldn't see my earthly dad, or am unable to see my heavenly Father, I simply must keep following his voice. It was a powerful lesson."

On another occasion when Israel was hunting with his dad, he fell over an embankment and slid down a steep hill. As his shotgun fell from his hand, he grabbed onto the trunk of a small tree. He remembers clearly that his father came to the edge of the hill, knelt down and reached for him, saying, "Son, just take my hand. Don't be afraid; just take my hand." Israel says, "I reached up, grabbed my father's hand, and he lifted me to safety." Again, this memory became another powerful image that remained with him. "And the mark of my father's hand has been upon my life all through the years. There is of course a spiritual parallel—the mark of the hand of my heavenly Father that is on my life."

Israel has vivid memories of his father's physical presence. "He was not a tall man, but he was distinguished–looking and had a presence about him that commanded attention. His hands were large and firm; there was a very special feel about my dad's hand placed on my shoulder." When Israel grew a little uncomfortable with hugging his dad, he says, "He would shake my hand, and his hand would envelop mine. I remember the firmness and strength of his hands. I've used that parallel also in sermons as I've talked about the strength and firmness and the safety that we find in our heavenly Father's hands."

It was during these outings with his dad, when the two shared in the lure and lore of the outdoors, that young Israel learned some of his most treasured lessons. He came to appreciate his father's wisdom, his patience, his strength. Sitting in a boat on an early Saturday morning provided opportunity for quiet fellowship and serious conversation. "He talked to me about being a young Christian," Israel recalls, "and what that meant in practical ways. Dad never made decisions for me, but he gave me wise counsel. Profound wisdom was transmitted in those informal times."

When Israel came to have pastoral responsibility in his first Salvation Army corps, he says, "It was to my Dad that I went for advice. He had beautiful insights into what it meant to be a pastor. His values were transparent. He believed in God, in himself, and in family."

PATERNAL ANCESTRY

Israel remembers his grandfather, Israel Gaither I, as a tall, well–built man. He has clear images of summer visits with him and his step–grandmother in Mocksville. Over a period of two weeks they would enjoy family reunions, the local park and picnic outings.

These summer visits to the Gaither home in Mocksville found the children surrounded by aunts, uncles and umpteen cousins. Years of separation has made it difficult to keep in touch with those cousins, but at the time of the 2005 London terrorist bombings, several cousins—out of concern—called Israel, then stationed in London. Though it was their first contact in decades, he says their early bonding melted the years of separation. A first cousin, Dr. Donald Meeks, who has lived his entire adult life in Canada as an educator, remained close to Israel's mother and other members of the family. His daughter, Melanie, in her pride of family heritage, is undertaking a study of the genealogy of the Gaither family name.

In the small community of Mocksville, Israel's grandfather was well known for his efforts to teach black children to read and write. His own parents had been taught to read and write by their slave owners, and they undertook teaching other black children in the community. At one point, local citizens mounted a drive to name the Mocksville Elementary School after Israel's great–grandparents. The effort did not succeed, but it signified the community's awareness of and esteem for the Gaithers' dedication to educating black children. That bit of family history remains a part of the heritage of the many Gaither descendants who live in the community.

"The name Gaither was taken from the family for whom my slave ancestors worked."

The family heritage is limited to a fixed point in history, beyond which genealogy cannot be traced. Israel records, "As in the case of many African–Americans, the name Gaither was taken from the family for whom my slave ancestors worked. If one traces the name associated with African–Americans, it all returns to the same root in the Winston Salem/Mocksville, North Carolina region. There is little doubt that white Americans who are known as Gaithers, deep in their ancestral past, have a link with my ancestors."

A RICH HERITAGE

When Israel went out for an evening, his father would say, "Remember your name. Remember who you are." Those words became a mantra, a watchword that Israel passed on to his own children.

"We were taught early on the expectation of respect for adults," he says. "There were occasions when an adult would see me with friends and speak to me about my behavior, then report what they observed to my dad. So I faced not only the discipline of my father but also scrutiny of adults in general."

Israel speaks of the indelible imprint of his parents and grandparents upon his life. "My father stood as a strong hero; he became the strongest male influence that has ever impacted my life. His influence was enormous as not only my father, but also as a model for what it meant to be a man as well as a Christian.

"I carry the name of my father and his father proudly. Having been named Israel L. Gaither III is a constant reminder of the rich heritage that is mine."

chapter **3**

Maternal Memories

The best monument that a child can raise to his
mother's memory is that of an upright life.
Anonymous

Israel acknowledges that his mother, Lillian Gaither, also had a significant influence on him and his sisters.

"I was impressed by the strength of my mother as a woman of conviction and strong belief. The Bible became instilled as, early in the morning, I would see mother, with her Bible open. Her powerful influence came through her Christian living before us as well as being as an exceptional mother. My

Israel with his mother, Lillian, and his sisters,
Kathy and Jacqueline

mother always carried herself with dignity and grace—and she still does."

Now in her 80s, Lillian lives with Israel's sister Dr. Jacqueline Gaither Respress, in New Castle. Israel says of his mother, "She too was a strong disciplinarian, although my father took the major responsibility for family discipline. Mom had very high standards for her children and yet at the same time was a protector/shield for us. I can recall many times when I misbehaved as a youngster that she warned she would report my behavior to my father. And that was sufficient, as the very thought terrified me."

The family remembers their mother as a wonderful cook. Her recipes have been passed on and relished by the family. Israel says, "I believe my mother could cook and bake anything and it always turned out just right."

As with Israel's father, his mother had many friends in the community. "It seemed in my growing years that she knew more people than any other adult I knew," he says, "and I saw the evidence of the love and respect her many friends had for her. While I recognize that I carry within me many of the personality traits of my father, I see in my sisters beautiful traits inherited from our mother."

Mealtimes were the axis around which the family revolved. These gatherings in the Gaither household were regular and ritualized. Israel II was always present for evening dinner. A substantial meal was prepared by Lillian, with the entire family always around the table. Sometimes extended family members or visitors would come, be invited to the table and become a part of the circle. "Each of our parents possessed a wonderful sense of humor," says Israel, "and both were great storytellers. Mealtimes for the family were and still are embraced by lots of laughter and recollection. I learned a great deal about who I am and where I have come from at the dinner table. My mother makes me proud to be a Gaither!"

The evening meal and Sunday morning breakfast were also worship times. Israel remembers, "It was a time of instruction, and Dad would always pray the longest prayer. My father was also a great storyteller. It was a time of bonding."

MATERNAL ANCESTRY

Lillian's parents, Vohu and Carrie Lue Johnson, had settled in New Castle during Israel's earliest years.

"My maternal grandfather was a full–blooded Mexican," he says. "My mother speaks of attempting to trace his heritage, but she was unable to access any information other than that he was an orphan raised in Diana, N.M. Mrs. Booker T. Washington took a special interest in orphan children, and Israel's maternal grandfather became one of the Washington's foster children. He was fluent in Spanish, reflecting his Mexican heritage. He married Carrie Lue Mitchell and migrated to Cleveland, Ohio, which they found discomforting, and so they soon moved to New Castle. Israel's mother, born in Montgomery, Ala., on Oct. 14, 1918, was just four years old when the family move took place.

Lillian's father, of a ruddy complexion, was often mistaken for a white man. He is fondly remembered as a man full of stories accompanied by a distinctive laugh. From both sides of the family, the Gaither children were blessed with grandparents who regaled them with colorful stories full of meaningful life experiences.

Israel's maternal grandmother, Carrie Lue, was quiet but had a warm sense of humor. She reared a family of three daughters and four sons. From that union came Israel's 14 first cousins. Raised in the same city, the Gaithers grew close to the Johnsons. The children often visited the Johnson home, where the pantry always held special treats.

> **"** *Early in the morning, I would see mother with her Bible open.* **"**

Israel has a special memory from his childhood of an overnight stay at the Johnson's home. He recalls waking to the fragrance of a typical Southern breakfast—eggs, ham, and grits. His grandfather also loved spicy foods, perhaps a legacy from his Mexican heritage. Israel's mother passed on to the family a love for spicy foods, which Israel admits he can no longer tolerate.

His last memory of his maternal grandfather is what all the family believes to have been a miracle. He was quite elderly when Eva and Israel met, and Israel holds dear the belief that he held on long enough to attend their wedding. He was at the wedding in a wheelchair, and Israel says, "I can still see his smile." One week later, he died, having been predeceased by his wife, Carrie Lue.

Miracles did not end with that generation. Lillian shares both a poignant and a blessed memory of a near-death experience. While dusting the top of a door, she fell off a chair. Unconscious, she was rushed to the hospital by ambulance. Israel was fishing when he heard his name and a message over the loudspeaker: "Your wife fell and broke her back." The two men fishing with him were preachers. They held hands and prayed, and Israel rushed to be by his wife's side. As Lillian was wheeled out of surgery, her husband walked in. The nurse could not get a pulse and exclaimed, "She's gone!" Israel uttered, "This isn't going to be. The Lord is going to heal her." He stood over her and prayed. Lillian opened her eyes; the first words to her husband at her bedside were, "I'm hungry."

"As I think about it," muses Israel, "I am really the sum total of the Gaither/Johnson influence. It's a rich heritage that I and my sisters deeply value and respect."

chapter 4

The Formative Years

*Remember your Creator in the
days of your youth.*
Ecclesiastes 12:1

I srael remembers that his father and mother always had time for their children. Sometimes the family would visit large amusement parks nearby in Pennsylvania and Ohio, but trips to the small amusement park in New Castle on summer Saturdays were a favorite with the children. The day would be spent on the rides, followed by a picnic.

FAMILY LIFE

"As a kid," reflects Israel, "I didn't think we were poor. There was always ample food on the table, deliciously prepared by my mother. I knew we were not middle class. I would define [our community] now, as I look back, as working–class. There were other sections of our city where the truly middle class and upper middle class lived, as well as poor sections of the community.

"We grew up in a humble home, in those days heated by a coal furnace, as [were] many homes in my neighborhood. I remember that one of my tasks as a teenager was to bank the coal furnace and add coal to the fire on those cold early winter mornings. My dad gave me specific hands–on instructions on how to bank the furnace, remove the ashes, and where to place them." Israel adds, "I hated it."

Living with a coal furnace also meant an extensive spring cleaning. "[It] was a challenge. We had to literally clean the entire house. We used a sort of clay to clean the walls. It would take, as I recall, several days for the house to be completely clean of the soot that accumulated over the winter."

Each of the children had chores around the house; Israel's was to ensure the lawn was kept tidy. It was very small, but to Israel it seemed to take forever to cut with the hand mower. His dad would become frustrated because

Israel would often stop to have a glass of soda or lemonade. His father would have to come out and prod his son to get on with it.

The Gaither house was tight for seven people, Israel says, "but we regarded it as a loving home, and it had all the conveniences we felt necessary at the time." He remembers their first television set; the family had to sit right in front of it on the floor to view the very small screen. It was black and white, but his father purchased an acetate sheet with different colors on it and placed it over the screen. "And presto! We had color TV!

"Celebrations—birthdays, holidays and especially Christmas—were always special in the Gaither household," recalls Israel. "Our parents provided a special touch for each occasion. In our home we did not usually have dessert following a meal, but on birthdays, a special cake baked by my mother was always prepared."

As a preteen, Israel's sister Carmilla made a special request for a birthday cake with white batter, vanilla frosting, and loaded with coconut bits. Israel says, "So we finished our meal—and I mean finished it because we always had to eat everything on our plate, including our vegetables. I had an aversion—and still do—to peas and carrots for that very reason. The birthday cake came out with the candles lit and placed in front of Carmilla. She had tucked her peas in the left side of her jaw—still whole. So when she blew out the candles, inevitably, the peas came spilling out all over the cake. I remember everyone practically falling off their chairs in laughter."

The subject of girlfriends did not come up directly between Israel and his dad. "But he was wise enough to know that when I was out with my friends, no doubt girls were present. I think he also knew that there were a couple of girls with whom I was especially close, and I can recall the awkward father–and–son discussions we had. My dad used to say to me when I would leave to go out with my friends, 'Son, don't forget your name. Your name is Israel Gaither.' What he meant was, 'Don't embarrass me.'"

SPORTS AND PALS

Israel grew up in an integrated neighborhood, with mostly African–Americans, or "colored people," as they were known in those days. He knew many neighbors in the community—both black and white—but his friends were predominantly black. That changed when he entered junior and senior high school, where he had more white friends.

Israel's early years bordered on the edge of the Civil Rights movement. In his teen years his interest in sports attracted him to activities at what was then called the "colored Y." It was vastly different from what was known as the "white YMCA." The "white Y" was a fine building, with a swimming pool, indoor gymnasium and game rooms. The colored Y, on the other hand, was a large, old house with a billiard table and space for table games. The basketball court was outdoors. On cold winter days, he and his friends would shovel snow off the concrete surface so they could play.

" The 'Colored Y' was vastly different from what was known as the 'White YMCA.'"

Other than the separation of the two YMCAs in the town, Israel has no recollection of experiencing segregation, but he realizes that life was different for blacks and whites "Looking back as an adult on those years, of course, I recognize that there was a subtle 'Jim Crow' segregationist attitude that prevailed."

Israel's favorite activities were sports–related. In addition to hunting and fishing, he played baseball, basketball and football. Interest in music and an appreciation for reading also began during his youth. Fondness for these activities continued through his growing years.

Israel has warm memories of his preteen and teen years. A large vacant lot across the street, several hundred yards from the Gaither home, became the gathering place for both baseball and football games. For baseball, large flat stones were used as bases and a white powder made the foul lines. Today when he returns to New Castle, he drives by that location, now a well–developed playground for neighborhood children.

During football season, one block on the street where he lived also became a football field. The telephone poles, linked with overhead wires, became the goal posts; a field goal simply meant kicking the football over the wires. Often the game would be held up to allow oncoming vehicles to pass. Also, once in a while, a ball would bounce off the windshield of either his dad's or a neighbor's car and, Israel says, "We would hold our breath hoping not to get into trouble."

Another vacant lot one block behind the Gaither home, next to railroad tracks, was a great location to play football. Israel remembers "coming out of many 'sand–lot' games on that field bruised and battered."

Several blocks away was the West Side Elementary School, an easy walk from home. At the rear of the school playground was a basketball court, another gathering place primarily for black teens.

In junior high Israel played on a Little League team from the west side of town. As a young teenager he became eligible and played in the Pony League, a program that brought together youth from all over the region. He wore his Little League and Pony League baseball uniforms with pride. But his father's strict standards permitted no sports on Sunday. He recalls that in his last year of Little League, he was nominated to the all–star team but was not allowed to play because the game was on a Sunday. He was extremely disappointed but accepted the values that were dominant in his home.

In high school he played intramural basketball. In that era the New Castle region produced some outstanding players, older than him, who went on to play professional basketball and football. They set good examples and were heroes to the boys in the community.

Among his friends, Israel began to be known as "Izzy." His father often referred to him as "Iz." When growing up, on the basketball courts and among school friends, "Izzy" seemed more informal and easy than the formal "Israel." The nickname followed him all through his life, even to the office of the Chief of Staff, for those closest to him. In a 2004 sermon before an American congregation in his home territory, General John Larsson related an anecdote concerning his Chief discovering a place in London for discarding excess items. Larsson said "Izzy" used this experience repeatedly to illustrate that sanctification needs to be a ridding of excess items in a person's spiritual life. Earlier, General John Gowans referred to Israel as "Izzy" as he conducted his installation as territorial leader in the USA East. Thus the familiar name came to achieve international coinage.

But mother and sisters did not acquiesce to this shorter version of his given noble biblical name, which means "prince." To them he will always be "Israel Lee," with retention of the family name "Lee."

THE EARLY SOUND OF MUSIC

Vocal music became a major interest in Israel's early life. He was part of the concert choir at New Castle High School. For several years he sang in a mixed vocal octet and a men's quartet. His teacher, George Bentel, led the interracial choir that sang not only for school functions but also for civic events. Israel also auditioned and was selected for the state choir, along with several of his friends.

In a singing competition, Israel won first place with his rendition of "Deep River." In later years, as a Salvation Army officer, he sang the national anthem at a Pittsburgh Pirates baseball game before more than 30,000 fans. At that game, one spectator, when he saw it was "Salvation Army Night," remarked to his friend, "I knew a guy in high school who was with The Salvation Army." When Israel Gaither was announced as the soloist, the man said in amazement, "You won't believe this, but that's the guy I went to school with." A brief reunion and time of reminiscence followed the game.

In his early high school years, a pastor's wife, Edna Stevens, took a special interest in neighborhood youth and formed a community Gospel choir. Rehearsals were held at a nearby church, with 50 or so teenagers. Israel was selected to be the soloist for "How Great Thou Art," which was performed on a number of occasions. He was also a member of the Union Baptist Church junior choir, led by Kathryn Engs.

These experiences became early indicators to Israel that he had the gift of vocal music, particularly as a soloist. This gift that he would use over the years he had first offered to the Lord in his teen years.

Israel's dad was instrumental in forming a Gospel quartet that included his teenage son. "I remember being introduced to a white fellow who arrived one evening in a beautiful–looking car and he wanted to hear us sing. So we sang, and for the next several months he arranged for us to appear in different locations. It never got to the point where he became our agent, but I must say that we were very good! And of course, at that point, all the music was a cappella with very close harmony. We had a mixed repertoire, then known as 'soul' music." Israel would later be reminded of those days as he listened to youth and adult choirs in Africa.

On many mornings, on the way to high school, he and several others would meet on a specific corner at a set time, and as they walked to school, they would harmonize, singing popular music. One of the members, Joe Palmer, went on to sing with the well known group, *The Platters*. Israel says, "Those early years of walking to school and singing, harmonizing, again, were all used of the Lord to develop the gift I really didn't know I had."

FORMATIVE YEARS

For Israel and his friends, Pittsburgh was the "big city." In those days of no four–lane highways, it was about an hour–and–a–half drive from home. When he first became linked with The Salvation Army, he attended divisional youth events in the city that would later play a major role in his adult life. "The big thing for the kids in the division to do," he remembers, "was to visit the Pittsburgh morgue for a tour. Compare that to what young people do at divisional youth councils now."

Israel was a "B" average student in school. He enjoyed the stimulation of subjects that had human interest. "I've been profoundly influenced in my thinking and learning experience," he reflects, "as a direct result of my officership and exposure to people and places around the world."

In retrospect, he writes, "Reflecting on my growing years, particularly in high school, I recall them as years of forming good friendships and preparing me for adult life in ways which I at the time didn't recognize. There were teachers who were influential in my life. It is interesting now, when I have contact with my sister Jacqueline, who is principal of the Ben Franklin Junior High School, that the stories she tells reveal a much different era than the time in which I was raised."

Israel was introduced to public speaking in an unusual way. His uncle Bennie suggested that he enter a public speaking contest sponsored by a local organization. He filled out the application, auditioned and was selected. Along with other contestants, he had to memorize a specific speech. A woman in the community coached him in elocution and delivery. He spent an hour or more several times a week in her home in the days leading up to the competition. Israel won the regional level and went on to compete in Philadelphia for the state finals. Two contestants made it to this level; he came in second and won a scholarship. That money was ultimately used toward his budget for attending The Salvation Army Training College.

Israel reflects, "I learned many lessons in my teenage and young adult years. Some have come through my own failures, and they have shaped and informed me. There have been times of real doubt about my place, my role, my future—but I continue to learn the lessons of my faith and heritage and thereby continue to develop a stronger belief in God. If I had the power to do it all over again, I would change nothing, except that I would want to handle the more difficult experiences I've had in life in a better way."

When he wanted to work at a car wash, his father would not allow it. He later took his son to the crane company where he worked and asked, "Is this what you want for the rest of your life? See here what I'm doing. No. I want something better for you. You must go on to school and prepare yourself."

"The strong influence of my father kept me at arm's length from social evils," Israel says. "I never engaged in drinking or smoking, or even swearing—although I was tempted occasionally to use a few choice words! So I don't think I gave my parents the kind of concern that a straying teenager might possibly give parents in this era.

"But I was not a perfect child by any means. I often came under strong discipline from my father and mother. Candidly, I feared it most when it would come from my father."

Remembrance of his dad's dress style evokes a painful, yet humorous memory. "We always went to school dressed well, but there were times, especially as the only male child, when I would get 'hand–me–downs' from my father. There was one pair of pin–striped trousers that I inherited, and I hated them. I was in junior high school and my mother would insist that I wear those trousers. One day—I remember specifically that I knew the next day I had to wear the pin–striped trousers—I hid another pair of trousers in the brush along the path that I would normally take to school. The following morning, I got up, put on the pin–striped trousers and made my way to school, taking the usual route. When I reached the brush where I had hidden the other pair, I changed and then went on my way to school. Coming back home, for some reason, I thought I could just simply forget about changing. So I wore the other pair of trousers home, knowing that my parents would not be there when I arrived. What I didn't count on was the presence of my sisters, Carmilla and Judy. They saw me coming in wearing another pair of trousers and knew that the second pair under my arm—the pin–striped trousers—were the ones I should have been wearing. They couldn't wait to tell mother and dad! And I felt yet again the ability of my father to exact discipline.

Despite such moments, Israel has a great fondness for the place where he grew up. "My years in New Castle were wonderful," says Israel, "and I will always regard the city as my hometown."

But a dark cloud loomed over the horizon of Israel's life, and there would be no lightning rod to defuse the emotional charge of its shattering effect on the Gaither family.

PART TWO

Beginnings of the Journey

1956–1992

chapter **5**

Defining Moments

For whoever wants to save his life will lose it,
but whoever loses his life for me will find it.
Matthew 16:25

A defining moment came when 12–year–old Israel knelt in the church where his father was the associate minister. The Sunday School Superintendent knelt beside him and prayed for him. He shares, "That was the moment I consciously first recalled asking forgiveness. In a simple act of dedication he turned his life over to Christ.

The moment evokes the memory of Salvation Army Founder William Booth, who, when asked the secret of his life, told how as a boy he had knelt at a bare table and vowed that "God should have all there is of William Booth." His daughter, Evangeline, later said of her father's decision, "His secret was that he never took it back." For Israel Gaither, that same unbroken dedication became the secret of his dedicated life and ministry.

ISRAEL MEETS THE SALVATION ARMY

A family of Salvationists from Punxsutawney, Pa., had moved into Israel's neighborhood. One of the boys his age became a good friend and, with his parents, invited him to attend Army youth activities. That was Israel Gaither's introduction to The Salvation Army, a small step that ultimately would lead to his epic journey.

He enjoyed the Army activities and became more involved while at the same time attending the Union Baptist Church. He attended the Corps Cadet Bible study program and had his first experience of a Salvation Army camp at Corps Cadet camp. Years later he would say, "That camp was the hook that really fixed my interest in the Army."

Although not a Salvationist, Israel was spending most of his free time at the Army by the time he was in his mid–teens. He did not become a soldier (member) within the first several years of attending the Army, but the love and interest of the corps officers (pastors), Brigadier and Mrs. James Dihle, had a significant impact upon him. As his involvement in the Army increased, he ultimately made the painful separation, leaving the Baptist Church of his family and youth to become a Salvation Army member in the New Castle congregation.

That corps today sits directly across the street from the church in which Israel was raised. In later years when he and Eva returned to the area, he shares, "It was always an emotional experience. Driving down Grant Street, I would make a right turn into the parking lot of the corps rather than a left turn into the parking lot of the Union Baptist Church. And then, following the meeting at the corps, I would walk out of the front door and immediately across the street faced the church in which I was raised and baptized as a young teenager."

During his high school years, he applied and was accepted as a staff member at Camp Allegheny, where he worked for two summers. When asked what he did, he says that as a member of the maintenance staff, he "proudly picked up the trash." At camp he came under the tutelage of the divisional youth leaders, Captains Stanley and Cath Ditmer. "Experience as a staff member," he recalls, "opened my eyes and heart to another fascinating element of what it meant to be a young Christian, and I engaged all the more readily in Army activity. It was in this context that my second life–transforming decision took place in the summer of 1961 at Camp Allegheny. I remember it clearly.

"It was a warm sunny Sunday morning, and I remember exactly where I was sitting in the Tabernacle. I was moved deeply in my heart by the Holy Spirit, knowing with assurance that God was calling me to Salvation Army officership. It was not just a call to the ministry but a definite call to leave the church of my heritage and to be an officer. But I resisted. The presence of God, with me for the remainder of that summer at camp, causing me to think about my future as an officer, was nearly overwhelming."

Israel made no public commitment, did not share this calling with anyone, and struggled with it throughout the summer. The Ditmers saw the potential of the teenager on their camp staff, adopted him as a friend and protégé, and served as role models for him. Finally he felt led to share his struggle with them, and "they became very protective of me, especially Cath. I was developing a friendship with a female staff person, and I clearly remember Cath Ditmer saying to the girl, 'Leave Izzy alone. He's going to be an officer.'"

In that camp setting and in this very formative phase of Israel's life, Captain Stanley Ditmer became the first of the seven influential servants of the Lord who would emerge as encouragers and enablers on Israel's life journey. In retrospect, Israel would later acknowledge, "These seven men have played a very important role in my life."

CONFIRMING GOD'S CALL

> **"I could never question the fact that I have been called to be an officer."**

Israel felt he needed a confirmation of God's call and "prayed over and over again that God would prove to me that He wanted me to be an officer." At that young age, he dared to challenge God. "God," he prayed, "if you really want me to be an officer, you have got to prove it." Then something happened that became a spiritual precedent for the way God would deal with him in pivotal moments of his life and ministry. God gave him a revelation.

"One morning, while sitting on the porch in late August, prior to the re-opening of high school, I received a letter from a friend with whom I had served just weeks earlier on the camp staff. On the back of the envelope she had printed the Great Commission passage: 'Therefore go and make disciples of all nations, baptizing them in the name of the Father and of the Son and of the Holy Spirit' (Matt. 28:19). Before I opened the letter, when I saw the back of the envelope with that passage, with its challenge to go into all the world, I knew that was the confirmation I'd been praying for."

Young Israel could not envision what God would have in store for him through the phrase, "of all nations." He would later reflect, "Little could I know that some 40 years later I would have the joy and privilege of actually ministering throughout the world."

In retrospect, he shares, "That was confirmation of my call, and I have never to this day been in a position where I could question the fact that I have been called to be an officer. I have often said that I could do any number of things, but I would never be able to deny that I was called to be an officer. And it is more real and certain to me today than it was on that August Sunday morning."

A BREAK WITH TRADITION

The dramatic decision had to be broken to Israel's parents. He says, "I returned home that summer, talked to my dad and shared my feelings. When I said to him that I felt I had been called to be an officer, I was shocked at his response because he said, 'I already know.' I asked how he knew, and I will always remember his answer: 'The Lord has been speaking to me—and I have been watching you. God's hand is on you for this ministry.' The Lord had revealed that to him and he was just waiting for me to tell him. He was absolutely thrilled with my decision." Although it meant a painful parting from his family's church and his denominational roots, his father gave full support for his son "to do whatever the Lord wants you to do."

Israel credits his father's fundamentalist theology in preparing him for the conservative theological stance he would embrace as a Salvation Army officer. Following the announcement of his intention to become an officer, his father spent a great deal of time explaining the theology behind the sacramental practices of the Baptist tradition. "But," observes his son, "he was sensitive enough to help me understand the implications of those sacraments as one means of grace, and that they were in fact not the only means of grace to a member of the Christian family."

Throughout his officership Israel Gaither would embrace the Army's stance—all of life is sacramental, grace is mediated in direct communion with the Lord, without a requirement of ritual. Although not observed internally, Salvationists may participate in the sacrament of communion in ecumenical fellowship. Israel would return to his father's church, sit in the pew, or preach in the pulpit, and indubitably affirm, "I know the real presence of Christ as a reality beyond the observance of sacraments."

Israel looks upon this time as a defining experience in his life. "There have been some remarkable occasions in my life that I believe have formed my belief about who I am and what I ought to be doing. One of those was the transition from the denomination of my father's church to The Salvation Army."

The Trumpet Call Had Sounded

At the end of that summer, the struggle resolved, 17–year–old Israel Gaither said "yes" to God's call, with its far–reaching ramifications. It would take him from the rich traditions of the church of his childhood and family into the full–time ranks and life–calling of Salvation Army ministry. This step of faith would launch him on a spiritual odyssey that would stretch all the way from New Castle to around the world.

In saying yes to the Lord's summons he began to march to the beat of a different drum. He forsook personal autonomy to be led by God to serve in the infantry of the militant branch of the universal Christian church. In response to a question put to him years later, he reflected: "The surrendering of my membership in the church in which my father was serving as the associate pastor and becoming a member of The Salvation Army in New Castle, Pa., was a step of faith that served as the initial step that has led, by God's grace, to my life's calling."

He had clearly heard and responded to the trumpet call and marched toward an unknown future in which life would never be the same. The spiritual journey he commenced would be fraught with deep challenges but also with peerless opportunities. Whom God calls, He equips, and He blesses and uses beyond the most daring imaginings. Seventeen–year–old Israel Gaither yielded himself completely to the will of God, and from that moment never looked back.

chapter **6**

Beginning the Journey

If anyone would come after me, he must deny
himself and take up his cross daily and follow me.
Luke 9:23

When he returned from camp that summer, Israel broke the news of his calling to his pastor and corps officer at New Castle, Major James Dihle, who responded with enthusiasm. Following his enrollment as a soldier, he filled out a candidate application for acceptance as a cadet to be trained for Salvation Army officership. Signed by the candidate and Major Dihle, it was dated March 2, 1962.

THE CANDIDATE

In response to questions on the application, Israel stated he had never used intoxicating drinks or tobacco, and that he had plunged into all corps activity without reservation. He shared in open–air (outdoor evangelistic) meetings, was president of Torchbearers (a teen group), accompanied the person selling *War Crys*, witnessed to others, visited sick friends, sang solos and led singing, participated in holiness, salvation, and young people's meetings, and was a beginner in playing the cornet. He identified his race with the term used at that time, "Negro."

Cadet Israel Gaither

His "Account of Conversion" related that he had been attending Camp Allegheny for several years and there had affirmed Christ as his personal Savior. He recorded, "I enjoy and appreciate and love the Christian atmosphere of the Army. Also, in my corps, I have been to the altar to accept Jesus before becoming a soldier."

To the question as to what branch of Salvation Army service interested him most, he replied, "corps officer or social work."

"What is your conception of the aims and purposes of The Salvation Army?" elicited, "First to spread the gospel of Jesus Christ, trying to bring unbelievers to him. Secondly to help mankind when necessary, economically." Young Israel had perceived the unique integrated ecclesiastical and social ministries of the Army. He was early attracted to the Army's practical expression of a Christianity with its sleeves rolled up, a ministry epitomized in the Army's slogan, "Heart to God and Hand to Man." Having come from a celebrating, singing, and spontaneous tradition in a Baptist church, Israel felt at home with the Army's informal style of worship.

On the application, he listed his typing speed as 54 words per minute. Included in books he had read in the prior six months was the account of Army history in *Soldiers Without Swords, Don Quixote* and sports magazines.

Characteristics of his future ministry are seen in his statements: "I am very much interested in vocal music. I have sung in the school concert choir three years, mixed octet one year, and the boys' quartet. I am singing with the community choirs also. In addition I do solo singing. My main cultural hobbies are singing and public speaking, the latter for which I have received a scholarship."

The candidate application also called for a description of one's experience of holiness, to which the high school senior responded: "I know that I have the Holy Spirit dwelling within me. It is because I know Christ and do have the Holy Spirit in me that I want to do something for mankind, spiritually as well as physically." Israel came out of a holiness church tradition, had knowledge of sanctification from his dad's preaching, and had been exposed to the teaching and preaching of his corps officer, Major James Dihle.

The questionnaire also called for an "Account of Call to Officership." The candidate responded: "In the summer of 1961 at Camp Allegheny I received the calling and knew God wanted me to become a Salvation Army officer. After returning home I told my parents of my desire to become an officer. My father and mother were happy to hear of my desire. I informed my corps officer and now am in the process of applying for entrance into the training college."

The sincerity of Israel's commitment was reflected in his answer to "Account of Efforts Made to Win others to Christ." "In general, I have tried to live a Christian life, so that through my actions alone, people will know Christ is in my life, and I have talked to others about Christ."

The official papers were stamped as approved by the territorial candidate's council on April 2, 1962, just one month from the date they were sent, and signed by the territorial commander, Commissioner Holland French. The expeditious one–month processing time, much shorter than for many candidates, gives an indication of the ready acceptance of the Army for the 17–year–old candidate from New Castle. In September of that year the accepted candidate became Cadet Israel Gaither, member of the 1962–64 *Heroes of the Faith* session,[1] entering The Salvation Army School for Officer Training in the Bronx borough of New York City, one month before his 18th birthday.

> *"His sense of humor was outright contagious as was his smile and joyous laughter."*

No one claims such a call to himself. It comes from God, who varies the giving of it from person to person. It begins not with "what I would like to do," but with "what God wills me to do." The pages of the Bible and of Christian biography give witness to the varied call of God to individuals. Isaiah heard it in the temple, Amos in the field as he was plowing, Matthew as he was writing tax receipts, Peter as he was mending his nets by the seaside, Paul as he was persecuting the Christians. Augustine heard the call through the voices of children in a friend's garden. To Luther it came literally with a bolt of lightning. To William Carey came a world vision as he mended shoes in his cobbler's shop. William Booth found his destiny among the poverty–stricken on the streets of East London.

Israel Gaither was but one in a line of succession of an innumerable company, among the well known and the obscure, whom God has called in unique ways. At a summer camp, in a spiritually incandescent moment the Spirit of God spoke to him with a clear accent. His commitment to full–time Salvation Army officership was a surrender to God's call and will. The certainty of that calling would be the spiritual compass that would guide him throughout his lifetime.

CADET DAYS

What was life like for Cadet Israel Gaither and his peers at the training school in the Bronx? Some who lived there and served in that intimate company share their reminiscences and reflections.

---

[1]Each session of cadets is ascribed a particular name.

"He was an outstanding basketball player."

Retired Commissioner Ronald Irwin's leadership, as then–Field Training and Intelligence Officer for men cadets, brought him in regular association with the young cadet from the small town in western Pennsylvania. He writes: "Even in his training days, he gave proof of his communication skills in the pulpit, his openness and ability to establish rapport with others, his sensitivity to human needs, and a standard of personal conduct not always evident in young cadets, ingrained no doubt as a result of the strong influence of his parents and the Christian home they established. It was obvious he had a good and an inquiring mind and the potential for productive service."

Commissioner Todd Bassett, writing from his office as USA national commander of The Salvation Army in 2005 was a member of the "Proclaimers" session that came into the Training College during the second year of Israel's training. "Despite this being the early 60s and the immersion of our country in Civil Rights issues, Izzy Gaither carried himself with a dignity and a poise which has flowered and blossomed into the competent and capable leader he has become. Even then, as cadets, we sensed his passion to exalt his Lord and to proclaim the truth of His Word in clear and careful tones, whether singing a solo or preaching the Word of God."

Commissioner David A. Baxendale, who was then the Education Officer on the training school staff, remembers, "Among the new cadets was the young African–American, Israel Gaither, who had great potential. I mention 'great potential,' as his abilities were not particularly showcased or up–front but were like nuggets that had to be mined, and then became quite apparent—such as personal warmth, depth of character, straightforwardness and a holy joy. His sense of humor was outright contagious, as was his smile and joyous laughter that made you want to join in and laugh with him! The men cadets formed a chorus which I had the privilege of leading and we soon found Cadet Izzy had not only a marvelous tenor voice but fine control and mellowness that attracted listeners for years to come as he sang his Savior's praise. He stood head and shoulders above all the others in his vocalizing."

Paul Baxendale, a session mate, recollects some of the less serious side of their training days. "Izzy and I played on the football and basketball teams. He was an outstanding basketball player. On Mondays when we had free time, we found places of interest in New York to visit and often went with a female cadet. It was required in those days to wear full uniform on our day off, but I became friends with the local pizza dealer around the corner from the school. He allowed Izzy and me to go down to his basement, hang up our uniforms and put on private clothing. We just had to buy a piece of pizza before we headed out.

"Izzy by habit sat on the very first row for the morning 'half–hour of prayer power' meeting. One day he was late, slipped in the side door and sat on the second row. The officer in charge said, 'Let us pray.' As usual Izzy bowed his head low like he had every morning on the first row, but being on the second row, he banged his head hard on the pew in front of him and yelled out really loud in pain. Unfortunately, everyone started laughing while the officer was trying to lead us in prayer. Izzy was in my brigade [groups that went out for field work] for 10–day campaigns twice. The first year Izzy asked if I would mind him being my roommate for the campaign. I said, 'You got to be kidding, I'd be honored!' We never discussed it beyond that but I just thought that he, being African–American, was concerned that some might not want him for a roommate."

Lt. Colonel Ernest Payton, on the school staff at the time, tells of the cadets having had a good basketball team which, when the opportunity presented itself, played teams from the several Salvation Army youth centers in the greater New York area. While playing one team, which excelled in the use of vulgar language as well as in rough and tough playing, Izzy came to Captain Payton indicating his concern that the cadets would be playing with this type of group. The captain's response was that these personalities were the very individuals to which The Salvation Army was called to minister and that the cadets had the opportunity to witness by both word and example. Payton said that Izzy took the lesson to heart and thanked him many years later.

A Song and a Surrender

It was 1963, and 17–year–old Ed Forster had just received news that would lead to fulfilling his life's dream—being a sportswriter. A job offer had come from the sports department of the prestigious *Boston Record American*.

Ed was attending The Salvation Army in Somerville, Mass., when a brigade of cadets came to conduct a 10–day evangelistic campaign. The

Cadet Gaither renders a solo, accompanied by
Cadet Nancy Burke (Moretz).

accompanying officer was Captain Ronald Irwin, with Lawrence Moretz and Israel Gaither among the cadets. Ed attended the meetings, unaware that his destiny was "in the wings." The Holy Spirit planted a seed of conviction, a call such as had come to the cadets, who had left all else behind to obey the call of Christ. But the dream of being a sportswriter held Ed captive. His deep struggle ensued from the start of the campaign and continued all through the final Saturday night and until three o'clock Sunday morning, when he finally knelt by his bedside and asked the Lord to resolve his dilemma.

Ed recalls that among the brigade, Cadet Gaither "stood out as more polished, because of his father having been a preacher." He remembers clearly the prayer service on that Sunday morning, when as Cadet Gaither sang the solo, "O Man of Galilee," His struggle resolved, he knelt at the altar, put aside his dream of becoming a sportswriter, and surrendered himself to the Lord's call.

But like one of his spiritual forebears of old, who after having put aside writing tax receipts and going on to write the greatest story ever told, Ed found that God had a greater purpose for his pen. He ultimately would write and send out the good news to all the world. As one of the Army's premier penmen, he authored a book and contributed to several others. He served an apprenticeship as an editor in the Army's national publications in the USA, then as editor in chief for the Army in the Canada and Bermuda Territory, and later as editor in chief at International Headquarters in London. In 2006 Major Ed Forster was appointed U.S. national editor in chief and national literary secretary, overseeing the largest publication output in the Army world. In this position he also oversees the production of the Army's Crest Books, which will add this title to its growing roster of Army volumes. This vast ministry had its genesis when Cadet Gaither's solo was used by the Lord to speak to his heart.

In the interim between Israel's cadet days and Ed's editorial roles, Majors Ed and Flo Forster had become corps officers in Pittsburgh. The Gaithers, as headquarters officers, attended the corps where the Forsters pastored. In that capacity they then ministered to the one who had years before ministered to Ed with his song.

NEW DIMENSIONS

Israel considers learning the value of community to have been one of the vital lessons from his cadet days. He had always enjoyed his privacy and did not find it easy living in the crowded dormitory of the training school. But he discovered that "disciples are best created in community. Other cadets helped me understand who I am, what I am to be, and the importance of other people in life supporting you." His fellow cadet, Larry Moretz, became like a brother, and their paths would closely intertwine in the coming years.

Oliver Wendell Holmes made the seminal observation: "Now and then men's minds and hearts are stretched by a new idea and never shrink back to their original dimensions." Two years of training with his fellow cadets and staff was stretching Israel Gaither. He would never return to his original dimensions.

chapter 7

Eva Shue

*A wife of noble character ... is worth
far more than rubies.*

Proverbs 31:10

Eva Dorothy Shue, the young woman who would become Israel Gaither's life partner and in the words of the popular song "the wind beneath his wings," made her entry to the world on Sept. 9, 1943, in Sidney, Ohio, a small community surrounded by farmland. Her parents, of German and Irish descent, were born and lived their entire lives in Sidney. Eva's mother, Merle E. Shue, who lived into her 90s, remained a strong and feisty personality, a venerated Salvationist stalwart in the Sidney Salvation Army corps (local church) until she was Promoted to Glory on June 16, 2006.

When Eva was growing up, a family of seven was a financial challenge for her parents. She remembers her father working two jobs—at a local factory and a funeral home—to ensure the family was properly cared for, and her mother holding jobs from time to time.

Eva acquired her love for the Army's Girl Guard program, a Christian scouting program within The Salvation Army, from her mother, who served for many years as the Girl Guard leader for the Sidney Corps. Under her tutelage Eva achieved the highest rank, that of a General's Guard. Years later, when Eva was appointed to the International Headquarters in London, she became World President for the Army's Scouts, Guides and Guards. On taking office she looked up the "World Book of Honor" that records all General's Guards, and finding her name, copied the page and sent it to her former Girl Guard leader.

Merle Shue, a faithful Salvation Army soldier, rang the Christmas kettle bell for 50 years, sold weekly *War Crys* at the bank and on the tavern route. In 2005, at age 90, Merle was still leader of the Home League women's group, although not as active as she once had been, given her physical condition. A lifelong Salvationist, Merle made the Army the center of life for the family. In April 2005, a surprise 90th birthday party with family, friends and corps members celebrated her life and legacy. One year later she suffered a stroke, following which Israel commented, "Eva's Mom is doing remarkably well. An amazing near–92–year–old gem of a mother–in–law."

Merle and Eva joined a succession of generations of the Shues who had made the Army their church home. "I'm proud of my Salvationist heritage," says Eva. "My Army journey began with my great–great–grandmother Davis. As a fifth–generation Salvationist, I'm from a long line of faithful soldiers who have proudly worn the Army uniform, and because of them I have inherited a wonderful Salvationist legacy."

Eva's brother Bill echoes her sentiment: "Mom was our major influence. She got us all to go to church at the Army. We enjoyed growing up in the Army corps. The family was at the Army in evenings as much as at home."

A "GRACE MOMENT"

In later years, a poignant moment would come for Eva in her relationship with her father. It was December 1998; she and Israel were making final visits with family prior to taking up appointments in the Army's Southern Africa Territory on Jan. 1, 1999. She remembers that as they drove away from her parent's home, she turned to Izzy and said, "I am not going to see my father again." Her dad was in good health as they drove away—but she had a clear sense of certainty about it.

The Shue family celebrates Merle's 90th birthday

Israel turned to her and reassuringly said, "Now, Eva, we decided we were going to be positive about this move." Eva responded, "Izzy, I am not being negative; I just know I will not see my father again."

Less than two months later, in mid–February, a call came to Eva and Israel in South Africa, half a world away, that her father was critically ill. Even though they immediately arranged to return home, the journey took nearly 30 hours.

When they arrived in New York to catch the final leg of their flight scheduled to depart in a very short time, Eva ran to a telephone to check on "Daddy." Her brother John told her the end was near and that other family members, as well as the attending doctor and nurse, were waiting at his bedside. She said to John, "Tell Daddy I love him." While she hung on, John went to the bedside. He shortly returned to the phone to assure Eva that he had given her father the message. In those brief moments, he had peacefully passed away.

Eva believes that phone call to have been providential, and that her father heard John say to him, "Eva says, 'Dad, I love you.'" She says, "That phone call, on February 16, 1999, in those anxious few minutes, remains as a 'grace moment' for me."

THE SIBLINGS

Eva's sister, Elizabeth Gross, or Liz, as she was lovingly known, was a diligent and capable worker, dedicated to completing whatever she set out to do. As the parents aged, she placed her own belongings in storage and moved in with the Shues to become the primary caregiver.

In 2000, Liz was diagnosed with cancer. The entire family was devastated. Israel and Eva took a flight home from South Africa to have some time with her. Eva carried a deep burden for her, for she once had loved the Lord, but her life had taken a different path from Eva's.

After being with Liz for a few days, Eva found an opportunity to bring up the subject of her sister's spiritual condition. Eva found that the Lord had already prepared Liz. She said, "Eva, I've been waiting for you!" Eva recalls, "I was able to lead her back to the Lord. In counseling her about her sincere desire for forgiveness and a restored relationship with the Lord, I asked if she had a Bible. I then had the privilege of giving my sister my Bible during the course of that precious time of restoration." For Eva, it was another sacramental moment.

Liz lived with cancer for 18 months. At that point, the Gaithers were nearing the end of their time in Southern Africa, finalizing preparations for their farewell and hoping to get home in time to see Liz. Eva shares, "I dearly loved Liz and desperately wanted to see her once more. But we did not make it in time, as the Lord received her on the Friday prior to the Monday of our scheduled arrival. I will forever miss Liz!"

Another sister, Carolyn Sue Fenn, reflects on her early life, "I hate to think of what we would have been without The Salvation Army. Our family had very little, and the Army gave us an outlet. We all learned to play musical instruments and went to band camp."

She says of Israel, "Sometimes he is so very serious, and yet we see the other side of him. It's unbelievable how he can be so humorous and make us laugh." Sue is impressed with him as a storyteller. She recalls his having told about what he said to someone who saw him coming off an elevator and mistook him for Colin Powell. Israel said, "Trust me, if I were Colin Powell, you wouldn't be this close to me!"

Candidate Eva D. Shue

Eva's younger brother, John, lived about an hour's drive from their mother. He provided the main care for his mother, giving her support and checking on her daily. He considers Eva his mentor in the faith and a model of Salvationism. He says, "My Christian faith is alive and well and always will be as an enduring legacy of the Army."

Eva's older brother, Bill, now retired, describes Eva as one of three sisters who often got the boys into trouble. It seemed there was a conspiracy of the sisters, as "All of a sudden, there's Dad, quoting what your sisters said, and that spells trouble for you."

Eva enjoyed life to the full. Her friends found her fun to be with. She had many talents and interests, including needlepoint, water aerobics, country–western music, roller skating, and of course a full program at the corps. Life in Sidney, Ohio was carefree and its days filled with adventures in friendship, varied activities and the maturing process.

GOD'S CALL

Eva Shue, like Israel, also heard God's call in a Salvation Army camp setting. At the age of 16, at the Army's Camp Glendale in southwest Ohio, during a weekend of camp meetings, Eva heard the voice of God calling her to service as a Salvation Army officer.

Two years later she filled out her candidate application for the 1962–63 "Heroes of the Faith" session. Her application identified her as a fifth–generation Salvationist, active in the total life of The Salvation Army corps in Sidney. She wrote that she attended open–air and indoor meetings, the youth programs, sold Christmas and Easter *War Crys*, prayed and testified in public, led singing, and owned and played a cornet. She was the assistant Sunbeam (a young girl's organization) leader, record sergeant, Young Peoples' Legion (a teen group) secretary, and a graduate Corps Cadet, having completed the six–year Bible study course.

Although totally involved in the corps, she had not experienced assurance of conversion until she was 17. "My definite conversion was only last November when the Lord spoke to me in a still, small way and I knew what I must do. So I went up and got saved."

"She complements Israel well, and together they make a first-rate leader team."

On the subject of holiness, she recorded, "I hadn't really thought much about sanctification until one of my friends who was going to training that year said, 'Eva, why don't you give your all, then I'd never have to worry about you because I'd know you have the seal of sanctification in your heart.' It wasn't that easy! I went forward and thought I had given God all there was of Eva Shue, but actually, I hadn't. It has been a long struggle these past couple of months, but with God's help I've succeeded, and He has all there is of Eva Shue."

She listed her conversion as having taken place at the Army in Sidney and identified "field" (working as an officer in a corps) as the branch of Army service that interested her the most. She wrote, "The main aim of The Salvation Army is to win souls. William Booth's idea was to help the needy, then get them saved."

Money earned as a "car hop" at a local restaurant was put in a saving account. So when she applied for training she could cover her entrance fee, travel expenses and incidentals.

To the question on "Efforts Made to Win Others to Christ," she recorded: "I haven't had much of an opportunity to win souls seeing as how I haven't been a Christian too long. But I've dealt with some of the young people in my corps while at the altar and the Lord has personally laid one individual on my heart. I've had many talks with her and I know that she is under conviction and one of these days I know she'll see the light."

Eva's brother Bill reflects, "We had some clue she was going to be an officer, by her attitudes, her relationships with people, always getting behind folk and nudging them in the right direction."

Her candidate application was signed Nov. 20, 1961, witnessed by her divisional youth secretary, Captain Wallace Conrath, and officially stamped "accepted" on Jan. 26, 1962.

Commissioner Todd Bassett recalls, "It was also my joy in earlier years to have been associated with Eva Gaither as a young person in the corps at Sidney, Ohio, where my parents were the corps officers. There has always been a radiant beauty that has shone forth from Eva's life."

She entered the School for Officer Training the same year as Israel, in September 1962. Of her cadet days she concludes, "It was a good time in my life, because of the people I met, and coming from a small town in Ohio to the big city of New York was absolutely incredible." She met and came to know Cadet Israel Gaither during their two years together in training, although the relationship never developed beyond that of being cadets in the same session.

This was the attractive, winsome, intelligent, and dedicated young woman who would soon capture Israel Gaither's heart. Her loveliness of person and spirit would cast a spell over him for which there was no cure! Little could either of them dream what God had in store for them, both of major challenges, and unparalleled adventures and fulfillment.

chapter 8

Against All Odds

*My grace is sufficient for you, for my power
is made perfect in weakness.*

2 Cor. 12:9

// **|** t was a time when it should not have happened—a black man interested in a white woman in the early 60s during the Civil Rights era,"
admits Israel Gaither of his courting Eva Shue. "No matter that it was
in the northeastern part of the country; it was not all that acceptable.

"We believed that God had brought our lives together and we understood
the test that it was for The Salvation Army, for there were no other interracial couples in the ranks of the Army as officers anywhere in the United
States. We didn't recognize the enormity of our relationship's impact on the
Army, nor what it would mean in the future. We continued our courtship,
knowing that we loved each other and believed that God had brought us
together."

THE RACIAL DIVIDE

Racism in the 1960s fomented a volatile mood in America. It penetrated society and even the church, so that 11 o'clock on Sunday morning became
known as "the most segregated hour in the week." Race provided quick
stereotypes; shaped where people lived and with whom they lived; determined where children went to school and which public facilities people could
use; and affected employment opportunity and access to wealth and health.

Race also entered into most people's choice of a marriage partner.
Race–mixing laws, prohibiting interracial marriage, had been passed by 30
states, and many stayed on the books until the Supreme Court threw them
out in 1967. Although these laws had not been passed in the northeastern
states, a prejudicial attitude toward interracial marriage existed there as well.
As Cornel West put it in the title of his 1994 book, "Race Matters."

People were torn along racial lines in the 1960s. In the South a black man could be lynched just for looking at a white woman. In the mid–60s a number of America's largest inner cities became infernos as race riots rocked America. In was at this time and in this milieu that Israel Lee Gaither and Eva D. Shue would apply to Army leadership for official engagement, as is the requirement for all Salvation Army officers.

One mixed–race Salvation Army cadet couple who, just a few years earlier, had sought to marry were quickly discouraged. The story is told poignantly by retired Captain Marilyn Chapman.

> In 1960 I entered the School for Officer Training in Chicago. There I met the man who was to become my husband. Near the end of the first year of training, after our relationship had been reported by a fellow cadet, we were called into the principal's office. (Just as a side note, Lionel and I were among the four oldest in our session.) Ostensibly it was on the basis of our having started a courtship, with the basic issue being that Lionel was black and I am white. The principal said there had been discussion and it was determined that there would not be any appointment where they could send us as an interracial couple. The other point brought up was whether we had considered what would become of our children if we had any. At that point we were asked not to have any contact with one another until a decision had been made. Within a day I was again called into the principal's office, with the Chief Secretary now present. I was told that I should pack and that my parents and the corps officer were on the way to pick me up. I was not allowed to say goodbye to Lionel since we had complied with their wishes and not been in contact. Within a few days after returning home, I learned that Lionel had been asked to leave the following day.

Following their summary dismissal, and encountering further discrimination and rejection within the Army, Lionel and Marilyn nonetheless married in December of 1961. The ceremony was performed by a friend because Army officers were not allowed to perform their ceremony, and in a friend's house, because Army property, even its churches, could not be used. Despite that treatment, the Chapmans maintained their active interest in the Army, sensing that officership was still God's call for their lives. After moving east to the New York area and rendering service as lay leaders, they were accepted in 1973 as auxiliary captains, initially a rank less than full captain not requiring the two–year training course, but that later can lead to the rank of a full captain.

The experience of the Chapmans throws a spotlight on the formidable obstacles to an officer's biracial marriage that the Gaithers had to overcome within the Army.

THE LEAP OF LOVE

In retrospect, it could seem Israel and Eva's life partnership was foreordained, when upon their commissioning as officers they were each appointed to the city of Pittsburgh, he to assist at Pittsburgh Northside Corps, and she to assist at the east side of Pittsburgh in the Homewood–Brushton Corps. Geography helped weave their destinies together through their respective officers–in–charge, Captains Garth and Irene Faulds at Northside, and Captain Joyce Herb at Homewood–Brushton. The officers were good friends who often visited with each other, and they included their assistants in their fellowship. The shared visits of their officers–in–charge enabled Israel and Eva's friendship to emerge. Thus began a relationship that would become a storied romance within The Salvation Army.

Young Lieutenant Eva came to appreciate her neighboring assistant officer's qualities. She found him "so kind and caring. I could easily talk to him. And he was always the perfect gentleman." Eva's warmth and friendliness, her inward as well as outward beauty, and her authenticity, all had irresistible appeal for Israel. Soon the two arranged for some rendezvous on their own—a drive in the country, an outing with nearby members of their session, and the occasional drive–in movie. A compatible and amiable friendship developed into a courtship.

They were keenly aware that they were crossing a strong dividing line in the culture of their day. As Eva looks back, she recounts, "Izzy and I both knew that our relationship would not be accepted by many of our Salvationist colleagues. But I must say that the loving response of others to our life together as husband and wife has been humbling and even overwhelming to both of us. We knew, without a doubt, that God had brought us together."

The developing relationship did not escape the attention of their divisional leader, Lt. Colonel John Waldron, who was acutely aware of the potential implications of a biracial marriage within officer ranks. So he placed them in appointments more than 200 miles apart. Only later would he reveal to them that the separation was to put their relationship to the test, to determine whether they would be prepared to go through the difficult days ahead of them as an interracial couple. But in the process, with "incredible phone bills," the distance between them only served to "make the heart grow fonder."

THE LEAP OF ACCEPTANCE

The Salvation Army and the public arena were not the only obstacles to be surmounted. The biracial courtship would prove difficult for the Shue family. They lived in conservative and primarily Caucasian southwest Ohio, which hugged the Mason–Dixon line, not far from Ku Klux Klan territory. In this area, as in the South, many people held antebellum views of black people, and mixed marriages were not just unknown but, to most people, unthinkable.

Eva recalls only one block in Sidney where African–Americans lived. She had one black friend in high school with whom she became close because the juxtaposition of their surnames in alphabetical order meant they often sat near one another in class. She says, "When now I look back, I realize how very important that was because it introduced me to a biracial friendship."

The time came for Eva to break the news to her family that she was in love with Israel, an African–American, and that they planned to marry. She readily admits, "I was scared to death to tell mother and father." She went home for a week, but kept putting off talking to them. On the final day of her visit, she knew she could delay no longer. When she announced her forthcoming betrothal, there was no joy. Eva's mother was openly angry; her father, although silent, turned ashen. Eva's delay until the last day to share her news with her parents further exacerbated the situation. The initial reaction of the family was nothing short of shock.

Young Eva that day traveled back to her appointment with a heavy heart. She says, "It was the most painful time we experienced in our officership." Tears accompanied her on the long return journey. Although a dark cloud had come over Eva's sky, a radiant rainbow would ultimately emerge from behind the dark shadows.

Eva's father was totally against the union. Her mother admits, "At first we were very upset; it was hard to accept. Today we would not want anyone to say anything bad. Izzy's the best." To the credit of the character of the Shue family, the son–in–law–to–be in later years would be able to say, "I never felt hostility, but only acceptance."

Brother Bill received a phone call from his mother, who announced, "Guess what!" Bill says, "At that moment, it caused quite a family uproar." Merle wanted to know what Bill was going to do about it. He responded, "If this is what she wants, there is little any of us can do to influence her at this point. If she makes up her mind to go this way, then nothing will change it." He talked to his pastor who advised him to be as supportive as he could.

But Bill did not attend the wedding. He did not meet Israel until 1999, more than 20 years after the marriage; the two had never been at the same place at the same time. He credits "Providence" for bringing Israel and himself together in Sidney at the time of his father's passing. Bill reflects, "Since meeting Izzy and getting to know him, I don't think Eva could have made a better choice for a life partner. He is a very talented, caring and genuine individual. I've been on Izzy's bandwagon ever since." His only complaint about his brother–in–law, he says, is that "sometimes I think his work ethic is a bit too driving!"

Eva's brother John said that when the news first broke, "It was a shock to the whole family. We had to overcome our resistance and learn to accept it.

Mom and Dad were very upset. After we came to know Israel, it was a lot different. I love Israel. He's a great guy. For the two of them to do what they have done, and what they will do, is amazing, and how they are spreading the Word of the Lord. We have seen Eva blossom with Izzy."

"Eva was accepted immediately into our family," Israel says, "and I into the Shue family. It was probably more difficult for the Shues given they had less contact in Sidney with black folk, but their love was immediately embracing, and I became a son. My father had a good chat with me some months prior to our wedding, when I indicated to him that I wanted to marry Eva. He talked to me about the reality of America in that era and what we might face. I can hear his voice calling me to understand that we had to live not only private lives but also public lives and that there could be rejection."

THE DILEMMA

The Salvation Army was not immune from the racial divide in the States. This was apparent in the appointments for black officers (referred to in that era as "colored").

Commissioner Ken Baillie, a friend and officer colleague of Israel and Eva during the time of their courtship, describes how the issue of the couple's engagement first emerged in Salvation Army circles.

> Lt. Colonel John Waldron wanted to mentor and encourage young officers and held twice a year Younger Officers Councils. We would suggest topics and speakers and he would give the nod. Like many Salvationists, especially young ones, we were forever wanting to remake the Army. Izzy was vocally in the middle of every discussion (as I was, truth be told). Eva remained more reticent, but when she spoke it was clear she had her own views and opinions.
>
> At one point Lt. Colonel Waldron called me aside, saying he wanted my opinion on something. That certainly got my attention. What young officer wouldn't be intrigued by his divisional commander asking for an opinion! In a side room he posed a question about Izzy and Eva. They had been dating for some time and had asked for official permission to get married. He observed forthrightly that their interracial relationship was potentially problematic and controversial, and he wanted to know what I thought about it.
>
> I recall asking him if they were successful in their individual officership. "Yes, definitely," he responded. "They are model officers."

"Then," I said, "I take it that the only—the only—question is the racial question."

"Yes," he replied.

"Then I don't think you have a choice," I said. "There is nothing I know in Orders and Regulations or Minutes which would make race a disqualifier for marriage."

The Salvation Army was not immune from the racial divide in the States.

That was a long time ago, when race was still an explosive issue in American life. The Civil Rights movement had started to push the envelope but interracial marriages were highly controversial. Izzy and Eva had been brave to date, and even braver to consider marriage. They were very much in love but they were not so star–struck as to be unrealistic or naive. They knew they faced all kinds of challenges. I recall clearly that their greatest concern was not for themselves but what their choice would impose on their children, who would have had no choice in the matter.

Lt. Colonel Waldron probed a little further, "What do you think the other officers will say?"

"I'm not sure I can speak for them," I replied. "But I can guess. Some older officers may be incensed. But our generation will be incensed only if the Army says no."

A faint smile curled at one side of his lips. "That's what I thought you'd say." And with that he got up and walked out. He never spoke of it again. But a few months later there was a marriage, and that marriage has lasted and prospered.

AN ADVOCATE EMERGES

Lt. Colonel Waldron, knowing of the painful struggle within the Shue family, made an unusual offer. It was gratefully accepted, and he, as Israel and Eva's divisional commander, traveled from Pittsburgh to Sidney, Ohio, in effect to be a "character witness" for Lieutenant Israel, whose integrity and leadership he discerned held great promise for the future. Merle Shue says that visit made the difference for the family and helped turn the tide for the couple struggling for acceptance of their relationship. Eva reflects, "I will always be indebted to John Waldron for that wonderful gesture. In the beginning it was very difficult for my family to accept the relationship—but they have over the years grown to love Izzy."

In The Salvation Army, husband and wife serve together as ordained and commissioned officers. This unique bonding and partnership in ministry has been one of the hallmarks and strengths of the movement. Consequently, single officers are required to file an application and receive approval for engagement and marriage.

On Aug. 31, 1966, Israel and Eva submitted their official Application for Engagement, along with a medical report, which was filed at Territorial Headquarters on Oct. 12, 1966. It brought out into the open what had up to this point been an unspoken, but ipso facto, non–acceptance of interracial marriage, both in society as a whole and within The Salvation Army. A biracial marriage had never before occurred, nor even been considered, among officers within the Army in the States. Some leaders thought that problems of finding suitable appointments and gaining community acceptance would hamper their ministry. During what would be an unusual extended period of processing, Israel and Eva were privately, albeit not officially, engaged.

In response to the application for approval of the proposed marriage, a letter from the chief secretary, second in command in the territory, on Feb. 15, 1967 to the divisional commander, Lt. Colonel John Waldron, advised that the matter of their marriage had been discussed at THQ "at great length and reviewed from every angle." Comments made reference to "problems that may face this fine young couple, including: (1) Mistreatment they may receive from some. (2) How well (if there are any) will their children be received? (3) We would want them to be aware, while it is not in keeping with Salvation Army thinking or practice, there may be some problems regarding their appointments. Some communities may not be prepared to accept them as leaders; however you can assure them we will do our best to place them where we believe they could render the greatest service to God and man."

What were viewed as extraordinary circumstances resulted in the highly unusual processing of a letter from THQ on the issue sent on Nov. 4, 1966, to International Headquarters (IHQ) in London. Lt. Colonel John Waldron entered his responses to some of the routine questions on the proposal.

> Question: Likely to succeed as a married officer? Response: Yes, if interracial nature of marriage does not lessen their acceptability, and if marriage is stable.
> Question: If marriage is agreed to later, are you prepared to recommend him/her for at least three appointments in your command? Response: Under normal circumstances would be glad to. However, this is his home division—might be better chance of success in totally new area. Some question whether mixed marriage would be accepted in Pittsburgh.
> Question: Your recommendation? Response: There seems to be no reason in O&R [Orders and Regulations] to decline

their request. Can only request approval with great care exercised in appointment.

Thus did their divisional commander "bite the bullet," in the midst of all the encountered concerns and resistance, with his recommendation for approval. No information is on file to record the response from IHQ.

On Jan. 11, 1967, the marriage proposal had been discussed with the territorial commander, with the following on record: "At this time the Territorial Commander mentioned there might be some family problems on both sides—progeny and complexions—and our inability to protect them from harm, hurt, malicious gossip or unkind speech, slights or worse. He also stated that no officer can be guaranteed goodwill or support in any city or town." The letter concluded: "Once they have been made aware of all the problems which may occur, we are ready to agree to the marriage of this fine young couple and wish you to assure them that we will be praying for them. We trust they will rededicate themselves to what may be an unusual challenge."

However, a letter from the field secretary (in charge of personnel matters) to the territorial commander revealed he was unalterably opposed to the marriage. Excerpts from his letter read: "I am attaching herewith the Application for Marriage forms, without my signature. In doing so I would like to reiterate the disastrous possibilities and effects which may result from this interracial marriage." Some concerns stated were "The influence upon other young people, cadets in training, other prospective officers and youth leaders. The ostracism which will be experienced. The long range consequences related to appointments, biracial children, etc., are endless."

That field secretary would, under normal circumstances, have been the one to give routine approval for the marriage. However the chief secretary, Colonel J. Clyde Cox, overrode the declination of the field secretary, and, in response to the advocacy of the young captains' divisional commander, Lt. Colonel John Waldron, signed his name approving the engagement and marriage. Some years later, he confided he had received hate mail from within the Army because of his advocacy and support for their marriage.

On Feb. 15, 1967, some five and a half months after submitting the initial application, official engagement was approved and the wedding date set for July 1, 1967 at the Pittsburgh North Side Corps. In a memorable ceremony, Israel's father, the Rev. Israel L. Gaither II, officiated, and the leader and friend who had made it all possible, Lt. Colonel John Waldron, led the service. Eva describes it as "a wonderful occasion shared by family, friends and session mates."

Lt. Colonel Waldron, in a letter of July 5, 1967, was quick to assure the territorial commander of the favorable response and outcome of the wedding. "The Northside Corps hall was well filled with friends, including most of the corps officers of this area. Mr. Shue escorted his daughter up the aisle.

Rev. Israel Gaither II performed the wedding ceremony.

A fine group of their session mates participated in the ceremony, and there was the usual air of festivity among them. Captain Gaither's father, Rev. Israel Gaither, officiated and handled it very nicely. As nearly as I can determine there have been no serious reactions."

"It was John Waldron," says Eva, "who played an immense role in the story of our married life." One of the Army's great visionaries, he became the second of the Lord's seven instruments for the enablement and progressive ministry of Israel Gaither within the ranks of The Salvation Army. The grateful couple later asked him to dedicate their two children, and many years later, Israel was invited to sing at John Waldron's funeral, attended by an overflow congregation in the chapel of his home corps in Oneonta, N.Y.

Mamie Podolsky, a soldier at Lieutenant Eva Shue's Homewood Corps, recalls the corps' support and response to their marriage proposal. "When they fell in love, we were very happy because they were both special to us, and what a joy it would be to have them as corps officers! We all knew that the challenges facing them were tremendous. There were not any interracial marriages in The Salvation Army at that time so they would be the pioneers. What faith! They took a lot of flack about their coming marriage, and our corps had all–night prayer meetings. They were both positive that God had called them into The Salvation Army and equally positive that God had put His seal of approval on their union. Their love and devotion for each other drew us in as a family, and as they submitted their request to marry, we fasted and prayed. We claimed the promise, 'No good thing will He withhold from them that walk uprightly' (Psalm 84:11). The request went through the chain of command all the way to International Headquarters. The final decision was left in Lt. Colonel John Waldron's hands, and he obeyed God and made the courageous decision. Victory!"

THE STILL ROCKY ROAD

The race issue, a most intractable divider of Christians, would not go away, even after Israel and Eva were married, with the blessing of The Salvation Army. He reflects, "In those early days it was not unusual for us to be together and not only feeling but seeing the stare of white folk as we moved around the community. There seemed to be more acceptance, though not entirely, in the African–American community." Israel shares a painful experience early in their officership.

> We experienced no overt racist attitudes within the Army but we knew they existed. We could feel it at times. There was one occasion when we returned to the School for Officer Training in the Bronx for our five–year review. During the interview with a key leader couple in territorial administration at that time, immediately on entering the room we could feel an animosity being directed at us. Literally everyone who had their interview prior to us extended their time—some significantly. The Spirit immediately moved me to be in control of my reactions, and I determined that I would not say anything except respond to questions. We took our places in seats in front of the desk. We couldn't see but had the feeling that the wife of the interviewing officer, sitting behind us, was communicating to her husband. The first few moments were extremely awkward, with dead silence, but I was determined that we would just wait to see what direction the conversation was going to take. The officer asked literally two meaningless questions that had nothing to do with our officer service and made no enquiry about our spiritual life or our marriage. Then he suddenly announced that the interview was over. We were not in the room more than five minutes.
>
> On exiting, Eva broke into tears. At that moment Colonel Peggy Hale, a highly respected single woman officer, was coming down the hall. She served at that time as the education secretary for the territory, and we knew her very well. She was one of the few officers during that time who was able to transcend racial divides. I see her now, coming toward us and embracing both of us with the question, 'What happened?' because she knew we had been in the interview. She took Eva aside to

comfort her and we made it through the rest of that week despite having experienced for the first time in the Army a feeling of hatred because of our interracial marriage.

Major and Mrs. Walter Bethel share the impact the Gaithers had upon them at the start of their Army ministry as well as the racism that persisted some years after their marriage. The Bethels went to the Army's training school six years after the Gaithers (1968–70) and were one of the first black married couples to enter that school in the Eastern Territory. For their 1969 summer assignment they were sent to the Pittsburgh Homewood Corps, where they would assist the Gaithers. Up to that time the Bethels had heard disparaging reports about the limited opportunities for black officers. "On commissioning weekend we met the Gaithers, the first biracial married couple in the Army," the major writes. "My wife and I did not go into culture shock or make a judgment call on their marriage. The Gaithers' marriage was not socially accepted in the black or white religious community. It was tolerated in the Army but not blessed by Army leadership. I had heard epithets about them, and I can only imagine how hard it must have been at that time being a black officer with a white wife and the battles they faced. When the Gaithers stepped into our lives, it was the beginning of the leadership we needed; the Lord knew this and sent them our way. They planted the seeds in our lives on how to serve the Lord in a black corps and among the people that were hurting. This summer assignment with the Gaithers prepared my wife and me for the Lord's work for the next 33 years."

The racial issue, in ways often unknown to the Gaithers, continued to haunt their career. Only in more recent times did they discover an exchange of correspondence that had taken place when, early in their career, they had been proposed as divisional youth leaders. A letter from the divisional commander where they would serve to the field secretary for personnel at the territorial level exposes the undercurrent of racial discrimination the Gaithers had to overcome.

I must confirm my initial reaction that this appointment would be totally unacceptable and would add complications to our administrative processes. In my judgment the mixed marriage would not be acceptable to the majority of our officers and soldiers and would, in fact, intensify the concerns of parents over relationships that might lead to comparable situations. This is still at the heart of much racial misunderstanding, and this fear is not about to go away. The proposed appointment might give encouragement to young people to pursue relationships that would cause great anxiety to their parents as well as threaten their future happiness and well–being. It must be remembered that there are only three corps predominantly composed of black Salvationists in this division. Soldiership of the other (37) corps is predominantly white and in many of our corps there are almost no blacks participating. Progress has been made in our racial relationships. This appointment could jeopardize this progress. The proposed appointment would not enable us to achieve the very considerable potential of our youth program. I therefore strongly urge that this proposal be withdrawn and must strongly indicate my unwillingness to accept this appointment to my divisional staff.

That appointment never took place. Instead the Gaithers were appointed divisional youth leaders in another division, Greater New York, where they received a ready welcome from Lt. Colonel Walter French and his staff and achieved high success in their leadership.

A friend of the Gaithers, Lt. Colonel Barbara Van Brunt, shares from a later period another incident involving a racial affront, to which Israel responded with a humorous twist. "The editor of our newspaper in Indiana, Pa., where we were corps officers, invited us to the Ice Capades in Pittsburgh and told us we could bring two friends. He took us to the top of one of the big buildings in Pittsburgh, to the Press Club Restaurant. We invited Izzy and Eva, never realizing that they didn't normally entertain black people at the restaurant. It became apparent that they weren't waiting on us as they were the people at nearby tables. To make a joke of the situation, Izzy got up, put a cloth napkin over his arm, and began serving our coffee and tea. We all had a good laugh and enjoyed the entire evening." Israel Gaither had long ago learned the secret that a sense of humor can redeem many an otherwise delicate situation.

The "racial divide," although now crossed by Israel and Eva, still separated African–American Salvationists from an equal role in Army leadership. For The Salvation Army, the biracial marriage was not the only issue. There were few black officers, and limited opportunities when it came to places to serve. Those places were so few, Israel says, that in those days, "you could chart the appointments of a black officer."

Racist policies and actions were emerging as points of focus within the Army just as they were being confronted in the world beyond the Army in America. Lt. Colonel B. Barton McIntyre, at that time the leading black officer in America, was a noted evangelist, who with his wife, made a significant impact in the territory. He was in charge of the famed Harlem Temple Corps and had the idea that it might be good if all the black officers in the territory could meet together during a forthcoming commissioning weekend. Black officers had not had opportunity to come together to review issues that would have an impact on them as citizens as well as Salvation Army officers. Israel was enlisted to help along with two other black officers—Captain Noel Christian and Major Abraham Johnson.

When the request was made of the territorial administration to conduct the gathering, the response made clear that it would not be officially approved or recognized; no official funds were to be used and there would be no support from territorial administration. Israel writes, "It was a devastating response, but we went ahead with the meeting, and the dialogue during that weekend launched the beginning of the transformation of long–held ideas and policies that clearly marginalized the nonwhite sector of Salvationists in the territory. It launched a change in attitude and policies related to ministry among minorities in the Eastern Territory. The McIntyres and the Johnsons of that day made it possible for the Gaithers and the black officers of today to be used in significant ways to further the Kingdom through the mission of the Army, and I salute them."

THE ENDURING LIFE PARTNERSHIP

The Gaithers' matrimonial bliss would not be without the normal post–honeymoon adjustments. As Israel and Eva moved into their quarters, Eva assumed her husband would carry out the trash because her Dad had always done that job. She soon discovered that Izzy did not automatically do that. She began placing the trash in strategic places; nothing worked until she put the bag right in front of the door as he was going out. He then got the message.

Almost 40 years into their marriage, Eva affirms, "Without a doubt Izzy has been the biggest influence on my life and helped to mold me into the person I am today. He is not only my husband and my life partner, but he is also my best friend. We enjoy life—doing things together.

"This became even more important when we moved to South Africa. We stepped out of the airplane into a new country, a new culture, where we did not know one person. It was just the two of us in those early months. And it was then that Izzy began doing some things, like shopping for groceries with me, that he had never done before. He would take me places where previously I would have driven myself. And I fell in love with Izzy all over again."

Life is lived forward, but understood backward. At the time, Israel and Eva were not cognizant of the internal difficulties relating to their marriage and appointments, most of which came to light during the writing of this biography. Israel says, "It's probably best we did not know for it may have discouraged us in our officership." In the long run the racial issue strengthened and contributed to their marriage. They were early led to pray about their relationship and become more certain of their love. The racial issue deepened relationships with friends who stood with and by them through the years. It paved the way for how they would enter into other people's situations and struggles. As a result, the bond between them became ever stronger and unbreakable.

"AGAINST ALL ODDS"

Anita Brown shares from her friendship and observation of the Gaithers as they "defied the odds." She writes, "As divisional youth leaders they defied the odds in my young African–American mind. They were an interracial couple serving in a predominantly white organization during a time when society and people were struggling to find a common bond because racial tensions were extremely high. I finally understand why it is this man, who has been my brother in Christ for more than 30 years, is a mentor and model of Christian ministry to me. His honesty, humanity, spirituality, integrity, compassion, passion, and love are all a faith–driven thing that comes directly from the hand of our Lord to the very heart and soul of his servant. I finally understand why he was able to look past racism and right into the eyes of his Savior. I finally understand why soldiers and officers from every corner where he has served, respond favorably to the mention of his name."

Colonel Joy Cooper, who served as secretary to Commissioner Eva Gaither when she and her husband were appointed to International Headquarters, offers another discerning observation.

> They rocked the boat when they fell in love. The first black and white USA officers to be married. What a good job the Army in the States had the wisdom to sanction the union. Even so, I understand that the going was tough in the early days, and not all officers looked kindly on the young couple.
>
> The white, pretty, fair rose and the dark, handsome hero. Would it work? Against all the odds? It did, because they sought His permission and approval.
>
> Theirs is a deep, true love. As Eva's personal assistant, I have witnessed them keeping the romance alive, with roses from him and special meals from her. Secret outings arranged by him (which I have had a part in) and thoughtful gifts from her.
>
> I well remember one of the first objects Eva unpacked and placed in her office when she arrived at IHQ was an exquisite china figurine, of a little white girl and a little black boy sitting on a seat, entitled "Perfect Harmony."
>
> They showed respect for each other, always considering each other's needs and feelings. They were truly in love and an example of a happy marriage to all who knew and worked with them.
>
> How was this possible in these days of shallow and broken marriages? Because it was GOD–ORDAINED.

chapter 9

First Steps of a Long Journey

*Do the work of an evangelist, discharge
all the duties of your ministry.*
2 Timothy 4:5

srael Gaither's Salvation Army career and ministry had a fortuitous, and no
doubt a providential launching. His 1963 summer cadet assignment, between the two years of training, from June 5 through mid–August, was at
Brooklyn Citadel, at that time one of the premier corps of The Salvation
Army. It hosted a full array of local officers (lay leaders) and musical forces,
then under the leadership of one of the Army's finest officer couples,
Captains Robert and Alice Watson.

The officers' small living quarters already included Lieutenant Judy
Lowers (Lt. Colonel Judy LaMarr) along with the Watsons' two children.
Cadet Israel was housed in the corps building, but often at the Watson home
for meals and times of fellowship.

The cadet and the captain spent time visiting the people of the corps and
worked together on every aspect of corps life. Robert Watson describes his
assistant as "capable and anxious to learn. In addition to an excellent working relationship, we formed a personal friendship that has lasted through the
years."

Cadet Gaither's apprenticeship in this setting proved to be a major season
of growth. "Brooklyn Citadel was a tremendous learning experience," he
says. "Captain Watson was a superb model of an officer. The corps was thriv-
ing, with many Newfies (Newfoundlanders). Corps Sergeant–Major (primary lay leader) Baxter Wheeler cared for me in a very practical way. It was
a new type of corps setting and experience, including a corps with a band and
songsters. The captain tutored and was most helpful to me."

One experience brought on some trepidation for the summer cadet. He
and Lieutenant Lowers were on an official trip in the corps station wagon
when another car went through the traffic light and badly damaged their ve-

hicle. "How I dreaded to make that call," Israel remembers, "calling Captain Watson and telling him we were involved in an accident with the corps vehicle. But when I called, his first response was, 'Izzy, are you okay. Is Judy okay?' The Captain got out of his sickbed at the time and came right away to pick us up." This "good captain" would surface again in significant ways during Israel's pilgrimage within the Army.

THE FIRST PITTSBURGH APPOINTMENT

On June 10, 1964, Israel Gaither was commissioned and ordained a Salvation Army officer and received his first appointment as assistant officer at Pittsburgh Northside Corps, with corps officers Captain and Mrs. L. Garth Faulds. One of the new lieutenant's first duties was to organize and lead the summer daily Vacation Bible School program. That he did, and its success merited the first published account of his Army activity, in the national *War Cry* of Oct. 3, 1964. It reported, along with a photo of the enterprising lieutenant with the young people, that 163 children had been enrolled with almost 100 receiving attendance awards, and an average attendance of 116 per day. Someone obviously had done an effective promotion, and had led the program successfully, even to the keeping of detailed statistics. Captain Faulds gave credit where credit was due, including in the article the statement: "Lieutenant Israel Gaither, assistant officer, directed the school."

The most important happening in the young lieutenant's life while at Pittsburgh Northside were the circumstances that brought him into proximity with Lieutenant Eva Shue. In that setting, their friendship was born, their destinies collided, ultimately to seal a memorable life partnership within The Salvation Army.

The leadership qualities of the young lieutenant did not escape the discerning eye of the divisional commander, Lt. Colonel John D. Waldron. He needed an officer for a special assignment, that of developing and opening a new corps in Aliquippa, Pa., where a corps had closed more than 80 years earlier. Lieutenant Israel Gaither seemed the right person for the job—he had initiative, was personable, and had vision and dedication. So, after a full year at Pittsburgh Northside, he received "marching orders" to go on June 30, 1965, across town to the Western Pennsylvania Divisional Headquarters, where he was assigned to "Special Work."

CHALLENGE IN ALIQUIPPA

Lieutenant Gaither inauspiciously arrived at Aliquippa in an old Chevy carryall. The town had been served by a Salvation Army Service Unit, comprising local volunteers who provide limited but helpful response to individuals in need. The lieutenant's mandate was to upgrade its status to a corps. There was no congregation, no budget, no building, nothing but a committee of a few volunteers and a lieutenant's dedicated initiative.

The enterprising Lieutenant rented a small room in a low–cost hotel, and in his high–collar uniform in the middle of a July summer, started out by walking up and down Main Street, meeting the business people and greeting people on the street. It was not long before Aliquippa knew that the Army had come to town.

Next, he found a former funeral home for sale and arranged for the Army to purchase it. In the exploring of its obscure nooks there was found a box of ashes. From that cadaverous setting, the lieutenant sought to birth and give life to a Salvation Army corps. Programs for youth were started, attracting some 40 to 50 teenagers with table games and other activities. The older teenagers, who came from working class families, became helpful assistants to the lieutenant. Major Ruby Smith from divisional headquarters, began a women's Home League program. Some families who attended the Army in nearby Rochester but lived in Aliquippa, transferred their membership when they saw that the Army had come to their home town.

> The impact of Lieutenant Israel Gaither had a wider sphere of influence beyond his immediate post.

The confidence of Lt. Colonel Waldron in his fledgling lieutenant's leadership was rewarded, just one year later, with the celebration on June 1, 1966, of the official opening of the Aliquippa, Pa., Corps. Lieutenant Israel Gaither was appointed its first corps officer. The Aliquippa Corps continues to this day, and many years later when the Gaithers returned from South Africa to the USA Eastern Territory as territorial leaders, soldiers Israel had pastored in Aliquippa were among those who welcomed them.

No one was more proud of Israel's achievement than his parents. His mother kept all the news clippings, saying, "I kept everything, you know how a mother is." She says, "My husband always said to Israel Lee, 'You are going to go way up some day.'"

Lieutenant Israel Gaither's life and ministry at that time already had a wider sphere of influence than his immediate post. Major Charles Kelly, then a teenager, recalls, "The first time I met Lieutenant Gaither was at a Teen Bible Camp at Camp Allegheny. I noticed that while he was all business teaching his classes, he had a more relaxed attitude with a group of young officers when playing a lively card game of Rook each night after the camp-fire program. I was surprised when later he showed up on a team of officers who were playing a 'challenge' game of basketball against the boys' staff. The lieutenant had a pretty hot outside jump shot, and the game gave me another look at the camaraderie that these young officers had, on and off the court. My lifestyle at the time was causing inner conflict with a growing sense of the call of Christ on my life. Inwardly, I was led to aspire for the type of lifestyle and camaraderie that I had seen displayed by Lieutenant Gaither, who was serious about life's priorities, while at the same time indulging in its fun and fellowship. Years later I realize that this encounter became a defining moment in my spiritual journey, ultimately leading me to embrace the balanced lifestyle he exemplified and to which Christ was calling me."

Return to Pittsburgh

Meanwhile, Lieutenant Eva Shue was making her own mark as a corps officer, first in charge of Erie Temple, a Scandinavian corps. While there, adding to her talent of playing the alto horn and cornet, she learned to play the guitar. Her interest in bowling led to organizing a bowling team in the corps. Her second appointment in charge, Pittsburgh Homewood–Brushton Corps, at which she had previously been an assistant officer, was a predominantly black congregation in inner–city Pittsburgh. Ironically, Israel in opening the corps in Aliquippa, had a predominantly white constituency.

One of the concerns that Army leaders had was where the young couple could be appointed once they were married. In fact, there had been the not–so–subtle suggestion during the process leading up to the approval of the marriage that there "may not be many appointments for you in your officer service." Israel reflects, "How wrong they were! In all of the interviews and times of counsel, we remained in prayer, just seeking the will of God, and we believed that it was His intention that we serve together as husband and wife as officers."

Following their exchange of marriage vows, Lieutenants Israel and Eva Gaither returned to the Homewood–Brushton Corps on June 28, 1967, to serve as corps officers. This would be the second of what ultimately would be four appointments for Israel and Eva in Pittsburgh. When they left for their honeymoon, Eva was the corps officer, and ten days later, when they returned to Pittsburgh Homewood, as was *de rigueur* in those days, Israel, as the man, became the primary corps officer, a unique challenge to Eva in their first years of marriage and corps appointment.

Lieutenant Eva quickly found that life would now be different from what it had been when she was in charge of the corps by herself. The main office Eva once occupied now became the private office of Israel, and he took custody also of keys to the official station wagon. Lt. Colonel Barbara van Brunt, session mate and bridesmaid, describes one incident that occurred during this adjustment period. "Eva had been the corps officer of the Homewood Corps at the time of their marriage, and then Izzy became the corps officer. One day shortly thereafter he dropped her off for a doctor's appointment and said he would pick her up. Well, he was quite late. Eva was standing outside the doctor's office impatiently waiting and contemplating that just a short time ago she was the corps officer, had the car and the money, and now she was stranded, no car and not a dime in her pocket to make a call. However, I knew she wouldn't want to be anything but Izzy's wife and through the years they worked out those little adjustments of the early days."

LASTING IMPRESSIONS

Corps Officer Israel Gaither, as he had with Major Kelly, left a lasting impact on another person by a seemingly simple act, this time upon a soldier (lay person) in the Army. The Gaithers had invited the Harlem Temple Band for a series of engagements at their corps, and among the young members who came was Ken Burton. He tells about that visit, a defining moment in his life. "One of my most impressive meetings with Israel Gaither was at a time when he did not even know me personally. He knew me to be a member of the Harlem Temple Corps band and that was it. It was around 1971. The band was the weekend guest at the Pittsburgh Homewood Corps. I was a teenager at the time and taking in all the Army had to offer. Although my grandparents were officers, I did not attend the Army until I joined the band at the age of 13.

"I was just really enjoying the trips, as young bandsmen tend to do. This young Captain got on our bus as we were about to depart to thank us for coming. He became emotional and spoke of how important our witness as bandsmen/musicians is and always will be. Also, of the work we had just completed over the weekend as God's work and how God had moved among the people. His talk on the bus that Sunday evening in Pittsburgh has remained with me to this day, and every time I play my horn or sing or conduct a note of God's music, I realize that it is for God's glory and not mine, to save others and to enhance the Kingdom of God."

Ken Burton, OF

Ken Burton went on from that defining moment to become, in

Israel Gaither's words, "truly one of the Army's outstanding lay leaders." Through the years he has given faithful service at Harlem Temple Corps, as bandmaster, corps sergeant–major and chorus leader. Honors accorded him include the William Booth Award, and Eastern Territory Man of the Year, an honor that was presented to him by General Eva Burrows. In 1978 he became director of the highly successful New Sounds for Christ contemporary gospel group. The capstone of his recognitions came in 2004 when he received the Army's highest recognition for service, when named to the Order of the Founder. Ken Burton's vision and commitment had been given a major spark by a young captain's powerful words and prayer on the bus. That man became his model—and friend—through the years. Ken Burton's endorsement of this biography graces the back cover of this book.

Mamie Podolsky, a former soldier of the Homewood Corps, tells of the ministry of her former Homewood former corps officers.

> Lieutenant Eva Shue had been appointed to our corps before her marriage. She came with all the fire of a new Lieutenant, a little slip of an officer on a mission for God. She opened her heart to us and we opened ours to her. She became my role model even though she was a few years my junior. There was nothing she wouldn't do for you if she could, including helping to move furniture. She was also a prayer warrior.
>
> Captain Israel Gaither came to the Homewood Corps, which was housed in a two–story building with a storefront. The second floor had been the officers' quarters, which was also used for the women's Home League and programs; the basement was the youth center. Under their leadership we were blessed with many children and outgrew these facilities. As programs expanded and attendance exceeded the limited facilities, the Captain arranged to purchase adjacent buildings to accommodate and further expand the Army's programs.
>
> From the beginning Lieutenants Shue and Gaither had a special place in my heart. They became not only a brother and sister in Christ but also role models and mentors. After the wedding they became our corps officers. Under their leadership the corps grew significantly, with young adults, several cadets, including Carmilla Gaither, the captain's sister. You name the activity; we had it—a tremendous midweek praise meeting, prayer and Bible study, Junior and Senior Songsters, Home League, plus all the community center activities, open–air meetings with flag and drum and the half–nights of prayer. We laughed, cried and prayed together. The captains not only preached holiness; they lived it. We were instructed in the wearing of the uniform as a testimony of a clean heart. I

wish I were eloquent with words so I could do justice to these two wonderful servants of the Lord.

AMID THE RACE RIOTS

Pittsburgh would not escape the rampant destruction and devastation of the race riots that erupted across America in the 1960s. Nor would the corps officer of Homewood be spared the smoke and fire of the suffering of those days. The May 18, 1968, *War Cry* published a photo and story of Captain Israel Gaither during the racial uprising in the city. The photo showed him packing and sorting food with volunteers, with this caption: "Many hands make light work for Captain Israel Gaither during racial disturbance in Pittsburgh. Salvation Army was a major source of food supply in Hill District." Another photo was captioned: "Captain Israel Gaither supervises sorting and packing of food." Army publications were not the only ones to take notice. The following article in a Pittsburgh newspaper was titled, "The Pittsburgh Story—People Helping People."

> Salvation Army canteens began rolling with the outbreak of violence. The presence of these Army vehicles in the midst of the debris and disaster was a welcome sight to weary firemen, police and National Guardsmen. Firebombed supermarkets and food stores meant a food crisis for residents and recalcitrants alike. The Salvation Army began to marshal its resources to become the major food supplier on the Hill during the emergency. The impact of Negro officers and Salvationists who manned food distribution centers will long be remembered. The Pittsburgh Story is a story of people helping people.
>
> Captain Israel Gaither, the corps officer at the Homewood Corps, was one of the Army's suppliers of goodwill and groceries in the riot area. A man who knows how to "keep his cool," the Captain's quiet efficiency earned him the respect of the Hill District residents. Women officers on DHQ staff led by Mrs. Lt. Colonel Waldron made 20,000 sandwiches in one day. That's a lot of dough! And Army personnel were waiting for the bread to come out of the ovens at the bakery. That's fresh! Teams came from Cleveland, ARC [Adult Rehabilitation Center] and other corps.
>
> "Well done! That's the least anyone could say of Salvation Army service during the recent racial disturbance in Pittsburgh.
>
> "Enough coffee was served to float the proverbial battleship! And who cares to disprove that the slices of bread that went into sandwiches alone were not enough to pave every

street in the Hill District where the violence was concentrated? It's common knowledge that the Army moved a mountain of supplies up on the Hill, but logistics are inadequate indicators of the power of love that made the supplies palatable.

Mamie Podolsky says of the captain's ministry during the riots, "My Dad died the same night Martin Luther King was killed. This sparked the civil disorders in Pittsburgh. It was a difficult time for everyone, especially my mother. There were uprisings and fires in our city and we were literally cut off from my mother's church and pastor. But not from Captain Gaither. Mom was not a soldier but he made his way to her home. There was a knock on the door, and when she opened it there stood Captain Gaither with his cap in his hand. He walked into her heart, made trips to her home to be a comfort and pray with her." Mamie adds, "Mom eventually became a soldier. We had times of sweet fellowship and Mom asked Captain Gaither to promise to preach at her funeral, which he did."

Israel watched from the Hill, where he lived, the inferno below that blazed from the buildings torched in the riots. The National Guard literally camped around the corps building. He witnessed fellow African–Americans who, out of frustration, were destroying and hurting their own community in random acts of violence. He himself felt a combination of fear, sadness and anger. This firsthand experience responding to those caught up in the riots seared its lesson on his psyche. He reflects, "It accentuated how deep was the divide [on[racial issues in our cities. This experience committed me more deeply to urban ministry." How often the Lord teaches his deepest lessons in the crucible of suffering!

A Soldier's Remembrance

How did the Gaithers fare in this their first appointment as married corps officers? What standards and foundations of their future officership emerged? How did they relate with their people? One of their soldiers from that time, Rev. Sharon Harper, now herself a minister, answers those questions from her perspective today.

> I first met Lieutenant and Mrs. Gaither in my early teens when they were our corps officers at the Homewood Corps. They both taught the people of the corps the art of love and compassion. Mrs. Gaither worked very closely with me and taught me that the most important qualities in leadership are love, understanding and hard work. She taught me how to play the tambourine and the importance of each movement and beat. We became the best, ministering in jails, nursing homes,

church services and open–air meetings. Mrs. Gaither made sure each child had proper uniform and that it was worn appropriately. She took notice of those of us that were unable to pay for the uniforms and gave us jobs to earn money to pay for them.

The Gaithers gave me a solid foundation. We were taught to memorize Scriptures, have daily prayer and devotions, how to lead a meeting and prepare a meditation, the importance of offering. and many more leadership qualities. Mrs. Gaither is an excellent speaker and always spoke words of encouragement; even when she was scolding us for something, there was an underlining layer of love. I can remember thinking that I wanted to be just like her. Captain Gaither spoke with such authority and power that I also wanted to be just like him. Even now, if you look at the way that I minister, you will see the two of them in me.

At the age of 14 I acknowledged the call of God in my life and immediately Captain and Mrs. Gaither began training me for ministry. I was given my own Sunday School class to teach and was taught how to prepare and lead in worship. Captain and Mrs. Gaither took me under their wings and taught me what lifestyle evangelism is all about.

When I was 15, Captain Gaither sat all of the teens down and spoke candidly about dating and the importance of choosing the right mate. He had us write down the qualities we desired in a mate, and then prayed with us. Years later when I called him to preside over my wedding, his first question was, "Does he have all of the qualities that you wrote down?" I had forgotten about that exercise, but when he arrived at my home he pulled the questionnaire out of his Bible and read off each item. My husband–to–be had all of the items on that list, and as of today we have been happily married for 32 years.

When I was in a college program, he would drive out of his way each Sunday to pick me up for Sunday school and church. During our drive he would encourage me to share the Gospel with my classmates, always talking about sharing the love of Jesus with everyone. His famous words to me when he dropped me off would be, "You may be the only Bible that your friends read." Those words followed me not only to school, but through life.

Captain Gaither always stressed the importance of holiness. I saw this not only at the corps but in his home also. Looking back at the times that I observed him during devotions, I realize that it was not a ritual; it was an encounter with our God.

There was another side to Captain Gaither that not many people could see. I had the privilege of being the babysitter for their first child, Michele. It was funny to watch him be intimidated by something so little. He seemed to be afraid of breaking her or something. It was strange seeing a man that was so in control and confident melt at the sound of an infant's cry. Watching him interact with her let me know that the "man of steel" was human.

The Gaithers have been a very special part of my life from youth until now. We have shared tears as well as laughs. We have shared physical food at well as spiritual food. When you get right down to the core of the life of Israel L. Gaither you find a man that gives honor to God and The Salvation Army.

In the very initial days of their officership, the Gaithers had a laser focus on mission and, by their love and leadership, planted seeds in the hearts of people they touched that blossomed into fruitful lives and service for the Lord.

chapter 10

The Making of a Leader

T he Gaithers' model of success in corps growth and ministry led to their appointment to one of the major corps responsibilities in the Army's Eastern Territory. On Jan. 27, 1971, they were appointed to Brooklyn Bedford Stuyvesant, commonly known as "Bed–Stuy." Here they would start out with an adequate and functional facility, a supportive constituency of local officers and musical forces, and a church that had an established position in the community. Bed–Stuy's congregation was mainly black, a rich ethnic mix of African–Americans and Salvationists who had come from Barbados, Jamaica and Guyana. In addition to the pastoral leadership, the Gaithers would be administrators for one of the Army's largest community centers in the New York City area.

"A Bit of Disquiet"

Lt. Colonel William LaMarr describes the Bedford Corps soldiers as "having a real sense of ownership. The young age of Israel Gaither was an issue to this corps accustomed to seasoned officers. There was also the issue of safety, interracial concern amid a psyche of riots in that community. But Izzy could overwhelm you with his competency. Those issues became secondary because people quickly realized he was a leader."

Even in this corps, with its black constituency and many of Caribbean descent, the issue of race emerged. The divisional commander, Lt. Colonel Walter C. French, encountered "opposition from several quarters, including the corps, when the appointment was announced. Soldiers of Bedford did not want a mixed–racial couple as an example; they did not want their black men marrying white women."

Captain Gaither's former corps officer trainer, Major Robert Watson, was now second in command in the division, and he was dispatched to the corps for discussion and prayer with the soldiery. Learning of the high quality of pastoral leadership the Gaithers would bring, and making it a matter of prayer, the Bedford soldiers were ready to welcome and give unqualified support to their newly appointed leaders. Robert Watson summarizes: "There was a bit of disquiet on the part of a few comrades of the corps when they learned they were receiving an interracial couple as corps officers, but it did not take long for Izzy and Eva to win their hearts and respect."

The Bedford corps had long operated on what was known as "colored people's time." Meetings would start late, end late; a laissez–faire approach to the clock. But the divisional leaders observed that "in short time after the Gaithers arrived, they had everything going on time and in order." On one Sunday the divisional leaders accompanied General and Mrs. Frederick Coutts as guests at Bedford. Lt. Colonel French, wanting to be prepared for whatever idiosyncrasies might prevail, asked the corps officer how the timing would work out. "Everything is fine, Colonel, all is going to be right on time," the young corps officer replied confidently. French reports, "The corps officer had the schedule so well organized; it all went as clockwork!"

Majors Allan and Marjorie Wiltshire recall important facets of the Gaithers' ministry at Bedford. "Brigadier Lebert Bernard, predecessor of the Gaithers at Brooklyn Bedford, had successfully encouraged a number of former Salvation Army officers from the Caribbean who had moved into the New York area to start a 'Former Officers' Fellowship' attached to their corps. These Salvationists took an active leadership role in the corps and were helpful in conducting meetings and revivals, and visitation. The Gaithers continued to minister to this group and encourage their unique ministry to God and the Army. They were responsive to his powerful preaching of the Word and faithful pastoral ministry and gave substantial support to the corps program."

Making a Difference

Captain Gaither, with a corps music group, conducted special meetings in Washing-ton, D.C., hosted by then–Captains Allan and Marjorie Wiltshire. When it was learned that the Wiltshires had requested a move from the Southern to the Eastern Territory, Captain Gaither and Lt. Colonel French were instrumental in negotiating the transfer in 1980. For the next 20 years until retirement, the Wiltshires and their family made a vital contribution in the Eastern Territory. Their daughter Margaret became one of the premier singers of the Army world. Later, with her husband, Captain David Davis, the couple would make a valued leadership contribution as officers in the territory. The Wiltshires acknowledge, "We owe a debt of gratitude to Izzy and Colonel Wally French for giving us the opportunity that helped us maximize our potential for ministry."

Shortly after the Wiltshires arrived at their first appointment in the East at Brooklyn Brownsville Corps, they organized a musical program featuring the musical groups Youth Unlimited from Washington and Ken Burton's New

Captains Gaither with YPSM Vida Gordon and
CSM Clement Jones

Sounds for Christ from the Harlem Temple Corps. Captain Gaither was chairman for the event. Allan Wiltshire records: "The young people did such a remarkable job in praising God. In retrospect, I believe that God gave Izzy a glimpse of what the future would hold for these young people in music ministry. He called both groups forward on that occasion and dedicated them to the ministry of God. It was a very moving time of consecration, for the Holy Spirit moved on the hearts of the young people and they responded by consecrating themselves to the Lord." A quarter of a century later the New Sounds for Christ holds the distinction as the longest–standing contemporary music group in the Army, with a national and international ministry.

One of the major achievements within the Bedford Corps during the Gaither years involved the Boy Scouts. Salvation Army corps often ran Scouting programs, and Bedford produced 19 Eagle Scouts, a number that may well represent a record for a Salvation Army center. The award is the highest in Boy Scouting and reflects excellence in both skills and character. Captain Gaither credited this outstanding achievement to his Scoutmaster, Clement Jones.

"LIKE ONE OF OUR OWN"

Lucille Grierson, who served at the Bedford Corps as leader of the youth singers and assistant young people's sergeant–major, remembers her corps officer with affection: "He is like my son. From the first day of our welcome to him, his messages were so powerful with lots of Bible references. I made a notebook of them. The song before his first message was, 'Fill my cup, Lord.' When he sang, the tears would come to him, and often in his preaching as well. He told us in one of his messages that when he was 4 years old, he ran to the platform where his father was preaching and said, 'Daddy, I want to help you preach.' His father put his hand on his shoulder and said, 'One day, my son, you will preach.' When you brought anything to him, he would say, 'Let's pray about it'—anything at all. It was a sad day when they left; it was like a funeral. Since becoming a commissioner, he doesn't think of himself too highly. He came off the platform at Star Lake during 2004 Labor Day Weekend meetings to meet the Bedford folk. He is like one of our own, a brother to us."

Ashley Crummey adds to the chorus of appreciation from the Gaithers' former Bedford soldiers. "We never had to make an appointment to see him. When he came to Torchbearers (16–30 age group), he was like an actor, played musical chairs, got right down to their level. He was a dynamic preacher, a Baptist preacher in Salvation Army uniform. No one was dozing when he preached. Visitation was done every Friday night when he socialized with young adults, a fellowship with couples. Mrs. Gaither was a strong leader; worked well with children, very friendly, willing to step in and help in the kitchen."

Olga Jacobs remembers a twofold attribute of her corps officer. "He was a man filled with the Spirit of God, and who was very firm too. You had to follow the rules."

Clotilde Gordon records, "God certainly smiled on the Bedford Temple Corps, when in 1971, he appointed two young captains, Israel and Eva Gaither, as pastors/administrators. Israel Gaither was an officer *par excellence*. He reverently magnified the name of Jesus, served humbly but vibrantly. The corps chapel was considered as holy ground, especially the penitent form (altar) and platform. He could be seen kneeling there, alone with his God, especially before the holiness meeting began, rededicating himself. This young captain was certainly chosen and anointed by God. How else could he have been such an outstanding Christian pastor and leader at such a young age! When he was here the anointing fell on this place over and over again."

> *"He could be seen kneeling there, alone with his God, especially before the holiness meeting began, rededicating himself."*

Lillian James was another soldier at Bed–Stuy under the Gaithers. "Captain Gaither was a no–nonsense spiritual leader. He was a strict, dedicated, loyal, intelligent and committed Christian, who always strived for the best in all of his endeavors. The captains worked diligently, relentlessly and upheld the highest standards of the Army for themselves and their comrades. Captain is a great holiness teacher. As I sat under his leadership and shepherding, I was blessed and I grew immensely in my Christian walk. Eva Gaither is an able and diligent assistant to her husband in the uplifting of the

Army's mission. They complement each other well. She performs her duties in a very professional and Christlike way. My family and I value their friendship more than we could possibly express."

Israel Gaither himself reflects, "I couldn't wait for Sunday morning when we had a full day at the corps." For him, preaching the Word, feeding his flock, was serious and sacred business. In preparation for his Sunday preachment, he would often go to the building on Saturday night and practice his sermon in the empty chapel.

A SERENDIPITOUS TRAINING

Commissioner Ken Baillie shares a unique experience when Captain Gaither planned a surprise and unconventional strategy at Bedford.

> I was stationed at the training college when the Gaithers were corps officers at Brooklyn Bedford–Stuyvesant. As the college coordinator for cadet field training, I was able to schedule myself to be the accompanying officer for brigades going to Bed–Stuy. It was enjoyable to spend time with the Gaithers again, and the corps was an inspirational model for cadets. I worked with the Gaithers to plan ministry activities that would benefit the corps and provide good training experiences for the cadets. Visitation was discussed as a possibility. Izzy suggested pairing one cadet with one soldier from the corps. Each pair would visit soldier families, new people, families of kids in the youth programs, etc., all in the corps neighborhood. This was Bedford–Stuyvesant—apartment blocks and storefronts, mostly African–American, with edgy inner–city life with drugs, crime and fear.
>
> "Visit in the neighborhood? Are you serious?" I asked.
>
> "Yes, of course I'm serious," he assured. "No problem. Your cadets will be paired with our black soldiers. It will be fine, don't worry."
>
> Many of the soldiers were Jamaican or from other Caribbean islands. Most did not live in the immediate neighborhood but commuted by public transport. Bed–Stuy was for black Salvationists, and a ride into Bed–Stuy was the price to pay to soldier where the action was.
>
> The first Wednesday came. We paired everyone up, gave instructions, handed out address lists, and sent everyone out the door. After a long afternoon, now well into the dark of a winter evening, the pairs came filing back in for a reporting time. Two or three cadets volunteered to speak. All were white. Each

told how fearful they had been to be walking around in a black, inner–city neighborhood. But they were so thankful to be paired with their soldier partners, who made them feel safe and who knew just what to do and say!

At that, one of the Jamaicans stood to give her report. "You felt safe with me? Oh, that's great," she exclaimed. "You want to know the truth? I and my Jamaican friends were very afraid. We've never done this before. We only agreed to visit around here because Captain Gaither told us we would be safe in the company of you cadets!"

Laughter all around, and relief. And a "Cheshire cat" grin on Gaither's face. But we did it again and again on following Wednesdays and Sundays. And all God's people were the better for it.

Bed–Stuy played an influential role in the making of Israel and Eva into the officers and eventually the world leaders they would become within the Army. Foundations were laid upon which they would continue to build. Eva speaks of the influence of their partnership in these early appointments: "Our two corps appointments together were outstanding—with wonderful soldiers who were partners in our ministry, and who played important roles in helping us to become who we are today."

chapter 11

The Next Generations

God sets the solitary in families.
Psalm 68:6 (NKJV)

A n unsurpassed joy came to Israel and Eva on Oct. 25, 1969, at the birth of their first child, Michele. It was love at first sight, and suddenly, the Gaither home resonated with new sounds and sights. Michele, as children often do, would teach her parents some of their deepest lessons—of love, patience, tenderness, forgiveness and responsibility.

A DAUGHTER REMEMBERS

From her formative years, Michele remembers her grandfather, Israel Lee Gaither II, as a quiet man, "but when he preached, he just rocked the house, in a sing–song style. He always dressed immaculately and wore white patent leather shoes." She adds, "Grandmother always looked gorgeous. They made church special." Michele recalls that at her grandfather's funeral in the church he pastored, there was "an overwhelming response, with people standing outside looking in the windows."

Of her grandparents, the Shues, Michele says, "They are down–to–earth, fun loving. Grandmother Shue came to our house when our parents were away and it was great fun being with her."

With a six–year age disparity between Michele and her brother, Mark, Michele says, "As a teenager, I tolerated him. He was little. My family was full of teachers on father's side, so I would play as teacher and make him take tests." In their adult life, sister and brother maintain close contact with each other.

Michele recalls that when the family lived in Queens, N.Y., "There were tons of kids on the street we knew as friends. They constantly came to our house for food. It seemed that Mom was feeding the neighborhood. Her spirit was always giving."

Summer vacations were spent at Dune Beach in Rhode Island. The Gaithers' daughter remembers, "Going to the beach was a big thing with our family. It was an awesome time because Dad, who takes so seriously his work, came to the beach and did not leave all day. We would take a packed lunch, and Mark and Dad would ride the waves together. Another summer highlight for my Dad and me was our enjoyment of seafood."

Michele came gradually into the faith; her journey confirms the adage that "God has no grandchildren." Each person must come to the Lord individu-

Grandson Isaiah with Michele [2005]

ally. She remembers the family always had prayer and devotions around the table after the evening meal. They would each read a card from the "promise box," and she says, "It never failed that one of the cards would relate to something going on in the family. Dad always stressed the importance of the Bible, and we would find the passage and encouraged to make it a part of our everyday life."

"Fun and family times epitomized our family. We have so much fun, with laughing overarching our times together."

Michele says of her father, "He is not just my Dad. He is my mentor—in my job, leadership challenges and difficult situations. We're a tight family. I talked to my mom several times a week, even when she was in London."

The daughter of a mixed–race marriage, she has encountered some prejudice, even at work. She found racism at Asbury College and Seminary where she had served, to be "more subtle. People seem stunned when they find out I'm African–American." But Michele had learned well from her parents the lesson of coping with grace in a divided world.

Another memorable day in the life of the Gaithers was Jan. 20, 1998, when Michele and her husband, Kevin, presented them with the crowning joy of their first grandson, Isaiah Highland Sparks. Like many other grandparents, Israel and Eva took one adoring look at God's gift to them of this precious bundle and capitulated. Life for Israel and Eva would never be the same again.

When the Gaithers went to South Africa, Israel and Eva sent a video each month. They did a "Mr. Rogers," singing, "It's a beautiful day in the neighborhood." They would say, "Hi Isaiah," and then read a book to him on the video.

A Rich Heritage

The Salvation Army was a strong influence in young Michele Gaither's life. "I'm thankful to God for The Salvation Army," she says. "I am the person I am because of The Salvation Army. For me, high school was very difficult, but the Army was my world. I went to camp and on overseas mission trips. Salvationists like Fred and Christine Honsberger came into my life at the most crucial time when I was a teenager."

Israel passed on to his children the mantra he had received from his father: "Remember who you are. Remember your name." It was not intended as haughty, but as a reminder that they represented the Christian heritage entrusted to them. Michele remembers that when she became eligible to wear the Salvation Army uniform and put it on, "it was more than just getting this cool suit. It was not just a Salvation Army ritual; it stood for something."

Michele's relationship with the extended family was deeply meaningful. "My dad's sisters played huge roles in my life. They are an inspiration to me. When Aunt Carmilla died, my dad was devastated, and it was a humongous blow to me. I had spent an entire week with her, and literally camped in bed with her. Grandfather was never the same after his two children died."

Michele had often wondered about the Mocksville, N.C., area where her dad had gone as a boy for a vacation every summer with his paternal grandparents. One day she had an unforgettable experience.

> When I came home and told the following story, my parents couldn't believe it. Driving in North Carolina, I saw a sign for Mocksville. I had never been there, but that day we drove to Mocksville. We were looking for my great–grandfather's house, which was near a church across the street from the school.
>
> We went into a nearby store and learned that a Gaither worked there. We asked, "Is the person white or black?" The response, "She's black." I thought, "Probably one of my relatives." When I finally found her house, I held up a photo of my grandfather. She said he looked just like her uncle Frank. She then called her cousin, who took me over to the plantation where my ancestors were slaves. We walked through the main house and the slave quarters.
>
> On the other side of the tracks, we found my great–grandfather's church. We couldn't find the house. To a neighbor who came out, we said, "We are trying to find my great–grandfather's house; did you know the Gaithers?" We were led to the house and found that all that was left was the chimney. So we ripped a brick off it.
>
> About 50 relatives gathered around. Historical information on the family was gathered. Across the street was a school that

was going to be named Gaither Elementary School because my ancestors would come back from their slave owners (who were very humane and taught them to read) and teach the others in the black areas how to read and write. This encounter with my roots was an awesome and deeply moving experience.

Today, Michele Gaither Sparks is Director of Communications at the Gatton College of Business and Economics at the University of Kentucky. Following in the family tradition of education, she also had taught journalism at Asbury College where she earned her B.A. and Master's degrees.

A Son Enters the Family

Another memorable day in the lives of the Gaithers was March 25, 1975, when the Lord gave them the gift of their son, Mark.

Mark shares the discussion that he was told ensued at his birth. "My mother thought they should name their son Israel Lee Gaither IV. My dad would have none of it. So they selected the name Mark with the middle name Lee, carrying on the family name tradition. Now their grandson, our son, carries the family's Christian name, 'Matthew Israel.'"

Captain Veronica Demeraski often cared for 8–year–old Mark when his parents were away. Israel, strict disciplinarian that he was, would say to his son when leaving him off, echoing his own father, "Remember who you are." Then, to Veronica he would say, "Give me a full report on the weekend." Her response: "I'm not going to do that; kids are kids!"

Young Mark was a member of the singing company led by Captain Demeraski at Pittsburgh Temple Corps. She was teaching two–part singing, with Mark learning to sing the low part. A short time later, then–Major Gaither was ministering at a corps and arranged for his family to sing a selection. They started the song, and suddenly Mark was singing a lower part instead of the expected part. Major Gaither stopped and had them start over again, only to have Mark again sing a lower part.

Mark recalls, "So in the quartet, I started singing low, real low, and my sister started giggling. Dad stopped and had us start over, reminding us that we were in church. The same thing happened. Everyone was laughing. He was mortified. He made us sit down, and that was the last time we did a family quartet."

The major's frustrated effort reposes as one of the humorous moments in the family archives.

An Indelible Imprint

Mark, like Michele, was strongly influenced by The Salvation Army. As a young person Mark had been actively involved with The Salvation Army Corps in

Grandson Matthew with Amy and Mark [2004]

Pittsburgh and Manchester, Conn. He says, "Some of my closest friends are people from The Salvation Army. The Army camps were influential, and friendships I developed have continued. Mom was my Bible teacher as Corps Cadet counselor and Bible Bowl teacher. I played in the divisional youth band, Pittsburgh Temple band and Manchester Citadel Band." Taking a page from his dad's life story, Mark sang solos in elementary school, and enjoyed singing in Salvation Army Songsters (choir).

"I had always been exposed to the Christian faith," says Mark. "That's all I knew. I gradually grew into it. As I learned more, my faith grew. I cannot pick a time, but I really got serious at Asbury College, and there was challenged, and I look at that as the big moment." Mark graduated from Asbury College in 1997, majoring in health and physical education, and earned his Master's degree in sports management from Robert Morris University. He was captain of the college basketball team and president of The Salvation Army Student Fellowship in 1996–1997. He remembers with pride that his dad was invited to speak in a chapel service during his senior year.

Mark now serves as a physical education teacher for grades 9–12 in Ringgold High School in Monongahela, Pa., and head coach of its varsity basketball team. There he is often a surrogate father to boys from one-parent families. "I really enjoy working with young people, especially under-privileged kids who don't have strong role models. You wouldn't believe the backgrounds many of them come from and how they look up to me as their coach, as a role model and in a mentoring capacity. I learned from my parents' example the need for helping others. It's not the paycheck, but what we can do to make a difference in their lives. High school kids are at such an impressionable age. They look up to us.

"Dad taught, don't do anything to compromise morals and belief. Remember who you are and whom you represent. You represent God, and remember you're a Gaither, and if you mess up, that's not going to be a good thing. We knew what was expected of us; for me always to be a gentleman, specifically to my mother, talk to her the right way, just the way he talked, in his manner. He was very stern and what he said was the law. We knew what was expected; he set rules, and we were to follow them. The worst words out of my mother's mouth were 'wait until your father gets home.'"

Mark remembers, "Mom was always interested and involved with us at public schools. Family devotions were observed after dinner. The biggest impression was how Mom and Dad interacted with each other. Theirs was a very loving relationship; obviously, they were a team. From observing them, I learned how I want to treat my wife Amy."

> *"I've always been very proud of my father. He's my hero."*

Israel's preaching left its mark upon his son, who says, "When Dad got up to preach, I thought it was God. One of most amazing times I heard Dad preach was at Granddad's funeral. It was with power. It was an incredible sermon, at the House of Prayer.

"I've always been very proud of my father," Mark readily acknowledges. "He's my hero. I've known he was going to have a huge impact on The Salvation Army. We are so proud of him. We know he has a great vision for The Salvation Army, and it's just an awesome responsibility he has now to impact it."

FAMILY MEMORIES

"On Christmas Eve," recalls Mark, "The Advent story in the Bible was read, then 'The Night Before Christmas.' We put cookies and milk out for Santa and his reindeer, and went to bed early so we could get up early. Somehow Michele always convinced me to sleep on the floor in her room. Dad set the rule that we could not come downstairs before 5:30. So we would sit on the steps, just looking at gifts, waiting. Dad would take his old sweet time getting downstairs, lighting the fire, while mother said, 'Hurry up!' Then we would open our gifts, one at a time. Every year a big present would be kept hidden in the basement or the garage—so we would open all the gifts and think that was it. And then, 'Oh wait a minute.' He would go and bring the big one out for each of us. He did that last year with Isaiah (age 7), having a bike for him in the garage."

One Saturday a month was set aside for Mark and his dad to do something special together— a fishing trip, a visit to the Basketball Hall of Fame, a Yankees or Red Sox baseball game. Mark fondly remembers between his sixth and ninth grade years the early morning fishing outings with his dad and granddad. As they sought to lure the denizens of the deep in Pymatuning Lake in Pennsylvania, Mark was cautioned to keep absolutely silent lest any reverberations alert their quarry.

One of the anvils on which Mark's young manhood was forged was the basketball court. One night in the Pittsburgh Corps gym, Major Gaither and Captain Kelly went to check on their sons. Young Chip Kelly and Mark had become close friends; later, each would serve as best man at the other's wedding. When the dads displayed some hoop skills of their own as they outshot the lads in a simple follow–the–leader game, a challenge floated through the air:, "Want to try a real game of ball?"

The gauntlet flung down, in order to put the proper parental respect back into these two upstarts, the dads quickly set a time: "Friday night, here in the gym. Come and get schooled." That was the first of a number of such games, in which initially the parents managed to prevail by mental strategies. Major Charles Kelly reminisces, "What started as a natural rivalry became opportune moments for us to invest ourselves in the lives of two of the most important people to whom we could minister—our sons. Years later, the joys of that first victory of our sons over their dads still echoes as one of the moments of pride between student and teacher, father and son."

Mark also remembers the hard–fought basketball games he and his dad used to play at Camp Allegheny against Major Kelly and his son Chip. Mark credits his dad's interest in sports as having contributed to his choice of profession as a physical education teacher.

Amy, who in Israel's words became a "daughter–in–love," shares her husband's pride in his parents. "We know that they are going to have a powerful world ministry, and many will come to know the Lord through them. We see how affectionate they are. They have one of the most healthy marriages I've ever seen."

Amy's earliest memory of her future father–in–law was of a most unusual encounter. She and Mark had been dating in Wilmore, Ky. and came to Michele's for Thanksgiving, a day associated with big football games. So the Gaithers decided to have their own football game. Amy tells of the happening. "All of us were outside throwing a football around. Mark's dad threw a long football pass to me. I ran so hard to catch it that when I caught it I was flipping over the mailbox. And of course he was mortified. But then when everybody realized I was OK, they started clapping for me. On this, my first holiday with them, my flip caused Dad to laugh so hard, after he was assured I was not hurt."

Mark and Amy presented Mark's parents with their second grandson, Matthew Israel, on Aug. 3, 2004. "He loves having grandkids," says Amy. "Dad gets so excited about them."

Amy discerned the true values imparted by Izzy and Eva as parents. "Our parents never talked about money as a priority," shares Mark. Amy adds, "They raised great kids, very unmaterialistic, loving and kind. My mother said, 'See how a man treats his mother, and that is how he will treat you.'"

Amy observes: "Mark and his sister get along so well; they never butt heads. I never saw siblings get along like they do. In seventh grade, he earned $500 from his paper route, and he gave it to Michele for college."

Mark explains: "I did a paper route during seventh and eighth grade. When Mom would drive, she would get out of the car and help deliver so we would get home faster. But when Dad drove, he read the paper as I delivered, and it took longer to do the route."

Regarding his parents' biracial marriage, Mark says, "Their mixed racial marriage was something we never thought about." "Because they were the first generation couple in the Army, some people had problems with it, even people who were their friends."

GOD'S SPECIAL GIFTS

With the Gaithers serving overseas in recent years, first in South Africa, then in London and traveling around the world, they nevertheless bridged the oceans and miles apart from loved ones with phone calls. In South Africa phone calls were expensive so they called home once a month and the families called them once a month. In England the phone rate was but five and a half cents a minute which enabled them to have frequent and unhurried conversations with Michele, Mark and other family members. Eva says, "We were able to keep in contact and of course e–mail was wonderful." T–shirts purchased by Grandma Eva from journeys around the world augmented the wardrobe of the children and grandchildren.

With the advent of their first grandson, Isaiah Highland Sparks, followed by that of Matthew Israel Gaither, Israel and Eva's nuclear family took on a new and exciting dimension. They quickly learned the culture of grandparents—that your grandkids are really awesome and their intelligence is off the chart!

The Gaithers feel great pride in their children—and they know their children

Grandfather with Isaiah and Matthew [2005]

support their ministry. "Michele and Mark, our children, are both beautiful gifts," says Israel. "I will never forget our welcome meeting as territorial leaders for USA Eastern territory. Following the installation service conducted by General John Gowans, Michele gave a beautiful tribute representing Mark and their spouses. Then turning to the General, and with tears in her eyes, she said, 'Thank you for bringing my parents home!' But three weeks later we were appointed to IHQ. Having just returned from South Africa to serve for only 103 days in leadership of our home territory—and having heard the heart cry of Michele—it was a very difficult decision to accept the appointment to London.

"But God used our children to ensure we obeyed the leading of the Lord. They said, 'We don't want you to go, but if this is what the Lord wants, you must go.' It is that level of support from our children as well as the larger family that has always been there for us throughout our officership."

Israel and Eva have not been spared the tears and heartaches that accompany the joys of parenthood. As Christian philosopher Victor Frankl, himself a survivor of the concentration camp, reminds us, "Suffering is an ineradicable part of life." That truism often is proved in family life. However, the times of personal adversity that came to the Gaither family forged stronger bonds of mutual support and sustaining love. Their own heartache also opened doors of ministry such as on one occasion overseas when an officer mother came to the altar to pray, with a heavy burden on her heart for her adult child back home. The woman shares that Eva knelt next to her, and when she revealed her burden, Eva responded, "We too have gone through that experience," and it became a moment of encouragement and solace.

A reciprocity of both blessing and ministry resonates between Israel and Eva and their children. On one occasion when it was known her dad was confronting a troublesome issue, Michele called. "Dad, I understand you are having a difficult time. May I pray for you right now on the phone?" That became a sacramental moment, among many others in the spiritual bonding Israel and Eva have with their children.

One of the darkest days in Israel's life was when he received news of his father's death. In those moments, Mark, attempting to console his father, said to him, "I know how much you loved your father and what he meant to you and want you to know I feel the same love for you and that you mean the world to me."

In that moment, Israel received back something precious that he had been giving out to his loved ones through the years.

Edwin Markham's famous words speak a deep truth to our human condition:

> There is a destiny that makes us brothers.
> None lives to himself alone.
> What we send into the lives of others,
> comes back into our own.

chapter **12**

Four Sisters

> *A ministering angel shall my sister be.*
> Shakespeare ("Hamlet")

srael Gaither II had passed on the gift of vocal music to all five children. Carmilla, the eldest sister, who was named after her paternal grandmother, inherited the best portion of the gift. She had followed Israel into Salvation Army officership and served in its ranks for a brief period, then moved out into the banking field.

THE STORM CLOUD BURSTS

In the prime of life, Carmilla was diagnosed with cancer. During her final days of struggle, as Israel sat at her bedside, she looked at him and asked, "Israel Lee, am I going to die?" He looked at his beloved sister, who had been so full of promise, who still had so much to contribute to the life of others, and words came with difficulty. But with conviction, he said, "We may leave here physically, but we don't die spiritually." The cancer claimed Carmilla's life at the age of 31.

In Israel's dark night of the soul, a profound spiritual experience took place. During the long drive from New Castle to New York through the late night hours, with a broken heart, he challenged God, "Why this waste? Why should such a young and promising life be allowed to be so cruelly snatched away?" Israel came from that bedside, and from Carmilla's funeral, feeling within his heart, "I must do something more; life must matter."

In retrospect, he shared with a reporter in Sweden his resolve from this trial: "That night when I was driving the long way back to New York I said to God, 'My life has to mean something. I'm going to make sure that my life makes a difference! Wherever you lead me, I will follow, because I absolutely have to do something. I want my life and my testimony about God to leave tracks and marks that make a difference. "

In a *War Cry* article of Oct. 4, 1980, titled "The Mystery of His Will," Israel revealed his heart's anguish and resolution in the loss of Carmilla.

> She was lovely, young and talented, with a strong commitment to the Lord. Suddenly, a routine physical exam revealed that she had contracted cancer. Immediately, prayers, hope, trust were all activated, believing for divine intervention and a total cure.
>
> Divine intervention did occur, but not as her family or a host of friends would have desired, for two years following that initial pronouncement, she rushed to Jesus. Her fine, sensitive soprano voice that only months earlier sang to witness, "I am bound for the Promised Land," was stilled and only the memories of a loving sister and faithful daughter remained.
>
> As always in times of such tragedy, even the believer cries, "Why must it be? Why must it be for even those fully committed to Him? Was it surely God's will?" What are we to make of the disappointments and tragedies which inevitably occur during the believer's sojourn?
>
> We learn the necessity of trusting the totality of our beings to the will of an all–knowing and almighty God. The family came to know even better the power, presence, perfection and purpose of the mystery of God's will—even in tragedy.

ANOTHER SOUL'S DARK NIGHT

Israel's next eldest sister, Dr. Judy McConnell–Jackson, had entered the teaching field, that to which Israel had first been attracted. She earned her Ph.D. and served as the dean of admissions and minority student affairs at Miami University in Ohio and as a professor of educational leadership.

But on a recruiting trip in Tampa, Fla., Judy in the prime of life at age 42, was tragically killed in an automobile accident. The Gaithers lived in Pittsburgh at the time, and word reached Israel while he was working late at the office. Eva had stepped out of her office on an errand to one of the downtown stores, and Israel sent a friend to look for her and let her know he needed to see her. She returned to the office, where Israel broke the tragic news. To his wife, Judy had become as a sister, and together, she and Israel wept over her loss.

The terrible accident brought a seismic shock to the family, as well to many whose lives Judy had touched. In her leadership role Judy had influenced many minority students to pursue their education. In the papers found after her death was another indication of her achievement, an invitation to become president of a small college in the south.

In this second long dark night of Israel's soul, he took from those deep losses what he called "a lasting legacy" left to him by Carmilla, Judy and his father—a legacy of a deepened faith and an extraordinary task for himself of trying to compensate in his own ministry for the lost ministry of his treasured siblings.

Israel speaks poignantly of these two tragedies in his family. "I have always considered that the deaths of Carmilla and Judy were, in human terms, untimely. Both of these women were in professions in which they were making a significant impact on people. Yet both were taken at an early age. The outpouring of love and affection for them during their funerals offered tribute to the impact of their lives."

The untimely deaths had a shattering impact on Israel's father. His son writes, "I am convinced that his demise was not merely due to age and failing health, but that deep within, he just may have given up. I remember him saying, following the death of Judy, 'Son, it's not supposed to be this way.' My mother and father suffered horribly as a result of the loss of their two daughters.

"Judy's death was devastating. Following the conclusion of the funeral and memorial services, I repeated the experience that I had following the death of Carmilla. There was a profound sense that I must live my life in the will of God that in some way I might finish what they could not. The loss of two sisters through heartbreaking deaths challenged me to rethink who I was, what I believed, and what I was meant to do with my life. It was a crisis of faith that deepened my life in Christ."

"There was a profound sense that I must live my life in the will of God that in some way I might finish what they could not."

Out of these dark nights of the soul came a light of conviction and consecration. Israel Gaither became a man with a mission—a now enlarged mission—with God's help to make a difference in his world. For Israel Gaither, mission as God would reveal it, would always matter most.

Jacqueline, Israel's sister, followed her brother's example of attending The Salvation Army's Camp Allegheny, and worked there as a waitress. She went on to achieve high academic standing and excellence, earning her B.S. in Education, a Master's degree in Education, and a school superintendent certification. At the time of this writing she is a doctoral candidate, and serves as principal of the Ben Franklin Junior High School in New Castle.

Education had always been a major emphasis in the Gaither family, going back to Israel's great–grandfather's teaching black slave children to read. Israel's four aunts on his father's side were schoolteachers. Jacqueline says, "We were not permitted to think about not going to college."

Jackie married Torrence Respress, who was called to the ministry under the mentoring of Israel's father and became the successor to the pulpit of the church Israel Gaither II had founded. Torrance further developed the life of the church and implemented a transforming of the physical edifice.

When it was suggested to Jacqueline that Israel was "the Jackie Robinson [the first black player to break the color barrier in professional baseball] of The Salvation Army," she rejoined, "No, he's the Colin Powell of The Salvation Army—his look, speech, demeanor, speaks with authority."

Mutual admiration abounds among the Gaither siblings. Kathy, Israel's youngest sister is on the staff of Yale University Hospital in a supervisory position in the business department, making her impact as a professional while fulfilling her role as a loving mother. "I'm blessed to have Kathy as a sister. In fact, when I left New Castle to enter the School for Officer Training Kathy was a child. I'm convinced that when I returned for the Christmas holidays and summer breaks, she probably thought I was a distant relative rather than her brother! But the beauty of the Gaither family is that distance has never impeded our love and appreciation for each other. Though few of the early years of my life were spent with Kathy in our parents' home, we yet have a strong connection with one another. And today, visits with Kathy are always rich with laughter and wonderful fellowship. Kathy has a keen sense of humor, as does Jackie. We speak with ease and mutual gratitude of our shared heritage. We are a very close family and I have found deep strength through my sisters. Each of them also reflects the heritage of our family. Having had the influence of four beautiful, intelligent and talented sisters in my life is a marvelous gift!"

Israel's wife quickly entered into that heritage. "Eva, from the moment we began our relationship," relates Israel, "was received by my sisters as one of them. It is a delight to see them interacting together. My sisters love Eva, and she really is far more than a sister–in–law; she is truly a sister. To my mom and dad, Eva is very much one of their daughters. Eva has shared the tremendous grief and pain that we have felt in the loss of Carmilla and Judy."

The heritage continues to the next generation. "Our daughter Michele has a number of the gifts and strengths possessed by my sisters," says Israel. "I readily see the Gaither/Johnson heritage in both my son and daughter Mark and Michele.

When Israel and his sisters get together, they reminisce about their younger days of friendly sibling rivalry. "I often tease my sisters—or I should say they put me straight—when I claim to have been the ruler of the house when Mom and Dad were absent, just because of being the eldest. If truth be told, when the four of them ganged up on me, there was no winning. One evening Mom and Dad were both away and I was given responsibility, as the eldest, for watching my sisters. We became engaged in a disagreement, and I like to remind them that they physically attacked me. I remember pushing Judy over the coffee table in the living room and watching it break apart. The next several hours we were all in fear and trembling, and the moment our mother and father walked in the door, they knew who was to blame for the broken piece of furniture. And I paid the consequences!"

MINISTERING ANGELS

For Israel Gaither, Shakespeare's words became prophetic: "A ministering angel shall my sister be." The two who were taken home, and the two who still share his life journey, continue to have a salutary spiritual impact upon his life and mission.

chapter **13**

A New Era for Black Ministries

*Speak up for those who cannot speak for
themselves, for the rights of all who are destitute.*
Proverbs 31:8

I t became increasingly common for leaders to call on Izzy for "extracur-
ricular" duties, outside the parameters of his appointments. During his
time as corps officer in Brooklyn Bedford, he was invited to address the
subject of "Black Theological Tendencies" at a Territorial Soldiers' Seminar.
He presented surveys on "Religion and Blacks" and "The Gospel to the
Ghetto," addressing black theology in both its negative and positive per-
spectives. He summarized, "We are facing a new generation of black
youth— youth that we must reach with the Gospel of Jesus Christ, a Gospel
that truly does liberate the inner man where it really counts! A Gospel that
enables one to see who he is, what he is, what he can become through Jesus
Christ. Black youth, like youth of any race, are seeking direction, stability—
and we have the answer! The task then is to become sensitive to the Holy
Spirit that we will know His influence and direction in all of our ministry.
May God help us."

Commissioner Peter Chang writes of his time as Education Officer at
the SFOT in Suffern, N.Y.: "Izzy had been invited to give lectures to the
cadets on one of the major issues of the day. In the early 1970s, liberation
theology was one of the hot topics. He not only understood the subject
matter clearly but also guided the cadets so very well. He did not teach a
hard line; rather, the application of the Army's mission in the context of
the ghetto."

Israel, who with his wife had experienced the pain of racism within the
Army, refused to become part of the problem but rather became part of the
solution. The young, successful corps officer now became the Army's most

eloquent spokesman on the race issue, helping the movement go forward into the new era with sensitivity and integrity.

BLACK MINISTRIES COMMITTEE

The Black Ministries Committee was established in the spring of 1977 to advise the Territorial Commission on Planning and Goals on all aspects of ministries within the black community. Comprising 13 members, primarily black Salvationists, Kenneth Burton of Harlem Temple served as chair, Captain Israel Gaither, then a divisional youth secretary, as vice chair.

The commission's mandate was to: (1) Review the impact of program, personnel practices and policy on black Salvationists and the black community; (2) Encourage the active participation of black Salvationists in leadership opportunities to strengthen ministries within the black community; (3) Promote the proclamation of the Gospel, the winning of souls to Christ, and the recruitment of soldiers to share in the mission of The Salvation Army.

Committee members became involved in a wide range of projects. The group made recommendations on such varied matters as candidate seminars, inner–city training programs, a bibliography of black literature, black–oriented brass and vocal music, the spirit of Salvationism in the black community, a black ministries newsletter and historical research relating to the black contribution to The Salvation Army in America. Originating with the committee was the concept of Salvationist ethnic booths to be featured in Heritage Hall during the 1980 National Congress, including the black heritage booth.

Months of intensive planning by the committee culminated in the celebration of Black Heritage Night in the Centennial Memorial Temple in New York City. Some 2,000 men, women and children from all parts of the Eastern Territory filled the temple to mark this historic event and to hear the dynamic preaching of Dr. Martin Luther King, Sr. Two black Salvationist musical groups, the Cleveland Gospel Singers and the New Sound Band, augmented the music of the Temple Chorus. More than 200 seekers came to the mercy seat in response to Dr. King's challenge and appeal.

"We were inspired, blessed and motivated by the caliber of Captain Gaither's leadership."

The committee's positive and proactive stance was having a salutary impact upon the overall Salvation Army.

"A CULTURE OF INCLUSION"

The committee was dedicated to the task of building a stronger, more unified Army. It stated its goal for "an Army rich in its cultural heritage and expression, yet one in its doctrines and principles, its aims and purposes. It rejoices in the unique 'Spirit of Salvationism,' which knows no ethnic or social barriers but joins together all Salvation soldiers as comrades of Christ united in one great purpose of taking the Gospel to all classes, all cultures, all peoples."

Marilyn Chapman, while a local officer in the Freeport, N.Y., Corps was appointed to the committee. She remembers, "There was difficulty in bringing members of the committee together at a convenient time for all. But that didn't stop Izzy. He was determined to get the job done. He came to our home in Freeport to get my thoughts regarding the issues before the committee."

Major Allan Wiltshire, as a corps officer, served on the committee, and considers it a forerunner of the Territorial Committee for Salvationists of African Descent, which would take committee recommendations a step further. He writes, "We were inspired, blessed and motivated by the caliber of Captain Gaither's leadership. He worked diligently and ardently, advocating a culture of inclusion in our dear old Army. He encouraged Major Norma Roberts to write the very first history on black Salvationists in the USA—*The Black Salvationist.*"

chapter **14**

Leaders and Models for Youth

*Don't let anyone look down on you because you
are young, but set an example for the believers
in speech, in life, in love, in faith and in purity.*
1 Timothy 4:12

The young corps officer of Bed–Stuy had proven himself as a leader, effective in both relational and administrative skills. He was now viewed by leadership as having potential for the next step of responsibility in the tier of Army positions.

When Israel was approached about what obviously would be a recognition of his accomplishments, to be divisional youth secretary for the Army's Greater New York Division, he had the temerity to ask his leaders, "Why are you giving me this appointment?" He wanted to be certain it was not because of his color. "I was not going to be just window dressing, or tokenism. I wanted to be sure they knew I could do the job." It was of course a rhetorical question, for he had earned the full confidence of his leaders who assured the appointment was by virtue of his merit.

Major Ronald Irwin, as territorial youth secretary, recommended the Gaithers as divisional youth leaders. He wrote, "The Gaithers were appointed due in large measure to their mission success at the Bedford Corps, and also because of the positive leader image of Israel Gaither to black Salvationists, particularly the young people. In addition, the Gaithers had a growing reputation as people of integrity who could be trusted by all Salvationists, regardless of color or ethnic background."

Upon receiving the new appointment, to be effective Sept. 10, 1975, Captain Gaither went to the divisional commander, Colonel French, and asked where they would be living. "In the divisional youth leaders' quarters, of course," came the reply.

"But you know where the quarters are located and the neighborhood," rejoined Israel, knowing that it was an all–white, upscale community on Long Island, within commuting distance by rail from the Gaithers' new offices in New York City.

"They are exceptional communicators, compassionate pastors, godly teachers."

"Yes," again affirmed French, "and that is of course where you will live."

To assure ready and deserved acceptance, French himself went to the neighborhood, talked to the neighbors, and apprised them on the new officers who were moving in, giving the highest commendation to their character and quality of life. He also "ran interference" with any who questioned the appointment of a mixed–race couple in this high–profile position with its potential impact upon the youth. As an advocate for the Gaithers, both in the present and yet in the future, Lt. Colonel Walter French, following in the example of Captain Stanley Ditmer and Lt. Colonel John Waldron, became the third in the sequence of the seven most influential Army leaders in the life and ministry of Israel Gaither.

The Expanded Parish

As divisional youth leaders, the Gaithers would be responsible for encouraging growth in youth membership, planning divisional youth programs, recruiting and preparing candidates for officership, and the Army's extensive summer camp program. In this high–profile position in one of the Army's largest divisions, they would leave their impact upon thousands.

Prior to their appointment, the Army's Star Lake Camp had been administered by the Social Services department, a departure from the usual arrangement in most divisions, of the camp staff and program being the youth secretary's responsibility. Colonel Walter French, in his confidence for Captain Gaither's ability arranged for him to be assistant director of the camp for two years to become familiar with its operation and large staff, following which the camp management was transferred to the mainline Army youth program, under the direction of the Gaithers.

Star Lake Camp hosted more than 2,000 campers each summer—with capacity for 450 campers and almost 200 staff at any one time. About 40 staffers were international youth recruited through the BUNAC [British Universities North America Club] program, which processes work opportunities for students abroad. The Gaithers would recruit and train staff, set up the programs, and operate four ten–day camp sessions, as well as the Army's

Star Lake camp staff, 1976 (Captains Gaither pictured 5th and 6th from left in first row)

best–known music camp, and a concurrent camp for adult Booth House clients. The camp is a community within itself, with responsibility for the safety, health, waterfront and nursing staffs, budget, and quality programs for all youth and staff involved.

Major Mark Tillsley was one of the youth who came under the ministry of the Gaithers. Speaking from his office as principal of the Army's largest School for Officer Training, Tillsley reflects on their influence. "As a young man, 16 years of age and new to this country, I was blessed to come under the influence of the divisional youth leaders, Captains Israel and Eva Gaither. Their cross–cultural savvy not only embraced the urban youth of the Greater New York Division but also helped this high school student from St. John's, Newfoundland, get acclimated to a very different setting. My love for the city, and my primary identification of New York as my home was largely influenced by the attitude the Gaithers expressed in their love for the young people. We have been part of the vast crowd of cheerleaders who have seen them develop in capacity and character over the past 30 years. They are exceptional communicators, compassionate pastors, and godly leaders."

A MISSING LINK FOUND

What impact did the youth leader, Captain Israel Gaither, have upon the youth who now were his "parish"? Major Raphael Jackson, at the time of this writing the divisional secretary in New Jersey, speaks to that subject.

> My beginnings were meager. I am the oldest of a family of eight children with no real father figure. When I was a young teen, we moved down the block from a Salvation Army corps and, after attending a music camp, I gave my heart to the Lord. My only role models were found in the Salvation Army—it was in the Army I found my purpose for life and my joy. The Salvation Army was a primary instrument the Lord has used for the salvation of my family. When my mother died while I was in training, I became the patriarch of my family.
>
> If I could identify a missing link, it was that all the leaders and role models in my life at that time, anyone that had positive influence, was white. We know that color does have its effect when no one that you respect looks like you. Many times I felt like an anomaly, a misfit. I also felt, rightly or wrongly, that I only had access to go so far, that there was only so much I could give or get from the Army, and that I would have to eventually move on. The fact that others like me had moved on to other churches or vocations seemed to reinforce this perception.
>
> Then the Gaithers became our divisional youth leaders in Greater New York. I definitely felt that now there were new possibilities. My first impression of Israel Gaither as a person was at a divisional reception he led. Here was a man who could one moment be gregarious and funny, and then be intense and serious. He had it all together—he could preach, sing and captivate an audience's attention. I started to realize how exceptional this man was.
>
> My response was if God would have me, I would be honored to be a Salvation Army officer. As I started to process my paperwork for training, I got the impression this man was no joke. I realized that he was multifaceted, that he traveled and functioned well in many different areas. As many have and continue to do, I noted and watched his progress as he moved "along the chairs"— it was as if you were watching some great documentary, stereotypes being challenged, preconceptions being disproved. Conversely, there were folks, both black and

white, saying that he was an anomaly, a blip, and so it would encourage me to prove them wrong, to show that he might be exceptional, but that this was just another aspect of who "we were," that you could not use one brush or tag to identify what a black man was and is.

Upon appointment to my first major operation, the Brownsville Corps, we had four day care centers, a combined budget of more than $3 million, but what was most frightening was that it had a significant black congregation. I didn't know what it meant to be the pastor of a black congregation with my white wife in the middle of Brooklyn Brownsville. I didn't know if I wanted to be there, if I wanted to succeed, if I wanted to be marked as a "black officer." I was going through an identity crisis. The Gaithers were in Southern New England at the time, and I wrote him a letter about my consternation. I thank him because he did not respond with any kind of clichés or even a direct solution, but in essence, told me that you have to give what God has given you to give and work out your own salvation.

Those five years in Brooklyn ultimately turned out to be so fruitful and satisfying because we were able to grow and develop gifts we had no idea we had, and we were able to see a large operation grow significantly.

After a stint as the area coordinator of Essex County, I was called and told that my wife and I were appointed as the divisional youth leaders of Greater New York. Two blaring facts were clear to me. I had for 20 years prayed that God would allow me to be a DYS, never daring to even dream that GNY could be a possibility. Secondly, that I would be in the appointment that once belonged to Israel Gaither! It was a humbling experience.

I am now in the position of being one of the senior black officers in this territory and am more cognizant of the responsibility and pressure this entails. Though I thank God that our ultimate role model is Jesus Christ, I am also mindful God calls us to be role models and mentors. The person that Israel is still challenges me not to be satisfied with the mediocre but to pursue to do the best with what God has given me.

Such was Israel Gaither's inestimable impact for God and the Army upon a young candidate and officer with much potential and valued leadership in the Army.

"VERY HIGH STANDARDS"

Lt. Colonel Tom Adams remembers when he was appointed as general secretary for business in Greater New York. "I arrived at the headquarters at what I thought was a very early hour to try to get ahead on my new appointment, only to find that our DYS, Captain Gaither, was already there and had done almost a day's work. This early start was a pattern that he maintained all his officership and allowed him to always be ready for the challenge of the day."

"I must admit," says Adams, "that this first meeting had me wondering what Izzy was all about, as he was sporting the biggest Afro hair style that I had ever seen. However, it indicated his desire to relate to the youth of the division. This reflects his attribute to make every effort to relate to those to whom God sent him. It should be noted that his Afro subjected him to the friendly banter of his divisional commander, Lt. Colonel Walter French, who insisted that full uniform be worn all the time when on official duty. An Army cap on top of all that hair was like a pimple on an elephant. But Izzy stuck to his guns. Time has taken its toll on Izzy's hair, and wearing an Army cap is not quite as difficult as it was in the old days."

Candidates and leaders, 1978 (Captains Gaither pictured on the far right of 2nd row with General and Mrs. Coutts, Col. French, Captains Klemanski, and Candidate Raphael Jackson pictured 2nd from left in back row)

Majors Guy and Henrietta Klemanski succeeded the Gaithers as youth leaders in August 1978, with Captain Israel Gaither remaining in the division as divisional secretary (second in command) and Captain Eva Gaither as Director of Volunteers and Women's Auxiliary. Klemanski remembers with gratitude their help with the transition.

"They warmly welcomed and encouraged us and became our mentors. I remember Brigadier Mary Nisiewicz, corps officer of Manhattan Citadel Corps, coming into my office on my first day there and she said, "Son, you have some big shoes to fill. I hope you are prepared to arrive early, stay late, and visit the corps like your predecessor did. We love them and they did a great job here." Wow, tall orders, but we quickly found the Gaithers made it easy to follow as we served together.

"We were amazed and impressed at the Gaithers' love for and commitment to people, be it fellow officers and staff, corps officers, soldiers or young people, and their exuberance in recruiting candidates. What a great opportunity also for us to learn the camping program and ministry at one of the largest and most complex camping operations in the Army world! We learned camp management from the Gaithers, including administration, discipline, hiring of staff, tireless hours of serving others and about needs of children coming from various cultures in the Greater New York area, and to see their lives changed.

"We were privileged to inherit upon our arrival 13 accepted candidates who had been well prepared by the Gaithers for entry to the School for Officer Training. We were appreciative of their spirit and depth, and willingness to help, even in costume as a clown at a Sunbeam Rally. We honor the Gaithers for their very high standards, honesty in leadership and integrity in presenting Jesus Christ through their personal and corporate ministry."

chapter **15**

An Able Administrator

Not lagging in diligence, fervent in spirit,
serving the Lord.

Romans 12:11

Israel Gaither had more than acquitted himself in the headquarters appointment as divisional youth secretary. With the recommendation of his divisional commander, Lt. Colonel French, he was three years later moved on to the next step on the leadership ladder, that of divisional secretary within the same Greater New York division, as of Aug. 28, 1978.

A UNIQUE AND EFFECTIVE STYLE

Arriving at his office very early in the mornings, Israel Gaither would spend the first minutes in prayer, Scripture reading and devotion, preparing himself for what the day might bring. Colonel French echoed what would become a familiar refrain of colleagues throughout his career: "No matter how early I came to the office I could never be there earlier than Izzy." Israel's divisional commander summarized his young protégé as showing "great relational skills, efficiency in administration, gifted in platform preachment, and as an accomplished soloist remembered for his signature song, 'Fill my cup, Lord.'"

Colonel James Knaggs recalls a memory of Gaither as divisional secretary. "He was always a prominent officer in the Eastern Territory. No matter where he went or what his appointment, he stood out. He was marked by the hand of God early, and we all knew it. Yes, the color of his skin made him even more distinctive, but he was known for his friendliness, sensitivity and integrity. His vocal solos and preachment, with a passionate theme, brought blessing. One evening, when Captain Gaither was the divisional secretary, we came to the music finale at the Star Lake Music Camp. Who should we meet on the road as the main parking attendant, but the captain. Humbly and gracefully, he welcomed guests and directed them to where they might best park their car or van. It was quite obvious that this was not a primary responsibility, although he performed the task in a first–class way." Major Peter Chang recalls having succeeded Gaither as divisional secretary. "I knew Izzy was a good administrator, but only then did I realize just how very good he really was. He dealt with issues promptly and thoroughly, documenting every detail. He was hard–working, starting the day before anybody else had arrived, and at such an unearthly hour in the morning, even beating the Long Island traffic."

Colonels Edward and Emily Fritz, in related leadership appointments, had opportunity to closely observe the Gaithers in the New York appointments. Colonel Fritz comments: "His skill in planning divisional events, including the weekly Friday Evening at the Temple services, was greatly appreciated. He is remembered as a team player, a passionate preacher, an inspiring vocalist, an adept organizer, an empathetic counselor, and an inclusive personality reaching out to others. He enjoyed sports but was not obsessed with them."

Eva Gaither made an impression on Colonel Emily Fritz. "Eva's energy and capacity for work, even at tedious tasks, amazed me. But it was our fun times together I cherish most." Emily also recalls Eva's response to a difficult time in her life. "I was one of 50 people injured in a fall from a deck collapse in Atlanta in April 1995. After 10 days in the hospital, I was airlifted and then put into an ambulance for the final leg of my journey home. Nursing care was provided for me daily for several weeks, and Ed each day brought home a delicious dinner prepared by an employee or officer from THQ. I soon learned that it was Eva Gaither who had organized this much–welcomed and thoughtful ministry. I thank God for enriching my life with their friendship."

> *"Eva's energy and capacity for work, even at tedious tasks, amazed me."*

Once Again to Pittsburgh

In the complex and weighty duties of his two divisional appointments in Greater New York, Israel Gaither had served with distinction. From there he was appointed, as of July 1, 1981, general secretary for the Western Pennsylvania Division, with headquarters in Pittsburgh. He was returning as second in command to the division he had left as a cadet and in which he had first served as a corps officer.

As the time came for the Gaithers to move on to this new appointment in their now fast–advancing career, Lt. Colonel French was told by a colleague on the receiving end in Pennsylvania, "It won't work here; we are too near the southern border." At each step of Israel's official journey the race issue emerged, at the time of his marriage to Eva, his appointment to Bedford, consideration of him as youth secretary, and now on the next step of the leadership ladder. And at each phase, Israel never reacted, never cried "discrimination," but handled the challenge with grace and dignity. He became a bridge for a new understanding, acceptance, and opportunity for minorities within the movement.

The appointment did "work," with the Gaithers once again endearing themselves and winning the high respect of their colleagues and all with whom they related. His expertise accounted for his being called to serve on national and territorial commissions, committees and planning groups.

Lt. Colonel William LaMarr, on the Western Pennsylvania divisional team with Captain Gaither, observed his astute leadership style. "He was responsible for our Allegheny County United Way budget. This complicated and challenging detail 'rolled off his back,' although he had no prior experience. Lt. Colonel LaMarr, then Izzy's subordinate at the Pittsburgh DHQ, acknowledged that there were two Gaithers. "There was Izzy your friend, and Captain Gaither the administrator, and never the twain did meet. In the office, Izzy your friend, almost like a light switch, said by his demeanor, 'You're here for business.' Yet even if you were chided, it did not carry over into your personal relationship."

FAMOUS FOR CAPERS

In this appointment Captain Eva Gaither served as the divisional Home League secretary. It was customary for the secretary's spouse to provide support, usually in entertainment at the annual summer camp for the ladies. In that role Captain Israel became famously remembered for his capers, bordering on Academy Award performances. On occasion he would don a wig and the costume of television's "Geraldine" on "The Flip Wilson Show," to

Preparing a pig roast at Home League Camp

the delight of hundreds of women who came to the Army camp for a holiday of fun and inspiration.

In the summer of 1983 at Camp Allegheny, the women's committee was scouting for some novel idea, and Major Veronica Demeraski shared that her brother–in–law, who was from Puerto Rico, "does pig roasts all the time, and the people enjoy it." So, dutifully, the general secretary arranged for a pig, set up the pit and fire, grunted and wrestled a pole through the cavity of the burnt–offering–to–be and took his turn as part of the human rotisserie, turning the pig all night until sunrise. The scene of this pig barbecue, with the general secretary doing his chores, and the fresh cooked pork that resulted, delighted the ladies and gave them an unusual story to tell the folk back home!

Major Molly Shotzberger recalls the event. "We had a Hawaiian theme to raise money for a special project; at the same time, the pig roast was taking place. Izzy was the auctioneer. About halfway through all the items he pulled out this very large beautifully decorated box. He said the item in the box was priceless, but it was a surprise. He allowed the bidding to reach more than $100, and then the woman who gave the last bid was escorted up to the platform. Of course everyone wanted to know what was in the box. Once the package was opened, the contents could be seen only by the woman, who began to scream and jump up and down, unable to speak. Izzy stood back laughing so hard he was bent over. Izzy the prankster had had someone wrap up the head of the pig that was being roasted for the luau. The poor woman thought she actually had to pay the money for the pig's head and was relieved when she was told it was just a joke."

On another occasion Captain Gaither and his fellow spouse–entertainers at Home League camp donned cowboy hats, with a plan to hold up the camp via stage coach. As a woman officer was leading devotions, Lt. Colonel Robert Strain, the divisional commander, was crawling up on the side of the platform and thought he heard the signal to start the surprise holdup. Bill LaMarr advised Izzy of the colonel's premature advance. Sensing a coup in this moment beyond what they even had imagined, Gaither responded, "Let him go!" Strain made his move, six shooters and all. Seeing their divisional leaders so out of character, the more than 400 women in the camp tabernacle erupted in hysterics.

Jon Walters, a session mate of the Gaithers, while traveling on business in Pittsburgh, had a standing invitation to stay at their home. He enjoyed their friendly hospitality and Eva's home–cooked meals. He remembers one visit that had an unusual twist. "It was prearranged that Izzy would pick me up at the Pittsburgh Airport outside at baggage. As I waited for him with my wheeled flight suitcase at my side, I opened my favorite newspaper, the *Boston Globe,* and read about my beloved Red Sox. Suddenly, a swift–moving individual ran past me, grabbed the flight bag and took off running. Another person waiting for a ride started yelling, and I ran after this light–brown–tweed–sportcoat thief, ready to pounce on and knuckle him! Yup, you guessed it, Izzy was the 'thief.' We laughed and laughed as we headed out to Tony Roma's for supper."

Bill LaMarr relates a story that became famous in the lore of Israel Gaither's time at Camp Allegheny. One late night at the office, Israel and his colleagues met in the parking lot and decided to go for a snack. Izzy suggested they could not do better than to go to his old stamping grounds in New Castle and get "Coney Island hot dogs" (considered an oxymoron by Bill LaMarr). So at midnight they headed to New Castle. The hot dogs were unlike any they had seen—served on a plate with "the works." The divisional commander did not make breakfast the next morning; he was sick all night. It is rumored that this eatery in New Castle still sells the Coney Island hot dogs, with chili, mustard, and "the works," and still there are those who make the 20–minute drive from Camp Allegheny to savor the spiced up frankfurters.

"Experience and Credibility"

Of the Gaithers' time in Western Pennsylvania, their senior officer and divisional commander in the latter part of their stay, now retired Commissioner Robert Watson, says: "Izzy and I were both early risers, so it was not unusual for us to schedule a private conference together to review personnel and other matters at 6 a.m. Understandably, things were rather quiet at that hour of the day, and we were never interrupted. We relied heavily upon the Gaithers' experience and credibility as the senior support officers at DHQ. I valued Izzy's counsel on many difficult issues. Alice and I drew strength from their fellowship and friendship during those days."

As a staff member and leader, Israel earned the reputation of getting done—on time and efficiently—whatever needed to be done. Whenever curmudgeons of red tape threatened to keep a job from getting a job done, Israel found a way around or through them to accomplish his task. He personified the definition of a leader as "one who when confronted by a problem, does not stop there, but finds a way through it."

"Israel took his God–given gifts," says his friend Major James Shotzberger, "and maximized them, as a good steward. With them he has sown seeds that have come back multiplied." In each succeeding appointment Israel Gaither was highly valued as a team member and effective leader. And from each new appointment he absorbed insights that contributed to his growth and preparation for further dimensions of leadership.

chapter 16

A Most Responsible Position

Now the overseer must be above reproach,
the husband of but one wife, temperate,
self-controlled, respectable, hospitable,
able to teach.
1 Timothy 3:2

A Salvation Army divisional commander in the USA holds one of the most responsible leadership positions, exceeding the responsibility of that undertaken in more than one–fourth of the overseas territorial commands of the Army world. The divisional commander is responsible for the oversight of the corps, service units, institutions, personnel, program, property, finance, and all related problem–solving and development within these categories. He is also looked upon as pastor to his officers serving under him. The position is directly responsible to Territorial Headquarters. It is the "top of the pyramid," next to the territorial hierarchy of The Salvation Army.

Major Israel L. Gaither was appointed divisional commander for the Southern New England Division, with headquarters in Hartford, Conn., effective Nov. 1, 1986. To Major Eva Gaither fell the leadership for Women's Ministries in the division.

"FOCUSED AND PRECISE"

Major Norman Wood, Gaither's second in command, remembers his leader as "focused and precise. He established guidelines and expectations for his staff and limited any possible confusion concerning areas of responsibility. He believed in good administrative practices and adhered to a schedule. He was a tireless worker, meticulous in detail. It was a challenging appointment because of limited resources, but it did not deter him in his vision for ministry. He had an engaging personality and participated in divisional events that contributed to a spirit of unity and camaraderie. He was not afraid to laugh at himself."

One experience during a men's camp program stands out. The heaving waters of the Atlantic Ocean were quite a contrast to the quiet waters of Pymatuning Lake, where Israel in years gone by had gone fishing with his dad. Wood, an outdoorsman, scheduled a men's fellowship deep-sea fishing trip, and Gaither was determined he would share in that experience. It would be Israel's first time on a deep-sea fishing boat. He was advised that in order to ward off seasickness, he should take some Dramamine® tablets, which while preventing seasickness can also bring on drowsiness. Norman Wood says, "We do not know for sure how many tablets were taken, but we do know that before the boat left the dock, Izzy was fast asleep and slept through the whole trip. I do not believe that he has gone on a deep-sea fishing trip again.

"Family values were extremely important to the Gaithers," recalls Wood, "and they instilled within their children the same values that had been a part of their childhood. They encouraged their son, Mark, to take a paper route both to teach him responsibility and also to earn his own spending money. Occasionally Mark would be ill or convince his parents that he should have a morning off. And Dad or Mom would assume responsibility for delivering papers. There were even occasions when Louisa and I could not assist our own son with his paper route, and the Gaithers would sub for him. Can you imagine a divisional commander subbing as a paper boy? We helped each other as needed. Now our son can boast that the Army's National Commander once helped him with his paper route!"

In addition to their responsibility as divisional leaders, the Gaithers were also active in their home corps. Eva was the Corps Cadet counselor for the Manchester Citadel Corps. The young people of that day still reminisce about their Bible study classes and recall times and events that tried their leader's patience. But Eva was loved, respected and held in high esteem by members of the class.

Eva was also creative, as reflected in the scope and quality of programs that came under her leadership. Major Louisa Wood says she felt privileged to learn under Eva's guidance how to plan and execute women's ministry events. "Both Eva and Izzy would be very involved," she says. "What fun we would all have when the divisional commander and his wife would let down their hair and participate in such humorous ways! Expectations were high, but they never expected anyone to do something they themselves would not do. This spoke volumes of their leadership."

Norman Wood adds, "We would highlight the dynamic preaching of Major Gaither. The division would prefer him to be the speaker for any event, rather than outside guests. Everyone would be challenged in their walk with Jesus after sitting under his ministry. He was concerned that the officers always be learning and planned many helpful and practical council sessions that would enhance ministry."

HIGH EXPECTATIONS

Majors Joe and Darlene Cramer, in their first experience as finance officers on divisional headquarters, wondered what their new divisional commander would be like. It didn't take them long to discover that "Major Israel Gaither expected your best for the division, The Salvation Army and, above all, for our Lord and Savior, Jesus Christ. We came to know him as Izzy, but when it was business, it was always Major Gaither. We were blessed by God with his vision for the division and for the officers under his command.

"Izzy was a stickler for the proper wearing of uniform. Once, when we were both arriving at the divisional office at approximately 5 a.m., I walked from my vehicle to the back door (about 25 feet) without putting on my cap. It was dark; I was carrying my briefcase and some other papers. But to be honest, I just didn't like wearing my cap. I thought nothing about it until we were in the building about 15 minutes and my telephone rang. As soon as it rang, I knew Major Gaither wanted to see me because there was no one else around. I picked up the phone and was told to come to his office. I immediately went and upon arriving was told to take a seat. Major Gaither proceeded to inform me of the proper way to wear a uniform, which included the cap. We had a discussion, and I would receive a memo reminding me to wear my cap.

"Major Gaither inherited some financial woes, at one point with DHQ unable to meet payroll. We had to make a presentation to THQ explaining our situation, how we got there, how we were going to get out, and how we were going to stay out of debt. It wasn't a pleasant experience for us. A plan was developed and Izzy worked hard at seeing the plan implemented. It meant cutbacks, watching program costs and developing new funding sources. It also meant the division would be visited on a regular basis by THQ staff to assess how we were doing and if any changes should be made. He made it through the tough financial times and when he left, the division was solvent."

Darlene Cramer remembers the divisional commander stretching her leadership ability with the assignment of planning a divisional world services ingathering celebration. "He affirmed me that I could do it, and said that he wanted to stretch my leadership abilities. With the guidance of Major Eva, the evening was wonderful, filled with God–given blessings from around the division! It was a great learning and stretching experience for me personally. Major Gaither saw possibilities in his officers that we might not have seen for ourselves. They both had a way of bringing those qualities to the surface to be used for God and The Salvation Army."

LEADERSHIP STYLE

Each Salvation Army corps community has an advisory board composed of leading citizens who volunteer their time and expertise. Thomas E. Desmond served as a member of the Greater Hartford Advisory Board and was its chair during Gaither's tenure. He owned an investment firm and his active community involvement included being president of 12 area associations and director of other groups. From a community and business standpoint, he assessed Major Gaither's four–year tenure and leadership in this capital city. "Israel's leadership style was exemplified by his strong interaction with the Greater Hartford Advisory Board. He respected the board's counsel, was an attentive listener to their suggestions and asked insightful questions as he explored the board's years of experience and knowledge of the Hartford area. Major Gaither's decision–making policy was based on reviewing the advisory board's input to his suggested changes or ideas." He adds, "Eva was an important influence to the success of the Hartford Salvation Army Auxiliary. Her gifts of listening and discernment were significant assets and blessings in their shared experience with the Hartford Salvation Army."

A Salvation Army officer lives a somewhat nomadic lifestyle, with major changes of appointments and cities, on average, every few years. Such changes can involve a dramatic, and sometimes even traumatic, transition involving leaving community and established relationships behind, and, for children, changing schools frequently. Appointment changes often were unilaterally decided by the divisional commander, subject to territorial approval. "Farewell" and "marching orders" were dispatched to the officer, who was notified of dates and the destination to which they were to proceed. Gaither, as a divisional and territorial leader, was remembered with gratitude for the then less–than–unusual practice of consulting with his officers about their appointments when circumstances would warrant. This proactive policy was considered by many a major and long overdue breakthrough in Salvation Army administration practice.

A RARE REVELATION

As divisional commander, Israel Gaither left an impact on many in unique and memorable ways. Colonels James and Carolyn Knaggs, as the assistant territorial youth leaders, were invited to the Southern New England Division to conduct a young adult retreat at Camp Connri in April 1987. They tell a remarkable story.

"Major Gaither had assembled a number of high school seniors who were applying for admission to Asbury College. He not only encouraged them but also opened doors for their eventual enrollment at Asbury and other academic institutions. We finished on the Sunday with a wonderful response at the mercy seat.

"As we concluded, Major Gaither was in the process of expressing gratitude to those who had helped through the weekend. It was here that he stopped quite deliberately and looked at Carolyn and me across the room. He then called us to the center of the room and asked the young people to encircle us for prayer. The memory is quite fresh in my mind as he called upon God to cover us with His grace and love, that we would be strong for the battle ahead and faithful throughout. His prayer demonstrated discernment available only to those who walk closely with the Lord.

"Who would have known that in only a few days our youngest son Joel would be tragically taken from us as a result of being hit by a car? Through the years, we have searched our souls for the presence of God through this most devastating experience and have taken great comfort in knowing that God was speaking to us through the voice and prayers of people around us. Izzy Gaither was there not only when we needed him but even before we knew we needed him."

Of that experience Israel says, "I felt led by the Spirit to pray for them, in one of those rare moments when God gives a revelation."

During his tenure as divisional commander in Hartford, Major Israel Gaither was appointed to Session 117 of the Army's International College for Officers (ICO) in London, Jan. 13 to March 7, 1988, for a study course with 24 delegates from around the world. That exposure, with its new relationships, engendered in Gaither a further awareness of the Army's response to people in other parts of the world. Israel's peers elected him president of the session.

Commissioner Doris Noland, also a delegate that year, shares her recollection. "He was a delight to have in the session and immediately endeared himself to us all. His dry, quirky sense of humor and his no-nonsense approach to difficult situations made him very popular with everyone, including the staff at ICO. He was then a new divisional commander and spent most of his free time handling divisional business long-distance. I was impressed with his depth of spiritual insight and while his mind was often occupied with the responsibilities he had left at home in his new appointment, he was very much present in the discussions and activities at ICO. Little did I know that ten years later our paths would cross again in a most unexpected way."

His ultimate word of disapproval was, "This is unacceptable."

DIVISIONAL LEADER IN PITTSBURGH

The next stop on what now had become a "fast track" for the Gaithers was to become divisional leaders in the familiar setting of their beginnings—the Western Pennsylvania Division, headquartered in Pittsburgh, effective Nov. 1, 1990. In this office it took two secretaries to keep up with Major Israel's workload. Those working as colleagues and under his leadership remember his penchant for memos. "You could not out–memo him," observes Major Sylvia Groff. "He would even send you a thank–you for a thank–you note."

His ultimate word of disapproval, according to Major William Groff was, "This is unacceptable." Upon hearing that from their leader, without question, officers knew it was back to the drawing board.

Bob Pease of the Pittsburgh Advisory Board speaks of Gaither's impact on this important arm of the Army in the city. "He is a kind man, a devout man with an open and sincere approach. He aided me with wise counsel for some difficult circumstances. Izzy's leadership while in Pittsburgh was exemplary. He approached every task with zeal and true joy from his work. His joy was contagious and staff and volunteers performed better and with more dedication because of his example. In everything that he did, he brought two essentials—his unconditional faith and his intellectual leadership. I consider him to be a true leader of men. His wife was as devoted as he, and in her own right gained the respect of all those with whom she worked. I consider him to be a spiritual leader, also a friend with no peer."

Major Kathleen Steele, in her words at the Gaithers' later farewell to South Africa, said, "When we were divisional youth leaders in Western Pennsylvania, I learned to love and to respect their leadership and learned a lot from them. One of the things that really strikes me was their example of servant leadership. During those long days of summer camp as divisional youth leaders, as the days get long and you start to get weary, it was not uncommon for Mrs. Gaither to come and say she was going to take care of the dining room, and for me and Hugh to go out to supper and have the evening together. That was just one example of their willingness to pitch in and their example of servant leadership.

"I also remember when we wanted to buy the first fax machine for Camp Allegheny. We were having a tough time on opening days without having required medicals on hand for campers when they arrived. We felt it would be helpful to have a fax machine for the day–to–day needs and to have physicals faxed to us from the doctor's office when campers arrived without them. We requisitioned one but it was not approved as the divisional commander felt it wasn't necessary. But his wife stepped in and told him that he should be there opening day and see the problem when we did not have what we needed that could be easily faxed. Without further ado, the fax machine was approved."

A MEDIA MOGUL'S MEMORY

Many in the Pittsburgh area and others who drive through tune their radio to KDKA Radio, where the Fred Honsberger talk show is the choice of most radio listeners between 2 and 6 p.m. Fred started as a news anchor and reporter and since 1990 has been in the role of talk–show host. He has won more than a dozen prestigious media awards, and also hosts his own TV show that airs daily between 10 and 11 a.m. He and his family are members of The Salvation Army Pittsburgh Temple Corps. This media "mogul" shares, in his inimitable way, his experience with Israel Gaither.

I have found both Izzy and Eva to be spiritual role models in my life. Both are centered on God, and that is what motivates and directs their leadership in The Salvation Army. The Army could not have better leaders!

When Izzy served as general secretary in the Western Pennsylvania Division, he would often participate in activities at Camp Allegheny. In fact, it has been tradition for DHQ officers to participate in a skit of some sort during Home League Camp. It was quite a sight to see him in costume along with the divisional commander, Lt. Colonel Robert Watson, dressed as women, complete with pantyhose! Anyone who knows these men should realize how amazing this sight must have been!

I remember the time that some unfortunate woman officer left her hat behind at Pittsburgh Temple Corps after a divisional meeting. Major Gaither left no stone unturned in an effort to find the owner of the hat. Several memos were issued to track down the poor woman. The effort not to make sure her hat was returned, but rather to inquire why the officer was not wearing her hat.

I also recall a very strange interview that took place later with Commissioner Gaither. It was upon his return from South Africa to lead the USA Eastern Territory. I was broadcasting my radio show from New York City on the first anniversary of the 9/11 attack. We had set up our studios in the Greater New York DHQ building on 14th street. I wanted to talk with Izzy about what it was like to be in South Africa when the attack occurred.

Before the interview, things were a bit awkward. Izzy and Eva came into the room. I don't think I had seen them since their return. I wanted Eva to sit in on the interview, but she said she just wanted to give me a hug, and left. Then, Izzy closed the door ... what was going on here? Was I being farewelled? Of course not; not even Izzy had that kind of pull. Oh well, on with the interview. Knowing the commissioner's fondness for Coney Island hot dogs from his hometown of New Castle, Pa., I suggested it had been a long time since he'd tasted one and then said they don't have any in New York City. He responded, "They don't have Coneys in London either."

That was a strange answer. How did London get into this conversation? How was that relevant? Afterward, I told Izzy how good it was to have him home and how we were looking forward to his and Eva's leadership in the Eastern Territory. To which he responded "Well, I believe there's something else in God's plan."

Wait a minute, he just got here. What could he possibly be talking about? Izzy seemed as though he wanted to say something to me. I wanted to ask, but didn't want to pry. If he wanted to tell me, he would. He didn't and we hugged and parted company.

All was revealed the next day. As I was driving back to Pittsburgh, I got the call from Captain Bill Bamford. Commissioner Israel Gaither had been chosen by General–elect John Larsson to be his Chief of the Staff. Izzy was right; there are no Coneys in London!

On another occasion, Izzy and Eva were special guests at their home corps, Pittsburgh Temple. Izzy wanted to sing a solo and asked my wife, Christine, to play piano. The song was "There's a Sweet, Sweet Spirit in this Place." Izzy wanted an old time "spiritual" feel to the song. Now, I'm not downplaying my wife's piano playing. She does a fine job with hymn tunes and the occasional offertory, but "pounding" the keys in the style of an old–fashioned revival meeting, well ... no. But the rehearsal was something to behold. Izzy encouraged Chris to go beyond her piano–playing limits. I saw his passion for the song being passed on to her. By the time the solo was sung in the holiness meeting, one would have thought Chris was a veteran of the revival tent. Not that people noticed her playing, or Izzy's singing. What those in attendance heard that morning was the Holy Spirit speaking to them through the music. And that is just what Izzy intended!

IN THE SCHOOL OF LIFE

Major Molly Shotzberger, a close friend of Eva's, shares a memory concerning her son Jim during this period. "We had just been transferred from

Pittsburgh to Toledo, Ohio. We had been in our new appointment for only 10 days when we received a phone call informing us that our son had been in a serious automobile accident. His leg was severely injured and he required immediate surgery. There was no time for us to get to Pittsburgh for the surgery. Izzy was called and he immediately went to the hospital to stay with him before the surgery and be there when he came out of recovery. This mother, who was so worried for her son, was comforted by calls from Izzy keeping us updated on all that was happening. She was also comforted knowing that her son was not alone. If Eva and Izzy are your friends, they are your friends, no matter what.

"The most important lesson he ever taught me was 'to choose my battles.' I remember asking his advice on a situation and he said, 'some battles are worth fighting; others you just have to let go.' I have carried that advice into my ministry and I am a better person today because of it."

Major James Reynolds, as divisional finance secretary in Pittsburgh, on one occasion confronted a delicate situation with the advisory board in New Castle, Pa., where Israel's preacher father was a member of the board. It involved the Army's policy of handling estates on a percentage distribution basis. The local board took strong exception that a percentage of a legacy that originated in their area would go toward support of area services outside of New Castle. As an 'unrestricted legacy,' besides an amount assigned to the local New Castle Corps, portions would assist with other Army funding needs. The advisory board felt the intent of the donor was to restrict the legacy for use (100%) in New Castle, versus the actual wording of the will, which was unrestricted and left to The Salvation Army in general. Major Reynolds explained that the Army legally could be guided only by what the actual will stated, which in this instance was 'To The Salvation Army,' rather than by ancillary comments from those who knew the donor.

Members of the board were unrelenting in their opposition and, near the end of the meeting, it appeared the majority of members would resign in protest. Major Reynolds says, "It was then that the elder Israel Lee Gaither II stood and made a calm and passionate plea for accepting the Army's position as well as loyalty to the overall mission of the Army." When he concluded, there were a few moments of respectful silence, and one by one, the majority of the board members went on to support the corps throughout their remaining time on the board.

The major observed something beyond the meeting that evening: "From that experience, it was evident where the son had received the qualities of leadership he had modeled to all with whom he met."

Indeed, the early foundations of Israel's spiritual nurture and training rendered inviolate his commitment to integrity and loyalty to God and the Army. The challenges confronted and overcome in his divisional appointments further honed the already sharpened skills for the next round of leadership appointments just around the corner!

Soul Mates

Cadet brigade: Israel (lower right), L. Moretz (top left), and P. Baxendale (top right)

The bridal party: Captain John Walters, Mrs. Captain Barbara Van Brunt, Captain Paul Baxendale, Mrs. Captain Ruth Pritchard, Eva and Israel, Captain Ronald Miller, Captain Joyce Herb, Captain Larry Moretz, Captain Barbara West, flower girl Robin Johnson, and ringbearer Kevin Barker

One of the interview sessions of Commissioner Israel Gaither with Colonel Henry Gariepy

Commissioner Gaither meets Archbishop Desmond Tutu

Mr. Esop Pahad, Commissioner Gaither, South Africa President Thabo Mbeki, General Gowans, and Commissioner Gowans at the presidential palace

General John Gowans installs Gaithers as USA East territorial leaders in
Old Orchard, Me. pavilion

Commissioners Israel and Eva Gaither in August 2006 had a 45-minute visit with
President George Bush. A warm and an intimate exchange on spiritual matters
took place in the Oval Office, concluding with the clasping of hands and prayer
by the National Commander on behalf of the President, the First Lady Laura Bush,
and for the nation

The General and his Chief of Staff

The Preacher (courtesy of the UK *Manchester Evening News*)

At an Army children's home in Korea

With Salvation Army officers in Korea

With "OKs" (officers' kids) in Russia

Lt. Colonels Rive, recipients of the Order of the Founder, flanked by the Gaithers
and the then territorial leaders, the Cliftons, in New Zealand

Israel's family celebrates his parents' 50th anniversary

Preaching the baccalaureate sermon at Asbury College

PART THREE

A Higher Level of Leadership

1993–2001

chapter 17

On to the Territorial Level

*Keep watch over yourselves and all the flock of
which the Holy Spirit has made you overseers.
Be shepherds of the church of God, which he
bought with his own blood.*

Acts 20:28

The progressive path of leadership on which the Gaithers were traveling
would now move Israel Gaither from the divisional to the territorial
level.

PERSONNEL SECRETARY

When Commissioner Ronald Irwin was appointed territorial commander for
USA East in August 1993, one of his priorities for addressing critical needs
in the territory was to select leaders in the areas of program and personnel.
His recommendation to the General, which was approved, was to appoint
Lt. Colonel Israel Gaither as personnel secretary and Lt. Colonel Larry
Moretz as program secretary. "Both appointments," he says, "were critical to
the mission growth achieved during my tenure as territorial commander
from 1993 to 1998."

Israel Gaither had been promoted to the rank of lieutenant colonel in his
last year as divisional commander, and appointed as the territorial field secretary on Oct. 1, 1993. The title of this position was changed during his
tenure to "secretary for personnel," and on June 12, 1994, Gaither was promoted to full colonel. The personnel office carried the major oversight in the
territory for its more than 1,700 officers—their appointments and development, and issues that might arise. Also, under the aegis of this office came
the ultimate responsibility for 12,000 employees in the territory. Israel now
occupied one of the most sensitive and responsible leadership positions in
The Salvation Army.

BEHIND THE SCENES

Some of the staff who worked closely with Colonel Gaither during this period take us behind the scenes to observe the more personal as well as the official side of the territorial secretary for personnel.

Carole Stollenwerk, who served as secretary to the colonel, gives a glimpse of both his personal and official office style. "He was a perfectionist in his output. He looked at issues from all sides, was fair, a good listener, proactive, and believed in longer tenures for officer appointments. He typed his own sermons and did lots of work in research. He was the only field secretary who never drank coffee; he always drank tea, with lots and lots of sugar, saying, 'Don't tell my wife!' He had a sense of humor, liked to startle people. Once when talking to a 5– or 6–year–old girl, seriously, in his deep–toned voice, he asked, 'Are you married?'"

Stephanie Elynich, who served as the second secretary in the personnel office, relates, "He was a very kind man, precise in what he wrote, organized, a hard worker. His hobby must have been writing letters. He wrote all kinds of letters, wrote to everyone. You would never get a form letter from Colonel Gaither. He would write letters to a sick child, and if the child fell off a bicycle, humorously, he would add, 'Don't ride any more bikes!' And there was never enough sugar in his tea. But what inspired me most were his sermons at staff devotions. Always heartwarming, inspiring."

Lt. Colonel Susan Gregg, assistant secretary for personnel during Gaither's three–and–a–half–year term, observes: "He loved apple pie and would ask, 'When is your daughter–in–law going to make her next apple pie?' He wasn't real patient at first but cultivated patience as he had to deal with dire circumstances. He was thorough in preparing cases for officer review board, wanted to know all background, be totally fair, with questions about families, school, and he encouraged consultation. He worked hard to move people into the right places. He was charismatic, open, and accepting. He enjoyed having fun, and loved to tease people."

"He worked for the mobility of black officers," Susan observes, "and was disappointed when they didn't measure up." Weighing in on this subject, Commissioner David Edwards adds, "Izzy did intentional movement of minorities as field secretary and chief secretary. His strategy was to open doors, provide opportunity of development and leadership for minorities, and to aid more minority officers to move into expanded opportunities of significant roles."

It was suggested by a close colleague that, "Colonel Gaither suspected there had been a 'ceiling' for African–American officers, and sought to address that, both while in the territory, and latterly in a world theater."

Lt. Colonel Margie Betts, who had worked as secretary for nine commissioners, observed, "He may not always have agreed with the territorial commander, but even when he did not agree, would gave his full support."

Commissioner Irwin remembers his protégé as, "meticulous and prompt in handling personnel issues. If he knew there was a problem somewhere, or an emergency or some sickness or death or misbehavior—he dealt with it promptly, doing what was right to protect the integrity of the Army while providing supportive counseling. He was compassionate in his dealings with officers, always fair, but at the same time, exacting appropriate discipline. He did not shirk from doing what was hard, but necessary."

IN THE HOLY LAND

During his time as secretary for personnel, Israel and Eva were the territorial leader representatives on a Holy Land education tour for officers. The objective was to visit biblical sites and study the culture, geography and background of biblical times. "The Gaithers were wonderful travelers and quickly became part of the group," observed Majors Ed and Darlene Russell, tour leaders. "They mingled as part of the group, rotating their seats on the bus so as to sit with each delegate during the trip." Israel and Eva led the worship at the Garden Tomb. The rainy, damp day could not dampen the inspiration of the setting or the Gaithers' earnest and affirming words.

Ed Russell describes a free day when he and his wife accompanied the Gaithers to Jerusalem's Old City to shop. "The way Izzy and Darlene went about bargaining with the shop owners, you would have thought that they were natives." Eva and Ed wanted nothing to do with the process. Izzy and Darlene wanted to buy their sons an olive–wood chess set and finally found the one they wanted. They haggled back and forth with the merchant for some time. Finally they negotiated a decent price, but Izzy wanted to get the price even lower. The seller in exasperation finally exclaimed, 'I'm done!' At that point the merchant gave up on them and sent them away. They shopped further but couldn't find a comparable set to the one lost in the bargaining. Izzy suggested that they go back and get the one they had let go. They returned, but now the seller

Israel Gaither with his favorite
Holy Land carving

wasn't interested. Darlene pleaded, and in response, with no credit to her bargaining partner, the merchant yielded and they had lovely chess sets to take home to their sons.

Of all the memorabilia from the Holy Land, Israel Gaither says he treasures most an olive–wood carving of Christ the Shepherd with a staff in his hand. It reposed in his office as a reminder that as personnel secretary, he was to be a shepherd to the people.

A Disagreement in the Family

On one occasion a matter involving Israel's father in New Castle came all the way to the Territorial Headquarters Finance Council. "My dad loved The Salvation Army," reflects Israel, "and had become good friends with Brigadier Jim Dihle through the New Castle Ministerial Association. In fact my dad said to me on one occasion, 'If I had known The Salvation Army as a younger man—who knows—I might have become an officer.' He was where he should be. I was proud on many occasions to stand with my father in his pulpit, he in his flowing robe and me with my 'flowing uniform.' I said to him one day. 'Dad, I put my robes on every single day, not just one day a week.' He replied, 'That's enough, son. I heard you, that's enough.'"

The elder Gaither's growing friendship with Jim Dihle over the years had led him to serve on the Army's advisory board in New Castle. Several years later he became the chairman of the board and held that position when Israel arrived as divisional commander for the Western Pennsylvania Division.

There was an occasion (referred to earlier) when the advisory board for the corps was in dispute with divisional headquarters over a legacy. His father had never engaged Israel in official discussions about the Army when he was home visiting with family. However, on one occasion following a wonderful meal Lillian had prepared, one by one, the family moved away from the table, leaving father and son alone.

"It was the perfect opportunity for him at one end of the table to lean forward (I'll never forget it), look me in the eye and say, 'Now son, let's talk about this legacy!' It was the only occasion on which my dad and I had any kind of disagreement over a Salvation Army policy. This occurred shortly before we farewelled to take positions at territorial headquarters in New York. The issue was still alive over the next year or so, and I remember one territorial finance board meeting when it surfaced again. I was serving as personnel secretary and Lt. Colonel Tom Adams was the secretary for business administration. The matter had now worked its way through divisional headquarters and was at THQ for resolution. Tom, my very good friend, with a chuckle, looked at me from across the table and said, 'Now Izzy, are you prepared to deal with this matter with your father?' Needless to say it drew laughter from the other members of the board."

CHIEF SECRETARY

When the chief secretary, Colonel Edward Fritz, retired in February 1997, officers from outside the territory were proposed to the territorial commander as possible replacements. Commissioner Irwin, taking the long view ahead for the territory, with the prospect that his successor, upon his retirement in August 1998 would likely be a non–Eastern Territory officer, advocated for IHQ to appoint Colonel Israel L. Gaither as chief secretary. Commissioner Irwin was confident that he would provide continuity and be an invaluable resource for the new territorial commander. The appointment was approved, and Israel Gaither became chief secretary, second in command for the USA Eastern Territory, as of Feb. 1, 1997.

Elevation to this high post, and Commissioner Irwin's prior influence in starting Israel Gaither on his headquarters appointments as divisional youth secretary, later as secretary for personnel, and now chief secretary, places Commissioner Irwin as number four among the seven instruments of the Lord who opened doors to ever–expanding opportunities of leadership and service for Israel Gaither.

Commissioner Irwin's successors, Commissioners Joe and Doris Noland, had reason to be grateful for Irwin's appointment of Colonel Gaither as chief. Joe records, "When we were appointed as territorial leaders to the USA Eastern Territory, we knew our time with the Gaithers would be brief, as the General had indicated that he had plans for them that would take them out of the country. Their knowledge of the territory was a tremendous help; his gifts complemented mine; and he adjusted quickly to my 'out of the box' thinking. Those four months were critical to my own indoctrination and made a smooth transition. During that period we were able to have in–depth conversations about the priority and importance of focusing on mission over method. Eva, like her husband, was able to handle difficult situations with grace and decisiveness. Both love people and people responded to them. When our retirement loomed in the picture, we were happy to know that the Gaithers were to take our place as territorial leaders. We retired knowing that the territory was in good hands."

As chief secretary, Colonel Gaither became a member of the Commissioners' Conference, which at the time consisted of the four USA territorial commanders and chief secretaries, the national commander and the national chief secretary. (In recent years, the wives of these members have also become a part of the leadership group.) The Conference meets three times a year at the Army's National Headquarters for extended discussion, policy review and decisions relating to The Salvation Army in the United States. It is the most significant single body for Salvation Army decision-making in the States and maintains an important bilateral relationship with the Army's National Advisory Board. Israel admits that at times meetings were frustrating, especially when he didn't agree with recommended policies or when there were sustained animated debates or strong dissent among the members.

Eva served on the counterpart national group, the Women's Work Commission, composed of the wives of commission members, who met separately in concurrent sessions. Israel's early training officer, Commissioner Robert Watson, who as national commander served as chairman of the Commissioners' Conference, gives his assessment. "It was interesting to watch the Gaithers bring the experience and wisdom of the years to the important discussions around those tables on issues affecting the work of the Army in the nation. They earned the respect of their peers and leaders, as well as those who came under their leadership during those days."

A "VELVET GLOVE"

As a fledgling and single corps officer, Israel had had an unpleasant experience during an official visit of a finance officer from DHQ in Pittsburgh. Rather than providing helpful guidance for the novice corps officer, the officer had dealt harshly with him about an oversight in the Army's bookkeeping system. At that time, Israel vowed that if ever he were in a situation in which someone needed either counsel or correction, he would do it in the spirit of compassion, or "tough love," and never in the acrimonious spirit that had been inflicted on him. Over the years he came to have many opportunities to fulfill that vow.

As chief secretary, he wore "a velvet glove over an iron fist." Daniel Diakanwa, a Salvation Army employee of African descent whose Army heritage includes his father having had the longest tenure as an African commissioner and territorial leader in Africa, shares an example. "I remember being summoned to the chief's office for a conflict–of–interest situation I was involved in, and he rebuked me with fairness. He wrote me up for the first time in my 16 years of service within The Salvation Army, and I accepted his reasonable sentence. I have known and observed his leadership for 26 years, and I have come to respect and admire this courageous man of God. Unlike many people of African descent, Israel Gaither is a man of faith and high esteem who is not intimidated by racism. He is both a thorough administrator and a pastor, a man of unquestionable integrity and dignity."

"Israel Gaither was very exact," observed Major Gary Miller. "This is the way it is going to be. At the end of the day, you will know where he stands."

From Major Lewanne Dudley comes another example of a gentle rebuke by the chief secretary. "When I was on the THQ staff as assistant territorial youth secretary, we were having difficulty making contact to secure information for our summer overseas mission team. I made contact by e–mail, dutifully copying the chief secretary. Well, Colonel Gaither was known to be one who strictly follows and enforces procedures. I was 'called on the carpet' for making direct contact instead of going through the chief's office! We did get the information needed as a result of the contact, but I got a little more than I had bargained for! I must say that the rebuke was not harsh, but gentle, and understanding of the situation in which we found ourselves. I was encouraged not to repeat this again in the future! This experience was helpful to make me aware that although we have easy access through Lotus Notes [the Army's closed e–mail system], we are still 'the Army' with regulations to be observed." At a later time, Major Dudley while serving in Nigeria would unabashedly add, "It is hard for me to adequately describe the magnitude of the pride and joy that I felt as an African–American when I heard the news of the Commissioner's appointment to IHQ as the Chief of the Staff!"

Authority without wisdom is like a heavy axe without an edge, fitter to bruise than polish. Colonel Gaither used authority to often smooth and polish rough edges and enhance the person and their role of leadership.

Captain Jorge Diaz remembers with gratitude, "When in an appointment in difficult circumstances, and not knowing where to turn, I picked up the phone and asked him for advice. He gave sound and godly counsel. The most impressive thing was that about a week later, the chief secretary was on the phone, 'Jorge, how are you doing? Has the issue become resolved?' I was able to say, 'Yes.' I was so encouraged by his interest and concern in following up our original conversation."

First and Lasting Impressions

The USA Eastern Territory's beautiful reception area has been enhanced for 16 years by Pat Murray, receptionist and self–described "director of first impressions." She shares a lasting impression the chief secretary made on her.

"When I was sitting here by myself late one afternoon, he came bounding through the door, stood at the elevator, called my name and said, 'Pat, do you know how great is this Army I serve?' He continued to expound the virtues of the Army, his mission and how much he loved the Army. He got on the elevator, the doors closed, and I thought it is

> *"I learned from them about surrender through pain."*

true that religion is not taught, it is caught, and how fortunate the Army is to have a leader who has such a passion for Christ."

A discerning observer, Pat took some lessons from further observations of the Gaithers at THQ. "In them I saw the meaning of 'faith in action.' And I learned about trust as the two of them entrusted themselves and their future to God. I've been very lucky to have Commissioner Gaither in my life, and I pray regularly for him as each day I see his picture on the wall with the other territorial leaders. I learned from them about surrender through pain. When surrender and pain came together, to witness their struggle to leave here, which was the height of their happiness, is to see the ministry of faith lived out at that level—very inspiring."

It has been said that no man is a hero to his valet, or perhaps either to his chauffeur. But Major Brian Figueroa refutes that axiom when it comes to the Gaithers. "I had the privilege of doing a fair amount of transporting them to and from appointments related to their preparation to going overseas, and to meetings, etc. No matter what time of day it was, even in the early hours of the morning, Eva and Izzy were always happy, vibrant, and enjoyable to serve with. One never felt uncomfortable around either of them. It was always a time of laughter, enjoyment, and serious moments of reflection for all that God has provided for us."

One year the New York Staff Band was invited to accompany the famous pop singer, Elton John, in a performance at Carnegie Hall. The event was the annual "Save the Rain Forests" benefit, a sellout concert featuring icons of the pop music scene. The NYSB was to accompany Elton John in "Abide With Me." Elton has a reputation for a counterculture lifestyle and there were those in the band who felt it would be improper for them to be on same stage. Other band members emphasized that the Gospels showed Jesus spending time with sinners. After much discussion, it was decided by the administration, including Colonel Gaither, that the band would not be a part of that event. One of the band members took the opportunity to sit down with the Chief to see if he would be willing to discuss the situation. "Being the exceptional leader that he is," writes Bandmaster Ronald Waiksnoris, "he was able to change his mind to allow the New York Staff Band to participate, with the understanding that it would be clear who we are and whom we represent." The band did perform at prestigious Carnegie Hall, playing "Onward Christian Soldiers" as they moved to the stage to accompany Elton John in a moving rendition of "Abide With Me." An insert in the program not only clearly explained The Salvation Army's mission, but also explained various third–world programs that the Army has that line up consistently with the concept of "saving the rain forests." Waiksnoris concludes: "On that evening, God's name was lifted up at Carnegie Hall, thanks to Israel Gaither's willingness to listen to all sides of the situation and make a good decision."

When Colonel Gaither himself spoke at public gatherings, he was sure to proclaim the Army's priority of evangelism and mission to serve others in his name. As chief secretary, in his dedication of the Hartford, Conn., Worship and Community Center, before a standing–room–only congregation, he declared prophetically, "We're going to exceed your expectations! How? With the power–plus of the Gospel and the ministry of social redemption!" He eloquently described the Army's mission. "The Salvation Army believes in possibilities, for transforming a person, a home, a community. We are a people who have great expectations. We dream big. We see people for what they can do and become. A people who are activists—our ministry is broad; we serve the whole person. A people who break barriers. These are the brilliant characteristics of The Salvation Army." He boldly claimed, to a chorus of amens, that "No barriers would be allowed to stand—not racial barriers, not economic barriers, not social barriers. This is a place where the disenfranchised struggle to survive. We can be used by God to be conduits of his grace. This house of redemption is set aside for the sole purpose of life–transforming ministries."

Each new appointment brought its unique challenges and opportunities and Israel Gaither as he went along, learned quickly and well.

chapter **18**

Shepherd and Pastor

*Be shepherds of God's flock that is under
your care, serving as overseers.*
1 Peter 5:2

The role of pastor to his flock did not end with Israel Gaither's leaving his appointments as corps officer. Upon assignment to headquarters, where he did not have the usual constituency of a parish, his pastor's heart nonetheless constrained him to encourage and minister to all who had need.

A strong element of encouragement has been a centerpiece of Gaither's personality and ministry. Many officers testify that his ability to empathize with others, to appreciate their concerns and trials, has been one of his most endearing traits. It is a gift honed by careful and prayerful response to people with hurts and heartaches. His antennae as a keen listener enable him to respond to the deep and sometimes hidden needs of an individual. The following testimonies from a sampling of such folk reveal Israel Gaither, a shepherd and pastor to the flock.

"GENUINE CARE"

Commissioner Anne Ditmer writes from her retirement home: "My husband Les Sharp and I came in contact with Izzy and Eva when we were stationed with them on divisional headquarters in Pittsburgh, with Izzy as our divisional commander. He was more than our divisional leader. He was our pastor. And what a good one he was! After Les' very serious and unsuccessful surgery in New York, I had to fly him home on a small medical plane. I was sitting up front with the pilot and as we were landing, there on the airstrip standing next to the ambulance, was Izzy in full uniform, waiting for his officer and friend. He climbed into the ambulance with Les, stayed with him until he was settled in his hospital bed at home, prayed with all of us and then left. Many visits in the last weeks of Les' life, and moments after Les took his last breath, Izzy was there for us, always waiting to embrace us with his love. We feel very blessed that he has been a part of our lives."

Major Betty Sharp, Les Sharp's sister, adds her note of gratitude for then–Major Gaither's pastoral ministry in that difficult trial. "Izzy became a pastor in the truest sense to our Les. He visited on a regular basis, always with Scripture, encouragement, comfort, prayer. That ministry did not end with Les. There were calls and letters to me, to my folks (then in their 80s and 90s). He attended to the comfort of my parents, put chairs for them at the head of the casket at the viewing and made sure they were able to greet all those who came. He arranged for them to be taken from the car to their seats at the cemetery, and saw them back to the car after the committal. There were private words and arms around the two of them before he left them, and the promise of prayer. There are not enough words to express my gratitude for his spiritual leadership, Christian example, genuine care and friendship."

Colonel Glen Shepherd, chief secretary in Canada, also speaks of Izzy Gaither's ministry of presence during a tragic time in his life: "In February 2003, when our son was involved in an accident that led to his paralysis, we saw up close the pastor in Israel Gaither's heart. For this we will always be grateful."

Major Blanche Reynolds tells of a difficult time when serving with the Gaithers in Pittsburgh. "Major Frances Long, with her daughter and grand-daughter, were on their way to a music program at Camp Allegheny. En route, the van Mrs. Long was driving went off the road, killing her. Her daughter and granddaughter were flown to the children's hospital in Pittsburgh, where they both died. Majors Gaither ministered and shared their love with the family and the entire division, as well as to an endless line of schoolchildren who came during visiting hours and to the funeral. In the days following the Gaithers made themselves available to the divisional officers and their children, consoling the family and others deeply affected by the tragedy."

"In my first corps appointment in Pittsburgh," writes Major Elizabeth Reed, who had earlier cared for the Gaither children, "who was there to greet me but Izzy and Eva. While there, a couple from Bermuda came, the husband in need of a heart transplant. I informed the Gaithers, and as a true pastor, Izzy was there the day of surgery and spent the day at the hospital with the family. He ministered to them and became part of their lives. The son, who was just 11 at the time, became a buddy with Izzy. The man is now the bandmaster of the Hamilton Citadel Corps in Bermuda and doing well, thanks to the prayers of many and the ministry of the Gaithers."

Israel Gaither's extended pastoral role is further revealed in the account by Lt. Colonel Gloria Hohn, while she and her husband were corps officers in Erie, Pa., serving under the then–Major Gaither as divisional commander. Her youngest son, Erik, as a high school student, had traveled with the divisional youth band to Canada. While there, he had an accident, dislocating his kneecap, and had to return home for surgery. Erie was a three–hour drive from divisional headquarters in Pittsburgh. But Erik looked up from his hospital bed to see his divisional commander, who had come to visit and pray with him. "There was no other business in the area to be attended to," she says. "He just came to the hospital, spent time with Erik, encouraging his spirit and his faith, and left. I tell you that it made a difference in our son's life."

Lt. Colonel Barbara Van Brunt, who had been a bridesmaid at the Gaithers' wedding, writes of her friend's ministry to their family in a time of deep need. "When our son Fred went through a serious illness that paralyzed him, he ended up in a nursing home in Ohio to learn to walk again. Eva and Izzy came home from Africa to see Eva's sister, who was very ill at the time and not expected to live. One day we were amazed to see them walk into Fred's room. They would have had to go a fair distance out

> *" Only if necessary, use words."*

of the way to make that visit. We were greatly touched and so blessed to see them and to have Izzy pray for our son, who since made recovery and re-members the Gaithers' ministry to him."

Major Molly Shotzberger relates a special touch of ministry when Gaither was her divisional commander. "At a Youth Councils in Pittsburgh, one teenage girl tearfully confessed to pregnancy. Izzy took her home so she would not have to face her officer–parents alone. He and Eva showed compassion and support as though she were their own daughter. Eva had a vital ministry with teens in the division."

THE MOST ELOQUENT PREACHING

A famous story of St. Francis tells that one day he said to one of his young friars, "Let us go down to the village and preach to the people." As they went, they paused to talk to each person they met. Francis stopped to play with the children, exchanged a greeting with the passersby, a word of encouragement to those in need. Then they turned to go home. "But Father," said the novice, "when do we preach?"

"Preach?" smiled Francis. "Every step we took, every word we spoke, every action we did, has been a sermon." Then Francis gave his now–famous words of advice, "Only if necessary, use words!"

Israel Gaither is well known as a powerful preacher. But for those who shared their story, and a great company of the unnamed, they will forever remember with gratitude his most eloquent preaching, that conveyed through an exemplary compassion and personal ministry.

chapter **19**

Marching Orders From God

Therefore go and make disciples of all nations.
Matthew 28:19

Israel's world was rapidly expanding. As his world view enlarged, his attention became drawn increasingly to global concerns of ministry. That development was abetted by opportunities of overseas travel and ministry. Reading on issues of leadership and the role of the church in the world further informed his view on the mission of the Army. Gradually he became aware that his preaching and teaching ministries were embracing more of a global view. "In fact I can recall going back through sermon notes and almost seeing the point at which I began to feel led of the Spirit to talk about the larger Kingdom mission picture. This had evolved over the years into some very strong feelings about the role of the Army as a missioning force in the world."

A quantum leap in the Gaithers' global awareness and development was "in the works." Their territorial commander, Commissioner Ronald Irwin, received a call from General Paul Rader asking if the Gaithers would be willing to take an overseas appointment. There was no indication where it would be or what they would be doing.

Commissioner Irwin made the enquiry with the Gaithers and immediately Eva said, "Yes." Israel was shocked. He looked at her and said, "What do you mean?" She responded that they had made that decision a long time ago when they committed themselves to officership, and there was no question but what they would go. Israel agreed, but as with his original calling to officership, he wanted some evidence that this was the plan of God for them. So they asked God, not to know where they were going, but to have confirmation that it was His will.

THE REVELATION

Over a period of months following that conversation with Commissioner Irwin, the Gaithers were led into contact with people from South Africa (they had never met a South African previously). One morning on arising, Israel had a revelation by the Spirit that Southern Africa was the location in which they would be asked to serve. He said to Eva that morning, "I know where we're going," and she asked, "Where?" He said, "I believe the Lord is calling us to Southern Africa." She was astonished and had difficulty believing it. But from that point forward they saw evidence that this, in fact, was the direction of the Lord.

They began some private orientation as to the ministry of the Army in that part of the world, even researching where staff lived. On one occasion they were in Newark airport awaiting the arrival of Israel's mother, who was coming to visit for a few days. Her plane delayed, they went into a coffee shop in the airport for some refreshments. Two women were seated at a table near them. Israel noticed a South African flag sticking out of one of their purses. An urge directed him to talk to her, to enquire about South Africa. Such conversations had already happened a number of times, and by now, Eva was a bit frustrated and said, "Please don't say anything to her. Don't ask her anything about South Africa." Israel said, "No, I must. I feel I must." So he engaged her in conversation. She knew about the Army and in fact was familiar with the very community in which they eventually would live— Edenvale. Israel took this as just one more sign that God was preparing them for the assignment.

Several days after he had this strong prompting by the Spirit that they would be sent to Southern Africa, he mentioned it to Commissioner Irwin, who then called General Paul Rader and said, "Izzy knows where he's going. He's told me he's going to South Africa." Rader responded, "Who told him?" The commissioner replied, "He had a revelation," to which the General asked, "Does that happen often?" Irwin records, "The General felt, as did I, that Israel Lee Gaither's revelation was confirmation that God's hand and leading were on the appointment and that it would be blessed and productive, as subsequent months proved."

When the Gaithers met the General in Old Orchard Beach, Maine, that summer of 1998, General Rader began the conversation by saying, "Izzy, I'm going to tell you and Eva something that you already know. I understand it has actually been revealed to you, and I just want to confirm it."

By this appointment, with all its momentous impact upon Israel Gaither, General Paul A. Rader became the fifth among the seven most influential leaders in the progressive leadership of Israel Gaither within the Army, and Paul Rader would continue to have an impact in Israel Lee Gaither's life story.

"THE MOST TRANSFORMING TIME"

Colonel Israel Gaither received his appointment to Southern Africa as territorial commander, and Colonel Eva Gaither as territorial president of

Women's Organizations, effective Jan. 1, 1999. With that appointment, he became the first African–American officer to serve as territorial commander anywhere in the world. It was also observed by an overseas leader, "that if Jesus doesn't come, Colonel Gaither will be the first African–American to sit on the Army's High Council."
History was in the making.

"That experience," he says, "and the actual time of service in South Africa, became the most transforming time in our lives, for it opened up in a remarkable way our understanding of other people, cultures and places, and the value of the Army as a gift to the world. Without the Southern Africa experience, we would not be the officers we are today, in terms of our own spiritual formation, our view of the role and place of the Army, not to mention my vision for what the Army can be and do in the future."

> *"Our service in South Africa became the most transforming time in our lives."*

The Southern Africa Territory includes besides South Africa—Lesotho, Mozambique, St. Helena and Swaziland. Its medley of people come from tribal, Dutch, Portuguese, Indian and Southeast Asian origins.

Linda Johnson wrote in the U.S. *Good News,* Oct. 23, 1998: "Just one decade ago, the appointment of an interracial couple to lead The Salvation Army's work in South Africa would have been not only unthinkable but also extremely dangerous." Israel Gaither affirmed, "We are going to a new South Africa, where people are free to move about and live as they please."

Under the rigid system of apartheid enforced by a white government until 1990, blacks, although representing 75 percent of the population, were forced to live in "tribal homelands," where conditions were extremely poor. All blacks and "colored" (Asian or mixed–race) people had to carry passes that identified them by race. Strict separation between races was enforced in schooling and in all public facilities. Mixed marriage was strictly forbidden.

Israel and Eva were journeying where the colorful diversity and ravishing beauty of South Africa rubbed shoulders with the deep suffering of its people.

THE PAINFUL PARTING

South Africa was a half a world away from family, home and all that was familiar. The Gaithers did not know one person in South Africa. For Eva, leaving behind family members was particularly difficult. For both Israel and

Eva, the prospect of leaving their home territory and moving to a place where they would be strangers seemed forbidding. But they had experienced a growing certainty that South Africa was part of God's plan for them and that He would prepare the way.

More than 1,000 soldiers and officers gathered on the final Friday of November 1998 at Centennial Memorial Temple in New York City for "A Celebration of Thanksgiving and Farewell." The program was punctuated with accolades and filled with surprises, including live fauna of South Africa. As the Gaithers were launched on their spiritual safari to South Africa, the soldiers and officers of the territory gave witness to their genuine affection and respect for these "home–grown" leaders. "I will be candid with you," Colonel Israel Gaither told the congregation that night. "We prefer not to leave. We haven't finished our work. But we have to yield to the will of the Lord. We cannot deny that this is what He would have us do."

At the farewell, Bandmaster Ronald Waiksnoris invited the colonel to play in the New York Staff Band. Israel donned the scarlet tunic, moved into the cornet section, and participated in the march, "Star Lake." That night he was also inducted as an honorary member of the NYSB.

Commissioner Joe Noland, territorial commander, expressed commendation for the Gaithers' contribution to the territory: "We celebrate their exemplary service and give thanks for who they are. Doris and I have only served with them for a brief time but have quickly discerned a genuineness of spirit and quality of leadership that is rare. They have never been confined to official responsibility. Israel's vocal solos often spoke more meaningfully than any words could; at the same time, he is one of the Army's most gifted speakers. His appointment is evidence of commitment to equality and of reconciliation in South Africa. It sends a powerful message—the right message."

"Extravaganzas she produced at Home League camps are legendary," lauded Commissioner Doris Noland of Eva Gaither's service as territorial secretary of women's organizations. She added, "And she usually managed to feature her husband in skits, including one in which he was a Spanish senorita. Through it all she managed to keep her family a top priority."

"We give witness of the saving power of Jesus Christ," affirmed Eva. "We've been given an awesome responsibility. We go where we know no one, not a soul. But we believe the Lord is there, preparing the way for us. We go in the strength of the Lord."

"Now Get Out of My Face!"

Israel's spiritual journey in those days gave credence to his powerful message for the evening. He and his wife would be going to a land that has "a possibility of becoming a rainbow nation of peace" but which still struggles with bias and deep cultural divides.

In this parting message to his home territory he shared his spiritual introspection. "I've wondered why God ever called me to be a Salvation Army officer. He knows how much I hate to pack boxes, to change houses." When he heard about a move that would take him halfway around the world, Gaither confessed crying out, "Lord, do you remember who I am?"

When he fell prey to this way of thinking, he said he heard God's loving response, "Israel, don't ask me that dumb question. I saw you before you were called. I know what is best for you. I'm not here to mess around with your life. I'll be everything you need. Now get out of my face!"

In his message that night he both affirmed and challenged the large gathering. "We've been captured by God's Holy Spirit tonight, redeemed and intended to be free. So every man and woman in this room can stand tall because of the possibility of being found. When you live in the light, ladies and gentlemen, you live with confidence. When you live in the light, you walk with an open freedom; you walk with your head held high. Because you live in the light, you live prepared; you live on guard. The believer is not shocked by the events around him or her but rather is always ready to give witness to the goodness and faithfulness of God.

"I may not have all the material possessions I would like, but if I have Christ, I'm rich, I've got joy. I may not have accomplished all the dreams I ever had, but in Jesus, joy and hope keeps the dream alive. This kind of confident joy keeps the believer safe and sound and preserved."

Israel scoffed at the idea that The Salvation Army has had its day in the sun, that it has passed its zenith. In his unquenchable optimism for the Army, he urged his hearers to believe with him that its best days lay ahead. He believed, under God, in the manifest destiny of The Salvation Army.

When the altar call was given, it was clear that the Gaithers' journey resonated with many facing God's call and their own struggles. People came forward in a steady stream.

Obeying the call to South Africa was a benchmark in their lives, and set an example of what it means to "go in the strength of the Lord." Their lasting legacy was not just one night of celebration but an ongoing challenge to follow Jesus—wherever He might lead.

The text God had used many years ago, scribbled on the back of an envelope from a friend at summer camp as an affirmation of God's call to Army officership, now became a reality for Israel: "Therefore go and make disciples of all nations." He had obeyed the call, and now he had his overseas marching orders from God!

chapter **20**

The Sand of Africa

Then I heard the voice of the Lord saying,
"Whom shall I send?
And who will go for us? And I said,
"Here am I. Send me!"
He said, "Go and tell this people."
Isaiah 6:8–9

he spiritual odyssey of Israel Gaither now took him and Eva on a pilgrimage across the seas to the southernmost country of the vast continent of Africa, a nation with no counterpart of geography, culture or people anywhere else in the world. When their plane landed on the soil of Africa, they were warmly welcomed by their new colleagues, and they stepped out into a new world that would change them forever.

South Africa

South Africa, at the southern tip of Africa, is prized for its wealth of natural beauty and resources and is the most highly industrialized and economically developed country on the continent. It was the last nation in Africa ruled by a white minority, having from the late 1940s to the early 1990s a white government that enforced a policy of rigid racial segregation called *apartheid*. Denied to the black majority were voting and other basic rights. Housing, education, employment, transportation and other facilities were segregated. Protests against apartheid often led to violence. In 1991 the government repealed the last of the laws that formed the legal basis for the apartheid system, and democratic elections were held in 1994. Nelson Mandela, a civil rights leader who had spent 27 years in prison, became South Africa's first black president of the country's first multiracial government. But apartheid's effects continued even after the laws were repealed, with many blacks and other nonwhites facing unofficial segregation and discrimination.

Black Africans make up 77 percent of South Africa's population, whites 11 percent. Some 60 percent of the white population call themselves Afrikaners, whose ancestors came chiefly from the Netherlands in the late 1600s. "Coloreds" (Asian and mixed–race people) make up 9 percent of South Africa's population. The average per capita income of black Africans is one–tenth that of whites. Some 75 percent of South Africa's people are Christians.

South Africa has sometimes been called "a world in one country." It is rich in geographic diversity, with seacoast, mountains, semi–desert, a wide variety of flora and fauna. It is also a land of extremes, with ultramodern cities like Johannesburg, and black townships where many live in shacks without electricity and running water. The diversity of the republic is seen most clearly in its people. Mandela has called South Africa "a rainbow nation." Eleven languages have official status.

The Salvation Army came to South Africa in 1883 into Cape Town. Today the territory has more than 400 officers and cadets and more than 25,000 senior soldiers. Services include traditional corps programs, hospitals, day–care centers, a home for battered women, and many other ministries including care for infants with HIV/AIDS. The Army has sought to address the scourge of AIDS which in Africa has taken from families a generation of men.

The Dawning of a New Day

Shortly before leaving for South Africa, the Gaithers were briefed at the United Nations by South African Counselor Peter Soul on political, economic and social issues facing the country. Soul himself would soon return to Pretoria and be available to the Gaithers as they began serving as the leaders of the Army's Southern Africa Territory.

In 1996 when General Paul Rader visited South Africa, he had participated in the nation's "Day of Reconciliation" and had launched the signing by Salvationists of *The Book of Reconciliation*. In 1997 the Army publicly acknowledged its failure to "stand up and be counted" during the years of apartheid and stated its commitment to develop programs and policies to "combat racism and strengthen what reconciliation has already taken place while aggressively partaking in our mission to reach the world for Jesus Christ." To Israel Gaither came the challenge to partner with the many who were committed to get on with building a new nation.

On Jan. 31, 1999, in Johannesburg, Commissioners Donald and Berit Ødegaard, East Africa territorial leaders, installed the Gaithers as territorial leaders for Southern Africa. The Army's famed Soweto Central Songsters were prominently featured during the programs of the day.

Shortly after their installation, Colonel Gaither wrote in *"The Territorial Commander's Column"* in the Southern Africa *War Cry* his gratitude for the "wonderful welcome" accorded them, and his initial impression of the Army he saw there. He emphasized the word "together" in their vision for the future.

"We will long remember," he wrote, "the vibrant testimonies, superb music and ready responses of people to the gentle urging of God for a deeper commitment of their lives to Him. My wife and I came away believing that we have a strong Salvation Army in Southern Africa! An Army that will move forward into a new century modeling what it means to work and witness together as one.

"Southern Africa has a Salvation Army of *praying* people ... Salvationists who are *proud* of their church and its role in their communities ... a Salvation Army consisting of people who strongly believe in mission ... Salvationists who believe and work for the strong *purpose* of this mission. As territorial commander I am so pleased that the vision articulated throughout the weekend with the watchword *Forward Together*, has struck a responsive chord in the corporate heart and imagination of the officers and soldiers of this territory. One more thing we saw and felt. This is an Army of *power* and *potential*."

A Secretary's Insights

When a vacancy occurred at the start of his time in South Africa, the new territorial commander made it a priority to secure the service of an efficient secretary, fluent in the languages of the territory and Army culture and able to relate to his unique administrative style. He found the perfect helpmate in Captain Marlene Hagar, who at the time was stationed at a country corps in the heart of South Africa. She had earlier caught his attention, and they had exchanged words at an officers' council.

In July 1999 Captain Hagar was called to THQ to interview for the post. She says, "It was a strange experience for me because never before in my five and a half years of officership did I have an interview for an appointment." She had heard that the colonel was professional and efficient and demanded the same from his staff as well. Two weeks later she was once again in his office, receiving a welcome as his private secretary.

Among hurdles to overcome at the beginning of their working relationship was the difference in accents—Gaither's strong U.S. accent and the captain's strong Capetonian accent. Hagar often had to put question marks on drafted letters at places where she could not understand what Gaither had dictated. She also discovered a difference in the usage of words in the USA and South Africa. On being asked by the colonel for a tablet, she seriously inquired, "Do you have a headache?" He said, "No, I don't have a headache, I want a writing tablet!" Throughout their time together in South Africa, they often laughed at such misunderstandings.

Few people know a leader better than his or her secretary. Captain Hagar shares her observations on Gaither.

There was no doubt when he dealt with any staff member or officer that protocol was of the utmost importance, and yet all found him to be personally interested in them. So we were able to see his professional and personal side in dealing with people. He knew every staff member by first name and, in South Africa, if someone calls you by your name in the workplace, it ascribes importance.

Then there is the efficiency side. When General John Gowans was to visit the territory, the very first planning committee meeting was held 18 months before the event. I remember making folders for everything from budgets, programs, participants, transportation, to bottled water for the services. I often heard stories trickling through from those who attended board meetings of which the Colonel was the chair and how people made sure that they had all the information at hand because he expected efficiency in the board meetings.

Today in South Africa people still talk about the dynamic preaching experienced throughout his years as the territorial commander. He kept his audience's attention every second he preached—he was and is passionate about preaching and often became emotional. When he gave altar calls people would flock to the mercy seat. I remember playing the piano on many occasions when he sang *"His Eye is on the Sparrow,"* and he sang like no other person I have ever heard because he lived through the song as he sang.

I saw a side of him that very few people saw. I remember keeping a constant stash of cookies hidden in one of my cupboards because of his sweet tooth. He knew exactly where the cookie tin was, but before coming into my office to help himself to a few, he would always stare down the passage where his wife's office was to assure she wasn't coming. One day, however, his secret was discovered when he was caught red–handed by his wife with his hand in the cookie tin. She reprimanded him for helping himself to my cookies, but I had to admit to her that I kept the cookie tin stashed away for him. It was actually a relief to him for his wife to know about the hidden cookie tin, as he felt more at liberty to help himself to the cookies after that.

His love for people extended to those who lived in rural areas in South Africa. He would return to the office telling me of the poverty he had witnessed, and he would speak with emotion as to the shock he often had at seeing how people lived in these areas. In turn the people in South Africa loved him because they saw in him a person who cared for them as people.

Integrity in the ministry was of utmost importance to him, and he often had to deal with officers whose integrity had slipped. He was known as the territorial commander not afraid to deal head on with matters that might otherwise be swept under the carpet. In South Africa there was a saying, "Rules are made to be broken." People had to learn very fast that this was not going to be the case with Gaither here. Being a man of high integrity, he expected those serving with him to be of high integrity as well.

He made a tremendous impact on not only the people in The Salvation Army but also on people in government and other circles as well. He was the very first black man, although an African–American, to take command of the territory. He is the kind of person that once you have met him and worked with him, your life will never be the same again.

"A Genuine Missioner"

Commissioner Jean B. Ludiazo, territorial commander of the Congo and Angola Territory, an African, shares his impression when Israel Gaither appeared on the scene. "My first encounter with Commissioner Gaither in Zimbabwe led me to ask, "Who is this man, an Afro–American with a special prophet look?" Although I had heard of him by several leaders, about his Christian character, boldness and mission passion, I had to now see him for myself. After some experiences together, I have no doubt to say that this man is a genuine missioner for Christ, a man of spiritual integrity, a man with destiny. In leaders' conferences, very quickly he strikes up friendship with people. I had the privilege to be on the same team with him during a visit to one of the corps in Harare. In a hall packed with spiritually thirsty people, he was the one to bring the final Bible message. Then what I was thinking of him was clearly revealed—he is a bold, passionate, and convincing preacher. His persuasive voice could penetrate the hundreds of people hanging on his magnetic words, and with no resistance, [they could] yield themselves to God when invited to step forward to the mercy seat. His influence on me, and ipso facto, the legacy to the Army, is that Israel Gaither will be known as a purposeful man focused on the mission, with a passionate flame to bring people close to God through salvation and sanctification."

Paul Heinamann, chair of The Salvation Army National Advisory Board in Johannesburg during Israel Gaither's tenure, reflects on his relationship with the territorial commander. "Early on I had many discussions with him to try and give him a feel as why we, in a country with abundant God–given talent, were still extremely short of skilled manpower. This was due to the lack of education and training of many of our people because of discriminatory policies adopted by previous governments. It didn't take him long to grasp and become sensitive to these issues. Izzy has his own opinions and views. He clearly demonstrated this at the time that a new national lottery was formed in South Africa, and as part of their philosophy offered financial support to charities. Izzy felt that it would be wrong to seek support from the lottery, and he had the support of the Advisory Board in this respect. He saw the lottery as an intrinsic evil, curtailing what we could do on our own, and he was concerned about the issue of integrity, with victims of the lottery already poor. It was also my pleasure to get to know Eva, who is a very warm and loving person. The two of them make a wonderful team and we will continue to think fondly of Izzy and Eva as friends wherever they are stationed to serve the Lord."

THE MANIFESTO

In his third month in office, he issued a *Vision and Call Statement;* in essence, his manifesto to the territory. It incorporated the theme for his goals in Southern Africa—*Forward TOGETHER.* Its purpose stated: "We will be a mission with the clear intention to share the Good News of the Gospel through every compassionate and ecclesiastical expression of ministry in the territory."

Twenty–one steps identified objectives for implementing key mission–initiatives, with evangelism listed as a first priority: "We will conduct all programs with evangelism strategies clearly integrated into the overall planning effort." Such an ambitious plan required organization: "We will realign structures, where necessary, to ensure mission effectiveness. We will be faithful stewards of our personnel, property and fiscal resources."

Leadership development became a foundational thrust: "We will engage leader development strategies to

The Gaithers and Nolands pray with a family at a new home provided by the Army in flood–stricken Mozambique.

ensure that future leaders are identified and trained for 21st–century leadership. We will create opportunities for the preparation of our young people for present and future key leadership service. We will embark on recruitment strategies that will result in growth in the number of soldiers and local officers serving within the territory."

The territorial commander, to move well beyond the status quo within the territory, decreed expansion as his final, 21st step: "We will develop innovative strategies that will result in the expansion of social and ecclesiastical forms of ministry. We will encourage and assist our young adults in the implementation of creative ministry that will attract and win people to Christ and the Army."

He concluded his extensive manifesto with the challenge: "By God's grace, wisdom and leading, let there be an energetic and enthusiastic response to this 'Call to Action,' and by doing so, ensure a strong mission–focused Salvation Army that is prominent and effective in Southern Africa's future. May it be so!"

After a little more than a year in South Africa, the Gaithers were promoted to the highest rank outside the office of the general, that of commissioners. In a group of international promotions announced by the General, the Gaithers were among six officers promoted to this rank. Included were Colonels Moretz and Clifton. For constitutional reasons, no two officers may be promoted to the rank of commissioner on the same day. Israel took this new rank on March 16, 2000, and Eva on March 17.

As he commenced the third year of his leadership, in a January 2001 *War Cry* article entitled, "Keeping an Eye on the Future," he challenged his people to "be relevant and not a relic of the past." He wrote, "'Forward TOGETHER' continues as our watchword. Salvationists must exalt the Lord in our worship, work and witness. Evangelize the lost, equip believers for effective service, enter lives and circumstances and bring healing and justice to our people. Engage in strategies that will pierce the darkness of sin and isolation, and expand the Kingdom through new corps plants and innovative ministries."

Reconciliation in the context of South Africa's history of racial problems loomed large on Commissioner Gaither's agenda. He enunciated his outlook, "The future is requiring us to expend more individual and corporate effort on reconciliation. Our mission pushes us into the horrible circumstances of the poor and disenfranchised—those who still carry the deep wounds of hatred and separation, no matter their color, language, ancestry, or place of abode. Surely repentance, forgiveness and reconciliation require our deeper exploration as a 'community in mission.' But we must first be truly reconciled among ourselves. I am calling all Salvationists to undertake prayerful, purposeful, intentionally deliberate acts of reconciliation. Salvationists of South Africa, by the signing of the 'Book of Reconciliation' and forever marking that day as historic, must now seriously regard that signal event as the beginning of a continuing process."

A Major's Observation and Bargain

Major Veronica Demeraski, a session mate and former associate, had occasion to observe from a unique perspective the leadership of the Gaithers in South Africa. She and Colonel Ian Smith came to the territory as the Army's international auditors, to look not only at the fiscal records but also at the complete picture of the territory. They reviewed missionary projects and held discussions with the chief secretary and the secretaries for social service, personnel and property. She reports, "There emerged the fact that Commissioner Gaither was developing the divisional commanders to manage their divisions, to see that THQ did not have to stand over everything, to instill in them courage and confidence, 'Yes, I can do this.' It was obvious that staff respected this approach although some were not convinced he could pull it off. Those from the old school considered that the divisional leaders needed close THQ oversight.

"I saw that South Africa was a first– and third–world mix, with its modern Johannesburg and its poverty–ridden Soweto, and the territorial commander moved in and out of these two worlds with ease. We saw him relate with staff at THQ and then with the common people, going from one culture to the other. What stood out most to us was that he was concerned and trying very hard to help South African officers to believe they were capable. For years THQ had made all the decisions, and it was hard to get them to believe, 'You can do things. You have the authority. You can fail and then start again.' He wanted to lift them."

Major Demeraski remembers that he had always been meticulously neat in his office, home and personal life. She was surprised to observe in their South Africa quarters that items were left around the house and that it looked very much "lived–in." When she inquired about this uncharacteristic appearance, the colonel replied that when they came to South Africa, they were counseled to put personal items out, not to have things stark. So wanting to identify with his people he did as South Africans do."

The major had reason to be personally grateful for her friend's bargaining skill, apparently honed in his trip to Israel. She showed interest in a wood hand–carving of African fauna being sold for about $25 and was advised by the colonel, "You have to bargain." She replied, "I won't, but you can!" She and Eva left to go window–shopping while the territorial commander argued and bartered on her behalf. When the group reunited, Demeraski found that her advocate had secured her memorabilia for $5!

Bridge Builders

The Gaithers had traveled to Mozambique during a period of recovery from a disastrous flood there. The Salvation Army had made a substantive

Opening the new library at Bethany Children's Home

response of food, shelter, and caring for families whose homes and belongings had been washed away. During his visit, Colonel Gaither offered words of encouragement to the stricken families, assuring that the Army was representing God in providing assistance to them. In parting he said, "God is with you; we are with you. So don't give up."

While serving in the Southern African Territory, they created "a bridge of hope" that spanned the oceans. USA East officers and volunteers crossed that bridge to South Africa, giving their time, labor, expertise and love. Those who couldn't make the journey offered their financial support. At the 1999 USA Eastern Territory Officers' Summit, an invitation was given to raise support for needy families in South Africa. The officers responded with a gift of $14,000. Eastern Territory personnel helped rebuild communities in Mozambique by supervising construction of 308 houses and starting fund–raising projects for local corps. Representatives from the Eastern Territory's Media Ministries Bureau traveled to South Africa with director Jeffrey Schultz to tape footage that encouraged contributions to the Army's World Services fund.

The Gaithers remember their reaction when they first realized the chasm between rich and poor in the territory. Commissioner Eva relates, "It was not so much a surprise as a shock! The initial response to seeing wealth and poverty in close proximity saddened and frankly even angered us. We had never seen people living in such desperately poor conditions, officers included."

She shared one of her most poignant experiences. "Our first visit to Ethembeni, our Johannesburg home for abandoned babies suffering from HIV/AIDS, left an impact that I will never forget. For the first time in my life I held in my arms a beautiful baby dying from AIDS." Her motherly instinct also influenced her leadership and ministry of the territorial family health programs, which aid hundreds of families in poor rural area township communities. She left her usual mark of creative leadership on divisional Home League rallies and women's leadership training programs.

Indeed, during their time in South Africa, the Gaithers became a "bridge over troubled waters" to many who suffered from poverty or disaster.

While overseas, they were encouraged by their large support force back home. In a letter to their family and friends, they shared their gratitude and gave an overview of their work in South Africa. "We are filled with deep gratitude to all of you for your indications of love and support this past year. You can't possibly imagine how important your contacts have been to us. Always, friends and family have communicated the right thing, in the perfect way, at the exact time of our need. In circumstances such as this—with separation from home, family, and friends—one depends on the power of the Spirit in a way never experienced in the comfort of the familiar.

"Our first year of ministry held two primary objectives. First, we had to get our minds, hearts, and arms around the territory. We needed to see and experience this country, and our people. That meant a great deal of travel, meeting the soldiers and officers, experiencing the richness of the diversified culture through worship, social experiences, listening and learning. In the process, we have seen all the regions of this territory in which we have an expression of ministry and mission. So we have a good sense of the vastness of the territory and the regional influences that impact our people. We quickly came to appreciate that we have two different worlds in which we live and minister: the first world of middle– and upper—middle class people with economic security, and the "third" or "developing" world, where our senses of sight, touch, and smell have literally been shocked. In reflection, we have also witnessed the joyous celebration of African worship with the natural, harmonious voices of our people producing music unlike any we have ever heard."

Eva shares a personal experience relating to their impact on the culture. "Izzy is a perfect gentleman, always opened doors, helped me with my chair, etc.—all the things that a woman loves. On one occasion in an executive officers' council, several of the Zulu women officers were sitting at a table, having conversation in their native tongue. I enjoyed a wonderful relationship with all of the leaders, so I asked them what they were talking about. In fact, jokingly I said, 'Are you talking about me?' Colonel Noreen Mzenda replied, 'Yes mama, as a matter of fact we were.' I began to laugh as she told me that they were going to tell their husbands to be more like the territorial commander and open the car door and help them with their chair. I said to the ladies, 'That's good, let me help you.' I went over to the table at which all of their husbands were sitting together and warned them that I would be watching to make sure they treat their wives as gentlemen should! Out of that light exchange those strong Zulu male leaders always made certain—in my presence at least—they were acting as gentlemen. And in fact they often wanted to demonstrate it! It was very unusual, given the culture of a male Zulu. It also taught me the importance of modeling what is right."

Prior to the Gaithers' arrival in South Africa, no separate records were kept at Territorial Headquarters of married women officers. One of the major efforts of the new personnel secretary (a married woman officer), was to establish personnel files for those officers, a huge undertaking that would take several years to complete. The effort underscored the value the Gaithers ascribed to the married woman officer.

In Pursuit of Excellence

A major area of concern to be addressed was in the field of community relations and development. Major Carl Schoch of the USA Eastern Territory, one of the Army's most skilled leaders in this field, traveled to Southern Africa for a two–week evaluation of the territory's status and needs in public relations. His recommendations included the reorganization of the department and expansion of its responsibilities. In response, Major Darren Mudge was sent from the USA Eastern Territory to serve in the new position of community relations and development secretary, along with his wife Major Lurlene Mudge as his associate. This change represented an expanded portfolio in community relations that would ultimately include oversight for legal matters. Major Mudge submitted a proposed plan to the territorial commander, which was returned with extensive editing and addenda. Israel was averse to importing an American system, and he "Africanized" the development plan for the Southern African Territory. He left the "how" to Mudge but clearly outlined his goals for the territory vis–à–vis the needs and impediments to growth that he had recognized.

Financial stability loomed high on the Gaithers' agenda for change. At one executive meeting Israel drew a wheel, depicting territorial departments as spokes of the wheel. "The hub is finance," he said, "and if the hub is broken, the wheel does not work." Then he added, "The hub is broken, and every department will be accountable for keeping within the budget." This set in motion the preparation and review of monthly finance statements, with strict accountability.

The new development department under Darren Mudge raised the profile of the Army in the country. A direct–mail company, an advertising agency and media company, along with expansion of the mail–appeal database was initiated with support donated by a Pittsburgh mailing service. During Major Mudge's three–year tenure the territory's annual revenue increased threefold, allowing for some of the goals Israel Gaither had set to be realized. Through contacts established with the U.S. Embassy and its ambassador in South Africa, funding was also forthcoming for various projects through USAID. The officer salary allowance, while still substandard, was raised during Gaither's tenure.

Fiscal stringency accounted for lack of the traditional infrastructure, such as department heads or a territorial business secretary. All but two divisional headquarters operated from an officer's living quarters with perhaps one secretary for staff. To help with the needs of the territory, Gaither called in resource people to assess and advise as needed. These included international auditors Lt. Colonels Larry and Gillian Bosh, who made seven trips in two years, and the Army's international legal secretary, Major Peter Smith.

One of the territorial commander's most dramatic innovations related to leadership development. A new Education Department was installed and a secretary appointed, with leaders and guest presenters conducting seminars for both lay and officer leaders. Gaither made it clear that he would not appoint someone based on color but on their abilities. He determined to identify officers and soldiers with potential, secure training and experience for them, then place them in positions of responsibility. Another part of Gaither's plan for identifying potential leaders was a weekend of testing by psychologists, funded by the USA Eastern Territory.

Placing younger officers into executive positions emerged as a paradigm shift. As a result, the territory experienced fresh ideas from those officers, who became passionate about their new appointments. Divisional commanders in their early 40s and executive officers in the same age bracket at THQ were a novel and salutary experience in the territory. Consequently today there has been a surge of national leadership with less dependence on overseas officers' support.

From his three years of service in the territory, Darren Mudge summarizes that Commissioner Gaither's approach was that territorial headquarters was for the purpose of supporting, rather than running the divisions, and he set about transferring "ownership" and decision–making to divisional leadership. "The elevation of divisional commanders gave them pride in who they were and confidence for doing things themselves."

Commissioner Israel Gaither had embarked on a challenging quest in pursuit of excellence for his territory. Major Lurlene Mudge observes, "He set very high standards, and expected excellence by his example and approach without having to demand it."

Advancing the Mission

In December 1999 Commissioners Ronald and Pauline (Polly) Irwin were invited for the commissioning weekend and executive officers' councils in Johannesburg. Ronald Irwin writes, "It was obvious to us that they were a breath of fresh air to the Southern Africa Army and that they had been embraced warmly by comrades there, both at THQ and in the field. Israel's platform skills enabled him to speak in terms easily understood, for he was culturally sensitive and aware of the long history of injustices as well as the need for spiritual healing. Under his ministrations in public meetings, there was a ready spiritual response at the altar. In discussions during my time in South Africa and subsequently, it became clear that his focus would be on leader development to assure the future of the territory and advance mission."

"The development of leaders of the future is the center point of my vision for the territory," stated Gaither. "Without competent, capable and committed leaders—no matter the color—the future will mirror the past! I'm not going to let that happen. It's about mission—not about me. It's mission that matters most!"

Israel Gaither argues his case for leader development as the key to mission progress:

> An aggressive and formal five–year "Leader Development Program," which will include a key leadership succession strategy, has been launched that has identified emerging nonwhite and white leaders who must be prepared for a better mission future. We are preparing nonwhite officers to assume, with full confidence and competence, key leadership chairs. Color over competence is not now, and never will be, acceptable to me—and it will never be the dominant influence in my leadership behavior.
>
> This is not the territory it once was. It is a new day for the Army and its mission in Southern Africa. And those now serving the territory are in the best position to appreciate the progressive changes as well as substantial progress to the mission, under the blessing of God, on so many fronts. I am determined that through God's wisdom and grace, the mission in this sector of the world will never again be what it once was.

Lt. Colonel Peck Koopman, a retired South Africa officer with strong European ancestry, served as field secretary during Gaither's time in South Africa. Koopman is described by Israel as "a tremendous man of prayer and lots of energy. I have said publicly and privately that God placed Peck in the field secretary's role just for me! He was the carrier of my vision of 'Forward Together' during our time in the territory. Peck and his wife Joan are very special people, and are saints." For his part, the colonel records:

> From the time I was appointed as assistant to a corps in 1960, I have had a burning passion for the expansion of the Field. I have always believed that God wants His Army to grow; that has been my passion. When the Gaithers and I met, there was instant spark and passion. The first meeting we had was in their home, informal, with other leaders. At the end we knelt in prayer and both Izzy and I passionately prayed for a forward move. He took me by the hand and said to me in a quiet corner, something to the effect that our hearts beat as one.

He always introduced me as "This is my Railton" (William Booth's first lieutenant and implementer of his vision). The most amazing thing for me was that Izzy trusted me and never refused me anything I wanted to do to promote and support the mission. Never did I ever hear a negative remark about anything that was related to mission. As Izzy said many a time, "We were together for such a time as this." Here I found my destiny in "Mission Matters."

We formulated over the next 18 months what we called Mission 2005, the objective being to double the Army in the territory by the year 2005. I set most of the objectives and Izzy gave helpful suggestions and encouragement. Some amazing successes were recorded, some bordering on the miraculous.

The annual corps review was adopted on the American principle, completely revised for the South African Territory, and followed by the new divisional review process. Another great advance was creating the annual consultation on moves, by the field and personnel departments. Izzy so elevated the importance of the divisional leaders, that most could not believe it. To those skeptical, I could assure with conviction, that things were different now.

Meeting South Africa's Giants

As part of the administrative oversight of the Army's mission in South Africa, Gaither both met and established a nexus with leaders of the community and nation. He had studied the nation's history and knew of its deep struggles and heroes.

When it seemed that black and white South Africans would engage in a cataclysmic confrontation, one man helped turn the nation back from the precipice and joined his people in the long walk to freedom and a nonracial democracy. Nelson Mandela, after release in 1990 following 27 years in prison, played the decisive role that led to South Africa's first democratic election. After his inauguration as president in May 1994, Nelson Mandela won the affection and respect of South Africans of all races for the manner in which he promoted reconciliation. Since retiring as president in 1999, he has continued to play an important role as senior statesman.

Dec. 4, 2001, in Johannesburg, became a red–letter day for the Gaithers and The Salvation Army in South Africa. Through the courtesy of Dr. Ivan May, a member of the National Advisory Board, special arrangements were made for Commissioners Gaither to hold discussions with the former South African president. General John Gowans and Commissioner Giséle Gowans arrived in South Africa two days earlier than scheduled in order to share in

Nelson Mandela creates a light moment for the Gaithers and the Gowanses.

the historic visits. Gaither observed that upon receiving the Army's party at his private residence, this world–renowned leader exhibited an extremely warm and gentle humility. As he rose from behind his desk, his tall, majestic frame seemed to overwhelm the beautifully appointed office.

"You know you are in the presence of greatness," reflects Israel, "when in the presence of Nelson Mandela." From the first strong handshake, it was apparent that not only did the Army leaders have the honor of being in the presence of a statesman, but also it was as if they were visiting a well–known friend, and members of the party were immediately put at ease. The territorial commander spoke of watching on television in the United States Mandela's 1990 release from Robben Island prison. He said to Mandela, "Watching that dramatic event unfold on the television screen, I never dreamed that God would give me the privilege of personally meeting you."

Amid an extremely busy schedule, Mandela generously set aside 30 minutes for conversation, in which the Gaithers presented an overview of key aspects of the Army's work in South Africa. The president spoke warmly of his appreciation for the work and mission of the Army, saying, "South Africa needs The Salvation Army." It was agreed that continued contact would be undertaken to follow up on specific matters, including flood emergency relief efforts and the ongoing ministry of the Army in Mozambique. It was evident that the Army had a friend in Nelson Mandela, with potential for assisting the forward movement of its mission in South Africa.

Treasured mementoes of the visit, arranged by Major Darren Mudge, were autographed copies of Mandela's historic autobiography, *Long Walk to Freedom*, for General Gowans and Commissioner Gaither.

The commissioner records, "Discussion was facilitated by the clear respect held for the Army by the immediate past president of South Africa. It was the uniform that made the meeting possible, not the individuals wearing it."

Israel shared the sentiment of Billy Graham, who upon meeting Winston Churchill, said, "I felt like I had just shaken hands with Mr. History." Gaither's secretary, Major Hagar remembers, "Upon his meeting President Nelson Mandela, he returned to the office and told me that he wasn't going to wash his hands again because 'Madiba' had shaken his hands."

In 1999 Thabo Mbeki, a former exile, took the mantle of national leadership from Nelson Mandela. Mbeki was identified in *Time* magazine (April 18, 2005) as "the most powerful man in Africa." As Mandela had helped unite a divided nation, Mbeki says he seeks to achieve something almost as difficult—to spark an "African Renaissance" that will bring democracy and peace and boost the continent's development.

On Dec. 6, 2001, two days after meeting with Nelson Mandela, again through Dr. Ivan May and now also through Mr. Esop Pahad, minister to the president, arrangement was made for the Gaithers and the Gowanses to visit with President Thabo Mbeki. Strict protocol was outlined, with a 15–minute time slot allotted for the visit. Spouses traveled with their husbands but were not included in the audience with the president. The Salvationist party was accorded VIP status, being picked up and transported by police escort to the presidential residence in Pretoria.

They were graciously received by President Mbeki. General Gowans described for him the international profile of The Salvation Army, and Commissioner Gaither spoke of the Army's work in South Africa. As he described the Army's work, the president's interest was piqued, especially when he talked about youth, and the 15

An informal conversation with President Mbeki

minutes quickly stretched to 45. President Mbeki indicated an interest in providing government aid to the Army's program for young people.

Then, to the surprise of the General and Commissioner Gaither, as they were taking leave, President Mbeki asked, "Would you like to see the renovations we are doing to the mansion?" The next minutes were spent on a tour of the extensive renovations, with Mbeki himself as tour guide! Then, as the Salvationists were leaving, with the breathtaking view of the Pretoria landscape before them, the president stood and waved goodbye. And he said to the Commissioner, "Next time you come, bring your wife!"

During that visit to South Africa, General Gowans conducted a series of meetings made memorable by his compelling messages and the significant response of dedication by the people. Far less uplifting was the General's tour of the apartheid museum, a moving experience to see such artifacts of the great suffering as ropes used in hangings and an isolation cell. The Gowanses' tour guide told them that she herself had survived six years in such a cell. The international leaders left South Africa with a keener appreciation for both the vibrant spirit of the Army and the travail in the history of the nation, from which Salvationists had not been immune.

Anglican Archbishop Desmond Tutu, celebrated cleric and 1984 Nobel Peace Prize Laureate, known as "the voice of the voiceless," became the primary church leader in South Africa in its struggle against the evils of apartheid. He preached that "There can be no future without forgiveness," and he wrote *The Rainbow People of God—the Making of a Peaceful Revolution*.

Israel, while in South Africa, was eager to meet this prominent leader, but the bishop's traveling and health had prevented a meeting. The Gaithers' time in South Africa expired, and they farewelled without having met Tutu. But later, during the bishop's February 2004 visit to King's College at the University of London, then as Chief of the Staff Commissioner Israel Gaither was among the congregation. He approached Tutu during the reception that followed in the Great Hall, and the pair engaged in a friendly conversation. Gaither later reflected, "It was a very special privilege having the chance to chat briefly with him following his preaching at Kings College."

"An African at Heart"

Warren Maye, editor of the USA Eastern Territory's *Good News*, himself an African–American, traveled with Commissioners Noland for two weeks in South Africa in November 2000. He recalls, "It was a unique opportunity to sense the day–to–day leadership of Commissioner Gaither and observe how he motivates, encourages, revives, focuses on people, as he moved among soldiers and cadets [and officers], whether in Mozambique recovering from flood, or in South Africa recovering from apartheid. I saw how he reacted with poise under pressure, giving hope and confidence in the Lord. Israel Gaither, who before South Africa looked upon the world as an 'African–American,' returned to the USA with a world view and a deeper sensitivity."

After three and a half years farewell orders came for the Gaithers to leave South Africa and return to the States, effective August 1, 2002. The Gaithers had made an indelible imprint upon the people there, and Africa had made its enduring impression

The experience and lessons of South Africa became indelibly etched upon the mind and soul of Israel and Eva.

upon their hearts. Eva Gaither remembers the land, the country and the culture of South Africa, but most of all, the people who became a vital part of their lives. "The people of South Africa will always live in our hearts and memory, including some with whom we closely bonded, both officer and lay Salvationists."

Israel affirmed, "We are humbled by the past three–and–a–half year ministry in a dynamic sector of the global mission. We are grateful for the sacred trust that has been given to us. If there is a message to be given, it must be— 'Mission Matters Most.'"

Major Mirriam Mavundla, who with her husband served on the THQ staff, offered her note of appreciation for Eva Gaither. "Thank you, Commissioner Eva, for recognizing the potential among women officers and for walking alongside them. Because of our history in South Africa, women tend to depend upon men or husbands. In your leadership you made it a point that women are encouraged to exercise their gifts and talents. Many women came out of their shells. As Africans we say, *Siyabonga Mama and Baba (Thank you Mama and Papa)* for coming to this part of the continent, South Africa. You made a great impact in the lives of officers and Salvationists. Our ministry has been enriched by your leadership."

When first approached about going to South Africa, Israel says, "We were not sure the appointment would work and said as much to General Rader. He was sure it would, and we had faith in him. He was right. It was amazing. As an interracial couple, we found that we were more comfortable in post–apartheid South Africa than we had been in America. In the early years of our marriage, it was common to be the object of people staring at us— but in South Africa no one ever paid any attention. But, given the horrible history of apartheid, we could not have been appointed to South Africa three years earlier. The appointment had been made at the right time, for the right reason."

Commissioner Joshua Ntuk, an African retired Salvation Army officer and former territorial commander in Nigeria, writes, "During his service in Africa, African leaders described Gaither as having a servant heart, a good friend of Africans, and relationship builder. He is an American by birth, but an African at heart."

A Song of Confirmation

At their farewell meeting in Johannesburg in 2002, following the haunting melodies and vibrant music of the territory's premier music and dance groups, Israel said, "I wish I could take with me the voices of South Africa, Mozambique and Swaziland. I will take them in my memory." With passion he preached on a Deuteronomy text, quoting from Moses' farewell speech, "Never forget." He challenged Salvationists never to forget their obligation to God, the miracles they had seen, and to pass on to future generations their love for God and for The Salvation Army.

Earlier in the meeting he had been invited to lead the territorial band. He picked up the baton and humorously said, "The first thing I need to know is what we are playing!" The selection was Commissioner Stanley Ditmer's "I'm in His Hands." Those present witnessed their leader's deftly leading the band selection. But the guest conductor, who as a youth had been mentored by the composer, and whose funeral service he would conduct in just a little more than a year, no doubt affirmed once again the song's truth for his and Eva's ongoing pilgrimage:

> *What though I cannot know the way that lies before me*
> *I still can trust and freely follow his commands;*
> *My faith is firm since he it is who watches o'er me;*
> *Of this I'm confident: I'm in his hands.*
>
> *In days gone by my Lord has always proved sufficient,*
> *When I have yielded to the law of love's demands;*
> *Why should I doubt that he will evermore be present*
> *To make his will my own? I'm in his hands!*
>
> *I'm in his hands, I'm in his hands;*
> *Whate'er the future holds, I'm in his hands.*
> *The way I cannot see, has all been planned for me,*
> *His way is best you see, I'm in his hands.*

Israel gives witness that the Lord at times has bestowed a revelation of his will to him. Significantly, "I'm in His Hands" was also sung in the first worship experience of the Gaithers in South Africa at the Johannesburg City

Corps, during the prayer meeting led by Major Ernest Jones. Israel says, "The singing of the chorus in that moment confirmed we were supposed to be there." Now, in their final meeting, once again the song by his mentor and friend had been selected. Israel in that moment made a "connection"; the two presentations of the song became spiritual bookends both of the Lord's confirmation of His will for them in their coming, and now, in their going.

THE SAND OF AFRICA

The experience and lessons of South Africa became indelibly etched upon the minds and souls of Israel and Eva. As he has acknowledged, Israel's time in Africa had a transforming impact upon him. He and Eva could never be the same again, and what they gained from their Southern Africa experience would forever resonate in their ministry.

The Lord's leading of the Gaithers to South Africa had been for them an epochal experience. It had led them spiritually where they had not gone before. They readily acknowledge that their time in South Africa was a turning point; it launched them into a new era, one in which their life structure had permanently shifted.

When David Livingstone, the famous explorer and missionary to Africa died more than a century earlier, his body left Africa, but a grateful people buried Livingstone's heart in African soil. The Gaithers left a big part of their hearts in Africa, but they also carried Africa within their hearts as they departed in July 2002.

There is a saying, "Once the sand of Africa gets into your shoes, you are never the same again." The "sand of Africa" not only got into the shoes of Gaithers, but also made its way into their hearts and souls.

chapter 21

"In One Accord"

They were all with one accord in one place.
Acts 2:1a (NKJV)

In the context of The Salvation Army's increasing diversification, its greater reliance on indigenous leadership, and changes and practices in the post–colonial world, the office of the General, the international leader of the Army, continues as a unifying influence for Salvationists throughout the world.

"ELECTION DAY"

The Army's 1878 Foundation Deed included a method of succession, provided under the Army's constitution, that the General would nominate his or her successor upon taking office. The nomination would be secret, and the successor's name put in a sealed envelope, kept safe by the Army's solicitor. On the death or resignation of the General, the envelope would be opened and the successor named.

The scheme was simple, but dangerous—a point made to the Founder in dialogue with the famed British Prime Minister William Gladstone, who said that the process did not allow for "calamity, incapacity or heresy." In 1904, William Booth arranged for an amendment to be made to the Army's constitution; it provided for the convening of a body of senior Salvation Army leaders, known as the High Council, should leaders become concerned over the fitness of the General for office. In 1929, when the first High Council convened, it revolutionized the means for deciding the appointment of the Army's highest leadership position, and since then, all succeeding Generals have been elected under those rules.

When the High Council convenes, by tradition at the Army's Sunbury Court outside London, it is "election day" in The Salvation Army. The High Council is the Army's equivalent of the Roman Catholic College of Cardinals, which meets to elect the Pope.

On May 6, 1999, the 14th High Council convened in London to elect the successor to General Paul A. Rader, who would retire on July 23. Those leaders who qualified for High Council membership included the Chief of the Staff, all commissioners except the wife of the General, and all territorial commanders. Coming from the then–104 countries and territories in which the Army was active, the leaders bathed the proceedings in prayer, supported by the prayers of Salvationists around the world. To this assembly came Colonel Israel Gaither, territorial commander for Southern Africa, a colonel just four months into his appointment.

The roster of the High Council reads like an issue of *National Geographic*, with delegates from such far–flung and diverse places as Australia and Africa, Japan and Jamaica, India and Indonesia. The leaders epitomize the internationalism of The Salvation Army—a spiritual bond that spans and transcends all continents, races, and cultures, and preaches the gospel in 116 languages.

Several characteristics of the 1999 High Council made it unique. It was the largest ever assembled, with 74 in attendance. It hosted the largest number of full colonels, including Israel L. Gaither. The gender balance of the membership had changed. Only two women had been members of the preceding High Council, but because of a 1995 change in the rules of membership, this time, there were 28 women. Of these, three were single officers and the remainder were married women commissioners, now considered "officers in their own right." For the first time at the 1999 High Council, a questionnaire was designed for candidates' spouses. New state–of–the–art conference facilities at Sunbury Court, designed to accommodate the increased number of council members, and with high tech interactive communication system, would be in use for the first time by a High Council.

Commissioner Robert A. Watson, USA national commander, a senior member of the Council and due to retire on Aug. 31, was elected president. His suggested theme, "With One Accord," was adopted.

A New Voice is Heard

"Knowing that Colonel Gaither could give a strong message with relatively little time to prepare," Commissioner Watson, in the early part of the proceedings, invited Israel Gaither to give the Sunday morning devotional message.

On that Sunday, many at that High Council, not having known or heard Gaither previously, could not have anticipated the passionate and prophetic message they would hear from a junior colleague. Commissioner Watson reported, "He did not disappoint us. God used him to prepare the hearts of the members of the High Council for the important discussions and decisions to follow." Indeed, following that Sunday morning sermon, a new voice had been heard, and a dynamic spiritual leader emerged on the international landscape of The Salvation Army.

His compelling message, taken from Exodus 18:19, was "Be Thou for the People God–ward." The following is an excerpt.

Mine is a sacred privilege to speak from the Word this morning in this hallowed setting. But I am reminded that just as God by His Spirit is found in this beautiful place, He is also present, right now, in the humble places in which Salvationists gather around the world to worship. Salvation Army halls—some of which lack the basic offerings that provide for even a reasonable setting—will find our people at worship, in humble places in which poor but powerful people gather to meet with God.

And so His Spirit reminds me again that it is neither the place nor the circumstances that make the difference—it is the believer who desires to know God, to celebrate God, to worship God, to give of him or herself completely to God, that makes the difference. So I am humbled at this sacred responsibility given me by our president.

I have sought the Lord's leading in an attempt to know what the Word has for us. And I am led to continue the focus on the significance of who we are in relationship to His calling and anointing for leadership of His people.

We would remind ourselves that in such an untidy world as this, we are first shepherds, leaders of the highest order, in possession of a divine call. So we engage in the worship of our Lord fully open to the moving of His Spirit. We come with a spiritual longing for more of God. For we want to be shepherds, pastors, leaders desiring to know the heart and mind of Christ. For how else can we lead in the will and intention of God?

It is not possible to provide safe, adequate, spiritual leadership without intimacy with God. Without deep intimacy we will fail the grand intentions of God for ourselves, our people, and our ministry. God forgive us for the times when we have operated from personal skill, ability, and knowledge.

I want to be a shepherd, desirous of knowing the mind of Christ! It is my primary need. In fact, as a leader of His people, I must, and you must, seek a higher level of intimacy than those we lead.

Look with me to the 18th chapter of Exodus, the King James version of the middle portion of the 19th verse, which reads, "Be thou for the people ... God–ward." This is counsel given to Moses by his father–in–law, Jethro, about who and what Moses was to be in the face of the tremendous organizational and personnel issues that came with leading the nation of Israel. In essence Jethro is advising, "Look, Moses, this is your responsibility. You are a representative of the people as you stand before God. You lead them on His behalf."

In this confusing and secularized age, what must we do? One thing I believe we must do in the communities of our leadership is to become the voice of redemption. I am believing for a Salvation Army that becomes the conscience of culture. For I believe we are in an age when another 'exodus' is needed. We need an exodus from warped values and benign acceptance of wrong. We need freedom from the shackles of secularism. Our people must be liberated by the power of Christ to be enabled to stand in purity and in confidence for that which is holy, and right, and just.

God stir us, shake us, causing a renewed Salvation Army to emerge with heightened passion to boldly speak the liberating power of Christ.

> *"God stir us, shake us, causing a renewed Salvation Army to emerge."*

In the hectic pace of our leader lives, listening for and to God is a discipline to be cherished. And the God–ward leader cannot risk not listening to God. For how can we communicate His intentions, if we do not hear from Him? And how can we hear from Him if we are not often alone with Him?

No doubt, you are, as I am, driven more than ever before to consider what is God calling us as a Salvation Army to be in the century to come. How can we better model the community of the Kingdom? How can we better impact corporately the world for Christ? Where is He leading me, as I lead His people? What else do you want from me, God?

Secondly, as revealed in Exodus 24:11–12, the God–ward leader has the privilege of leading followers into new and dynamic encounters with God. Here is an image of a privilege intended for the leaders of God's people in our time. We possess the potential of leading our people into experiences and encounters with God that will have a revolutionary impact on their lives and circumstances, so much so that they will never be the same again. The God–ward leader, by the power of the indwelling Spirit of God is capable of that kind of leadership.

From my place of leadership, I see people who need a new vision and a new visitation from God. They need to "see" God, experience Him in a way never thought possible. They need a dramatic encounter with Him. And you and I stand in a relationship to God that makes such a spiritual journey for them possible.

Our leadership of leaders is a profound privilege, for there are those who need us to model what it means to be a minister with passion. Too many are living insensitively on the edge of defeat. And the sheep who follow them will never realize their God–given potential in Christ if those who lead fail to reach their potential. So the demand for a model of a God–ward leader is urgent!

Thirdly, the God–ward leader quickly responds to meet God, even in the clouds of life's journey. Moses is summoned to go beyond the other leaders and the people. He is called 'higher up the mountain.'

The call we have received to leadership, I believe, is a higher summons, to a higher degree of responsibility, a greater accountability, with larger outcomes anticipated. You see, we are not only the appointed, but we are anointed leaders—shepherds, bishops, priests if you will.

The Lord called Moses into the cloud for his purging, renewal and instruction. God called him by name. And He talks to Moses about keeping the lamp burning, holy consecration, about worship and anointing. He prepares him for leadership.

He calls each of us to unique roles of leadership. And this is one more time to ready us for God–ward leading.

"THE WHOLE FOCUS CHANGED!"

Up to that hour of worship the High Council for the most part had been consumed primarily with the mechanics of rules and procedural matters. Commissioner K. Ross Kendrew of New Zealand describes how that sermon became a turning point for the conference. "My memory is of the days spent in highly technical debating of the matter of rules for High Council procedure. I wondered at the absence of focus upon the mission of the Army. Where were the delegate leaders with a passion for mission and for Kingdom growth?

"The whole focus of the High Council changed for me when Israel was invited to address the council during the Sunday worship service. Here was a man of passion. Here was a leader whose heart and mind were upon mission and Kingdom growth."

The invitation to the colonel to be the Sunday preacher, by his former captain and mentor along the way, unintentionally catapulted him to a new height of recognition and esteem on the Army's international scene. Thus Robert Watson, from earlier influence at the beginning of Israel's training as a cadet, then as his divisional leader and colleague, and now at this Army summit, became the sixth among the Lord's seven persons who had a major influence in the progressive development of the leadership and ministry of Israel L. Gaither.

Israel's preaching that Sunday morning was not only a defining moment for that High Council, but also left its imprint upon the colonel from South Africa. He would return from this summit a different person from the one he had been when he arrived. But a most awesome moment for him was yet to come!

chapter 22

The Nominee

Fear not, for I have redeemed you;
I have called you by name; you are mine.
Isaiah 43:1b

In an atmosphere of quiet reverence, each member of the High Council was invited to nominate any Salvation Army officer (except himself or herself) for the office of General. A two–thirds majority is required for election on the first three ballots. After each ballot, the nominee with the least amount of votes is dropped from the ballot. After the third ballot, only a simple majority vote is needed for election.

In 1999, the High Council nominated eight members for the office of General. Five agreed to stand as candidates; among them was Colonel Israel Gaither. With him stood Colonel Shaw Clifton (territorial commander, Pakistan), Commissioner John Gowans (territorial commander, United Kingdom), Commissioner John Larsson (territorial commander, Sweden) and Commissioner Earle Maxwell (Chief of the Staff, IHQ).

Shaw Clifton brought impeccable credentials: a degree in law, several books to his credit, exceptional platform skills, and service as an officer in Africa, Asia, America and the United Kingdom. John Larsson and John Gowans also had backgrounds of international leadership and were gifted platform leaders. "The two Johns" had become household names for their musicals presented around the Army world. Earle Maxwell, an Australian with notable overseas service, was well known and respected as an effective Chief of the Staff, second in command for the Army world.

For Colonel Israel Gaither, it was one of the most awesome and defining moments of his life, a recognition and honor the candidate from New Castle, Pa., could never have dreamed would come his way. Astonished, overwhelmed and humbled by his nomination, Gaither travailed through the night "with a fearsome struggle, resorting to solitude and prayer." He sought counsel from friends, felt led that God wanted him to make a statement at that gathering, then accepted the nomination. "It wasn't about wanting to be General, but about speaking what the Lord directed me to say. If I were to be nominated again, it would be the same—not 'running for election,' but having the opportunity to speak the message that God gives to me."

ANSWERING THE QUESTIONS

Since wives of colonels were not members of the High Council, it was necessary for the spouses of Shaw Clifton and Israel Gaither to journey to London for the remaining proceedings, and to answer questions posed to them. The Council adjourned while Colonel Helen Clifton traveled from Pakistan, and Colonel Eva Gaither made her way from South Africa.

After a day of prayer, meditation and preparation, the Council reconvened in full session to hear the candidates' replies to the 25 questions (actually 35, with subquestions included) that had been prepared by the Questions Committee and approved by the full body. Questions ranged from issues of health, family, spiritual gifts and testimony, administration, recruitment, mission, vision, uniform, strategy, doctrine and attitude toward changes. Each candidate provided a written response to the questions, with a copy to each member, immediately prior to his presentation.

1999 High Council candidates: Colonel Israel Gaither, Commissioners John Larsson, Earle Maxwell, John Gowans, and Colonel Shaw Clifton

Israel, with the other four candidates, remained in virtual isolation as they prayerfully prepared themselves for the questioning period. Following each presentation, the spouse of the candidate would give her written response to six questions prepared by the Questions Committee for the spouses. Those questions related to health, family background, role of the spouse to the General, platform ministry, spiritual journey and women officer issues.

The first question, in two parts, on the General Questionnaire for Candidates related to health. Candidates were asked to "inform the Council of your relevant health history," and "What do you do to maintain good health and to manage stress? Do you have the stamina to cope with the demands that will be made of you as the General, and do you have any difficulties with long–distance flying, eating food of various countries, and culture differences?"

He replied that he had maintained a schedule of full health examinations and that no concerns had arisen from those exams. He stated that he and his wife exercise moderately through periodic walking, which they believe also impacts positively on their levels of stress. He stated he had no difficulty with long–distance flying, is cautious with respect to diet, especially avoiding spicy foods, and previous and present cross–cultural dietary experiences had not proved difficult.

Asked what he saw as the role of the spouse of the General, he responded, "My wife will actively participate in the determination of her specific role. However, we also enjoy our team–ministry relationship."

In response to a question regarding spiritual gifts, he answered, "My spiritual pilgrimage has revealed, and I have been affirmed, as having several of the gifts from the combined 1 Corinthians and Romans passages: leadership, faith and speaking the Word. I humbly wish to use those gifts for His glory and the mission of the Army."

In regard to style of leadership, he said, "I operate in the consultative style of leadership although I am not afraid to make the final and/or independent decision when required. My leadership style is reflected in my attempt to use the 'team–ministry' approach."

Asked to tell of his experience relating to sanctification, Israel replied, "I stand humbly before you, grateful to God for the work of redemption and sanctification in my life. Early in my officership, there came an understanding of full consecration as I came to grips with certain matters concerning my relationship to God. Each privilege, particularly in key leadership appointments, has awakened a need for a deeper consecration. Although so often failing, I seek to live the will of the Lord in my daily life, and I know the certainty of his cleansing, the supremacy of his place in my life. I am at complete peace with God."

High Council members did not withhold hard questions of the individual candidates. A pointed question posed only to Israel Gaither was: "Having served only in the USA until your present appointment and having been in your present command as a territorial commander for only a few months, are you convinced that you have the background and experience to undertake the worldwide responsibilities of the General?" His response: "I have never been convinced of my adequacy for any appointment entrusted to me by God and the Army. In fact, some of the key leadership appointments entrusted to me, including my final divisional command, provided me responsibilities in a number of dimensions, which are greater than those which I now hold."

Should he be elected, his five–year term would expire five years before retirement age. The question was posed: "The term of office for a General is five years. How would you envisage your succeeding service as an officer should you not continue as General beyond that period?" His response: "I would be willing to step aside, if unable or unwilling to serve a second term, and assume an appropriate appointment and rank until reaching the age when I would become eligible for full USA Social Security benefits."

NOMINATION SPEECH

Each of the five nominees who stood for election addressed the High Council, identifying their perception and vision for the international leadership of the worldwide Salvation Army. Colonel Gaither, realizing he was little known by most of the Council members, after his brief introductory words, felt led to identify himself, "Who I Am," to those who would be casting their ballots. Secondly, he outlined in essence, "What I Believe," and finally, "Why I Am Standing." His presentation was spiritually autobiographical from which the following is excerpted.

> I stand humbly before you with thanksgiving to God for his redemptive work in my life, the cleansing and indwelling presence of the Holy Spirit, and a true determined desire to fulfill my calling for my entire life as a Salvation Army officer. I am confident of His place and call in my life.
>
> My desire to stand as a candidate for election does not result from any desire to promote myself. I state that in truth, on my honor, and in the sight of God.
>
> FIRST, THIS IS WHO I AM. A man who has found his place in life. You see, I believe that I must make a difference in the world. God has not called me to a "closet" Christianity. I have never fretted over the "next" appointment. My intentions have always been to be faithful "just where He needs me." That is not to suggest that every appointment [I have had] would [have been] my choice. I would never have chosen the significant responsibilities which have been afforded me by God and the Army, responsibilities for which I have never

thought I was adequately prepared. But I humbly and gratefully acknowledge that somehow, and for His reasons alone, He has seen fit to use me to make a difference in the lives and circumstances of at least some. As a result, I have grown to believe in who I am in Christ.

My confidence is rooted in Him, and I live convinced about His intention for my life. I derive my daily direction and sustenance from my early morning time of private worship of Him. It has been my practice for years, and He is faithful to me in every encounter. I do not have the gift of prophecy, but I can attest to the fact that there have been those times when God has remarkably provided revelation to me for specific circumstances beyond my capabilities.

THIS IS WHAT I BELIEVE. Let me tell you what I believe, about the mission of this great Salvation Army. I believe that God raised the Army for a singular purpose in the world that cannot be fully realized through any other organization or body of believers. It is my firm belief that God has a special role for the Army to play in the bringing in of the end of the age and the Kingdom of God. We are situated globally to be an effective agent in fulfilling the command of the Great Commission. That is, if we can convince and mobilize this great Army of Salvationists in a worldwide resurgence of effective evangelism.

I believe in the Army doctrine. When I made the change of membership from my father's church to the local corps, I left behind the sacred and beautiful sacraments in which I participated. I admired my father in his clerical garb. But as I indicated on Sunday morning, this uniform is my "robe." And I am proud to wear it.

While we are not sacramentalists, we do have our cherished beliefs and practices. They are sacred to us, and well they should be. Our ecclesiastical customs must never be set aside. And neither must we seek to imitate the practices of the conventional church. We are unique in Christendom. If I desired to be a minister, I would be pastoring a church. But I'm not. God called me to be a Salvation Army officer, and I have the privilege of preaching, pastoring and serving in a manner and for a purpose that caused my pastor father to comment on one occasion: "If I had come to know The Salvation Army at an earlier age, I just might have been an officer."

I believe it is incumbent on us to reclaim our corporate calling to evangelize with passion and relevancy. Those about whom God spoke to our Founder still exist in greater numbers than ever! But in too many sectors of our Army, we seem to be losing, or have lost altogether, our passion for reaching the lost with the pure Gospel! We seem more comfortable with offering physical food than spiritual nurture. We respond more readily to natural calamities than the spiritual disaster in which too many of our people still, seemingly comfortable, exist! The significant differences are being made in the parts of the world that stand as beneficiaries, in the shift of evangelical Christian presence away from the West, to Africa and Asia.

Somehow, through some creative means, we must find a way to sustain the mission in such parts of the world. A seeking of the mind and heart of God, coupled with the resources already at hand surely will reveal possibilities from which to capitalize on the potential for expansion! Unless we can find a resolution relatively quickly, I fear we will lose precious opportunities never to be regained. It may require a new way of doing business! Perhaps a shift in mission priorities will be necessary. The new millennium advances and must not find us crippled by our inability to "do something."

Here's something else I believe! There is a desperate need to revive our focus and commitment to meaningful holiness teaching! The notion of "living a life of holiness" still seems foreign to many Salvationists, nothing more than a nice phrase from the song book! It is not understood, and thus not thought to be vital!

I believe the Army is capable of emerging in the new century in such a fashion that we model what the Kingdom of God looks like! Here is the challenge that has come to my heart for a renewed Army! Challenge our youth with creative and dynamic mission possibilities, for they just might be God's answer to our need for renewal! If we can discover again the urgency of evangelism, substantial growth will follow! If Salvationists around the world would take the journey to rediscover our holiness heritage, a holy people will emerge. And a holy people after the heart of God will make a difference for Christ in the world.

I CONCLUDE WITH WHY I AM STANDING. I stand for election believing the Holy Spirit's revelation to me. In the early hours of Wednesday morning, He clearly revealed that I am to be available for this hour. This is not my preference. I would rather not be in this position. It has been an emotionally grueling experience! But I am compelled to stand.

I am aware of the number of votes cast for my nomination. In good conscience, just as some have declared they could not stand, so I declare that my conscience, sensitized by the Holy Spirit, requires that I reckon their trust in me. I must believe that those who cast their lot for me did not anticipate that their vote would be lost or wasted by any action I might take to step aside from their summons to me to stand as a candidate. My personal integrity cannot allow that, even though I readily admit to you that a battle has been raging within me.

I wish to acknowledge in an unnamed manner those of you who have stood by me. Some of you did not realize that through a simple word, a touch of your hand, an embrace, a look, you became God's affirming agent for me. Several of you have, in the private places of this beautiful setting, ministered to me—encouraging me to press ahead and fight the inner battle.

I also stand proud and humbled to be one among this company of the highly committed. I have come to regard you as far more than leaders. You are brothers and sisters in Christ. In a mysterious way over these days, you have become part of me. And so I speak to you from my heart about "who" I am; and "what" I believe; and "why" I stand.

I also stand because of others who are watching these proceedings from a distance. I indicated my pride at being numbered among you. I hope you realize that in more ways than one, this fourteenth High Council has done something historic. You have allowed, by your acceptance of rules and procedures, this man to stand before you. And with that, we corporately have sent a strong message to the world that senior leaders believe in the future. We have said that youth is valued. We have said that a black American cannot only be the first to sit among this group of world leaders as a full member, but he can be so trusted by some that they would risk their vote to nominate him. I tell you, we have sent a powerful message to our beautifully diversified Army of Salvationists. Yes, Mr. President, it is true—we are "in one accord." Our corporate action moves us beyond the ugly, tiresome barriers of age, and race, and ethnicity and language.

When we leave this place, in full assurance that God has directed us to the leader of His choice, let us also remember that we have, by the grace of God, done a worthy thing. A thing that could not have been done before. But it's time now, and we did not fail the God–given, precious opportunity.

Fellow leaders, comrade Salvationists, brothers and sisters in the Lord—this is why I stand. This is who I am. I have deep beliefs about my role and place in ministry that have been forged out of experience. I understand the challenge of being

black in a white structure. I know, with Eva, what it is to declare our love and then wait to see if The Salvation Army really
does mean what we say we believe. And despite the whispered
debate we understood occurred throughout the Army world
about the 'problem' of a white woman marrying a black man
as officers—God has ordered our lives.

And there was one man, who himself served on a previous
High Council; he alone would stand for us and with us. And
in this hour I declare by my standing—my tribute to him. I
honor him. For with my father, he too modeled what a priest
looks like.

I retire to my seat convinced that I have responded to the
call of God for this moment. And I am honored by your corporate trust in me. God give us a leader who will take us to renewal and revival! May it be so!"

[The reference, in the next to last paragraph, was his tribute to the late
Commissioner John D. Waldron, who, through his confidence, courage and
advocacy, had made it possible for Israel and Eva to have their marriage approved, and who officially encouraged the progress of the Gaithers in their
early years. Commissioner Waldron was, next to his father, Israel's primary
hero. In this moment, he sought, by standing as a nominee, to measure up
to that early confidence expressed in him.]

THE BALLOT

Although Israel Gaither's number of votes was inconsequential, and his
name was dropped after the first ballot, the High Council with its nomination of an African–American for the Army's highest office had made a powerful statement. Gaither went to that Council a virtual unknown to leaders
outside of America. He had been a territorial commander for only four
months in remote South Africa. He was in the junior ranks among the large
group of commissioners. Some saw the nomination of an African–American
to be a symbolic gesture, one that would send a message to the Army world.
But it left its indelible impression upon that Council, and upon the nominee,
and it catapulted Gaither upon the world scene of the Army. The one who
preached and was nominated would be more than a fleeting meteorite on the
horizon; he was, from that moment, a new yet fixed star in the Army's
universe.

The late General Frederick Coutts, recorder of the Army's official history
for a period of more than 60 years, had said, "The only thing predictable
about a High Council is its unpredictability." The 1999 High Council illus-
trated that statement in that on the third ballot one candidate received more

than half of the votes in his favor (40 of 74), enough votes to carry him into office if he retained that number into the fourth ballot requiring only a majority vote. But with low–vote nominees dropped after the initial ballots, this most mercurial of High Council voting reflected 'swing votes,' so that the fourth ballot resulted in a tie, and the fifth ballot was carried by three votes, the second closest election in High Council history.

In that final tally, Commissioner John Gowans, who had led the United Kingdom Territory since 1997, was elected to succeed General Paul A. Rader. John Gowans, who because of his age was due to retire in 1999, was granted a three–year extension to serve through November 2002. A charismatic leader, accomplished lyricist and poet and compelling preacher, he greeted the High Council's decision by announcing that he would work for the "total mobilization of the Army."

Colonel Israel Gaither was among the first to both affirm and hold in prayer the newly appointed international leader of the movement to whom he and Eva had fully dedicated their lives.

"He is a self–made man, overcoming both natural and artificial barriers both in and outside the Army."

In retrospect, Commissioner Joe Noland, then territorial commander in the USA Eastern Territory, acknowledges, "Both Doris and I felt strongly that it was time for a young General, and time to break tradition. It would have been revolutionary to have a young, non–commissioner elected as general and, in our opinion, Izzy fit the bill perfectly. It would have added a new energy and vibrancy so desperately needed."

Commissioner das Krupa, territorial commander of India Southeastern, shares an Asian viewpoint. "The acceptance speech given by Israel Gaither at his first High Council gave glimpses of his depth of knowledge about the Army, incisive mind and clear perception about the Church and world at large. A man from a nonwhite background in the first world and relatively unknown to the worldwide Army outside USA was quickly recognized for world leadership. I perceive him as a man of intense passion for evangelism, strong in convictions and [having] a businesslike approach. He is a no–nonsense man. Behind all the seriousness and intensity, he is equally sociable, approachable and humorous. He is at ease in dealing with complex issues and has decorum and courtesy in interacting with people. He is compassionate at heart and understanding, knowing the minds of people both from developed and developing countries.

Among his many skills, he is a gifted communicator and wise counselor. He can articulate his views well and speaks his mind. He is a preacher par excellence with zeal and eloquence. He is a self–made man, overcoming both natural and artificial barriers, both inside and outside the Army, through sheer determination and hard work. Eva Gaither is an unassuming and a quiet woman, most knowledgeable about women's ministries and has interest in providing support and resources to other women leaders. She is easily approachable and maintains humor to balance her seriousness in work."

Israel and Eva Gaither had "been to the mountaintop" and would return from the rarefied air of that experience with an invigoration of mind and spirit beyond what they could ever have imagined.

chapter **23**

A Grand Homecoming

"The Lord shall preserve your going out
and your coming in from this time forth,
and even forevermore."
Psalm 121:8 (NKJV)

The Gaithers returned from the High Council to their posts as territorial leaders in South Africa. After serving there for three and a half years they received word from General John Gowans that they had been appointed leaders of their home territory, USA East, effective Aug. 1, 2002. In taking the helm of their home territory, they would be assuming responsibility for one of the largest territories in the Army world. Its more than 1,700–officer strength was second only to the United Kingdom and Canada; its number of corps was the fourth largest; its more than 100 cadets is the largest group of officers–in–training in the Army world. The Eastern Territory's number of employees and its fiscal and community operations were without equal in the global Army. Now, more than ever, the Gaithers acknowledged their need to "go in the strength of the Lord."

The territory's annual camp meetings, held in the coastal resort town of Old Orchard Beach, Maine, had for more than a century featured renowned preachers, bands and soloists, and every Salvation Army General since Albert Orsborn (1946–1954) had spoken there. The camp meetings celebrate Salvationism and afford opportunities of witnessing to vacationers, who mushroom the local population of some 7,000 people to more than 100,000 in the summer season.

The Old Orchard Beach Camp Meetings' modern outdoor pavilion served as the venue for the Gaithers' welcome back to their home territory. Sharing in the installation events were the Army's new international leaders, the General and Commissioner Gisele Gowans; USA national leaders Commissioners John and Elsie Busby; the USA Central leaders, Commissioners Lawrence and Nancy Moretz; and retired territorial leaders, Commissioners Ronald and Pauline Irwin. The territory's chief secretary, Colonel James Knaggs describes the day: "The Gaithers' homecoming as territorial leaders was an extraordinary event. The camp meetings were at a high pitch throughout the weekend, with his installation and the renewed love affair with the Eastern Territory, USA. It was a defining moment of mission awareness. "

The Installation

General Gowans conducted the Gaithers' installation. His words, before the more than 1,000 gathered in the pavilion, both commended the Gaithers and defined the role they would now assume in their home territory. In response to each question posed by the General, the Gaithers responded with the words, "I do."

> It is with joy and confidence that I commend to you your new territorial leaders. I know them both to be wholly dedicated to God and to the great service for which He raised up The Salvation Army. Throughout their years of service, the Gaithers have demonstrated steadfast loyalty to Christ and unique gifts of spiritual leadership. The Salvation Army is a vital part of the universal church of Christ, and as such requires godly men and women to undertake its temporal and spiritual leadership. God has provided for that need, and we rejoice today in the appointment of Commissioners Eva and Israel Gaither as territorial leaders for the USA Eastern Territory.

General Gowans installs the Gaithers as territorial leaders in Old Orchard Pavillion.

The God who has called you into his service, the God who was with you when you signed your covenant as Salvation Army officers, the God who sustained you through the years, is the God who will empower you for the responsibilities now placed upon you.

Commissioner Israel Gaither, as the territorial commander, you will have the duty and privilege and care of all aspects of Salvation Army activity in this territory. Do you rely on the Lord to enable you for this task?

Commissioner Eva Gaither, you stand beside your husband in the leadership of this territory; you share his commitment in a deep and holy bond. Do you promise that the central aim of your service will be the glory of God and the salvation of souls as you take up your special responsibility as territorial president of Women's Ministries?

HERE IS THE WORD OF GOD. Do you promise to uphold the Bible as the divine rule of Christian faith and practice?

HERE'S THE ARMY FLAG, the yellow, red and blue, under whose folds you have fought for so many years. Its colors and its motto represent the essential themes of the Army's message—salvation through the blood of Christ, sanctification by the Holy Spirit. Will you make every effort to help Salvationists under your direction to hold those doctrines sacred and to maintain the integrity of that message?

HERE'S THE MERCY SEAT, to which sinners are called in repentance and where believers find the closer communion with God. Here the lost will be saved, here the disciple will be filled with the Holy Spirit. To this end, will you make the mercy seat the focus of your ministry?

HERE ARE YOUR PEOPLE, those gathered here are but representative of the officers, local officers, junior soldiers, adherents and friends of The Salvation Army in this territory. You are called to serve them in the name of Jesus Christ as you are also called to serve the unsaved, the unfriended, the unchurched. Do you accept their spiritual well–being as your responsibility?

In recognition of your willing response to the challenges presented to your new appointment, I now solemnly charge you in the presence of God the Father, Son and Holy Spirit to preach the Word of truth and to uphold its principles, to stand by the flag and to preserve all it represents from harm or disgrace, to raise up officer candidates to perpetuate and enlarge that ministry, to minister to the ministers, to provide pastoral care for the officers, to maintain the internal discipline of the

Army and to encourage that spirit of self–denial. To provide full opportunity for all the people of God, men and women together, to utilize their spiritual gift, fulfill their calling, and make full proof of their ministry. And to administer the work of The Salvation Army in this territory as trustees of its property and finances and social programs and its people, its well–being and its future development.

Izzy, Eva, my prayer for you is this, May God grant you much grace and wisdom in your leadership.

"MISSION MATTERS MOST"

Throughout the weekend, the new territorial commander emphasized what would be the theme of his leadership: "Mission Matters Most." He called on Salvationists to "dream heroic dreams," to believe they can "win in the fight for God against sin and evil." Gaither declared, "We, as the Army, need to be discovering and engaging new frontiers and new mission opportunities."

"What a wonderful blessing to be back home," said Eva. "We return from three and a half years of blessing in a beautiful country, where we met many, many beautiful friends, and where it was difficult to say goodbye. Now God is taking us on a new journey in our life. We look forward to the future and to what He has in store for us. Praise God we can put our trust in Him."

The newly installed territorial commander passionately challenged his congregation and the territory. The following is excerpted from his message.

I'm helped by what I read in the record of St. John's Gospel (5:30), the words of Jesus, "By myself I can do nothing." If it's true of the Savior, I must readily admit to you tonight that it's true of me; by myself I can do nothing.

Mission matters most to me. It always has. But in these last three and a half years there has come to me a new understanding of what mission really demands. Mission occupies more of me because of what I have seen and what I have felt.

I believe in the God–ordained purpose of The Salvation Army. For the mission is fundamentally about the Kingdom of God, the reign of Christ, in people and places, now and in the future. You will need to understand that I will be talking about mission very often, not because there is nothing else to say but because it is the most significant thing to be said.

I want to tell you something. The mission is not yet accomplished. We engage in spiritual warfare in a post–modern, post–Christian era. The Salvation Army in this territory must always have its spiritual eye on tomorrow, working for the way things ought to be.

Beloved, I call every Salvationist in this territory to be absolutely certain about our mission. A Salvation Army that is unclear about its mission has nothing to say to the world. We'll just be another social institution, another "do–gooder" agency in a corner of America, pleased with a distorted sense of who we are and why we exist. I promise you that on my watch, this will not become a federation of little Salvation Armies scattered and scurrying about, devoid of the larger call. That is not good enough. There is a divine genius behind the birthing of this movement. Our heritage must always inform our present and our future.

As an African–American, having now lived in Africa, I know something more about the value of roots and my heritage and its contribution to God shaping my life. We were out driving in a small African community, getting lost as we were making our way. I stopped at a traffic light in a small town. I looked to my left, and saw a man cross the street who looked like my father. I came away from that experience with a new idea about my heritage.

It's no different with The Salvation Army. The past informs the present and shapes the future. If you and I abandon the past, the future will be a blur. We'll be like a ship adrift at sea, anchorless. I want a resilient Salvation Army, one that is firmly attached to our roots. Not to the institution, but to the ethos, the values, the why's of our being. Are you with me tonight— a resilient Salvation Army, but not a rootless one?

Here's something else that I believe more than ever. The future demands a restless Salvation Army, not a resigning Salvation Army. This is not the time to give up, content with what we see in the present. We won't give up, no matter how hard it gets! We're not going to give up, because with Christ, we win! I don't like playing on losing teams.

> *" We are continually astounded at the way God mysteriously works in our lives."*

This time in the Eastern Territory demands that we be in a state of readiness, not in reserve. I believe we are ordained to occupy. There is more mission ground to take. Nothing less than winning is acceptable. Our place in the world is not to merely join in a battle already in progress. It is in fact to ignite war on the forces of evil. That's what it's about. We are a Salvation Army, and we are meant to go to battle.

Now hear this. I am ordinary—very, very ordinary. If I were God, I would not have called myself for this great mission. I'm too ordinary. But He knows more than I do. So I'm privileged to be called, as ordinary as I am, to an extraordinary task, to serve an extraordinary God. I gladly admit to you tonight in the words of Jesus, "By myself I can do nothing."

I require His anointing, I need His presence. I know something of what God is capable of doing. I must, I will, I promise you—that I will rely on him. By myself I can do nothing.

I covenant with God and our international leaders and you, Salvationists and friends of this territory, by His grace and through His anointing, I shall give all that I have for the extending of the mission—for one reason, and for one reason only, so that Jesus reigns.

An Initial Momentum

A quick series of platform ministry assignments soon was imposed on the new leaders. Just one year earlier the USA and the world had been stunned with the horror of the terrorist attack on September 11. The world, from that moment, would never be the same again. On the first anniversary of that tragedy, Sept. 11, 2002, Gaither spoke in New York City at a Memorial Service with the theme, "Fallen But Not Forgotten." For those gathered and remembering the several thousand innocent victims of that unimaginable tragedy, it was a comforting and memorable night.

At the September territorial welcome to cadets of the Bridgebuilders session, Gaither preached on "traveling light"—on the perils of carrying emotional baggage into ministry. He listed three emotional "bags" he believes must be discarded: discontent, doubt and disappointment. He reminded his hearers, "When you "dis" someone, you lessen their value. When you put *dis* in front of *obey*, you have *disobey*. If you add *dis* to *respect*, you have *disrespect*. Put it in front of God's appointment for your life, and you get *disappointment*. We need a Salvation Army that has shaken off all these bags."

Pointing to the cadets, he said, "This is bag–dropping time!" Turning to the congregation, he said, "Give us a Salvation Army that is able to confront the world—free—possessed by the power of God!" Many knelt at the altar to "drop their baggage."

The gauntlet for the territory had been thrown down at the Old Orchard welcome and installation. The Gaithers had established in this very first month a momentum of leadership, and the troops were motivated and ready to respond.

But very shortly would come another summons that would dramatically alter their lives and ministry in a way they never could have imagined, and would cut all too short their homecoming and ministry in the USA East.

PART FOUR

A Global Ministry

2002–2005

chapter **24**

Search for Consensus

If any of you lacks wisdom, he should ask God,
who gives generously to all without finding
fault, and it will be given to him.

James 1:5

A s retirement approached for General John Gowans, the High Council once more convened at historic Sunbury Court on Aug. 30, 2002. The record 87 members included 71 commissioners, 15 colonels, one lieutenant colonel; 49 men and 38 women. A record 19 members were of U.S. origin.

AN AGONIZING DECISION

Nominations were invited in the search for consensus in the voting process. Israel Gaither, now a commissioner, was again nominated for the office of the general, this time with but a couple of hours to decide to stand or decline. He had only that same month been appointed to his home territory, USA East, as territorial commander, and in that short time had been exuberantly welcomed and had galvanized the territory with his manifesto, "Mission Matters Most."

He resorted to prayer. In an agonizing searching of his heart, he sought to know God's will for this moment. He stood before his colleagues, shared his struggle and announced that he was led to keep his commitment to the territory that had welcomed him as its leader and the vows he had made to it. With pathos, he made known his decision to decline. Later, Israel says, he "took some heat" from colleagues who expressed their disappointment with his decision.

On the first ballot, Commissioner John Larsson, Chief of the Staff, received more than two–thirds of the votes from a field of three nominees and was chosen as the 17th international leader of The Salvation Army. Larsson brought to the office a rich heritage of Army history, proven international experience and leadership, and renown for musicals with enduring lyrics of praise and worship written with John Gowans.

Israel Gaither tendered his congratulations and support to the General–designate and returned to fulfill his mandate of mission for his home territory. (Or so he thought!)

THE "KALEIDOSCOPE OF PERSONALITY"

Representative members share their reflections on Israel Gaither's impact upon that 2002 High Council. Then Lt. Colonel Dick Krommenhoek, territorial commander of France, wrote his observation of "the kaleidoscope of Izzy's great personality."

> Getting to know and to befriend Izzy was a great privilege and doing so at the High Council revealed dimensions of him which I probably would not have experienced otherwise. Almost every day a new characteristic emerged, which one after another revealed the total kaleidoscope of Izzy's great personality.
>
> First of all there was this big smile and his genuine warmth when shaking hands and meeting Izzy's eyes. Distinctly I remember him saying: "Great to meet you, brother!" Now, for many obvious reasons, it would be highly unlikely that anyone in this world would suggest that Izzy and I were brothers when looking at us. Yet, Izzy's brotherly authority powerfully declared our brotherhood without a shrink of a doubt and with the wealth of his warmth, he convinced me instantly. If at that moment anyone would have asked me, Who is this person standing next to you? I would have answered: "This is my brother Izzy, can't you tell?"
>
> Within seconds this newly acquired "relative" had managed to communicate to me that I was included and important.
>
> Izzy is a great communicator, who brilliantly uses this gift to convince. This becomes very apparent by the fact that when Izzy speaks, everybody listens.
>
> During the High Council in 2002 Izzy communicated through his musical skills as a vocal soloist. He has a fine tenor voice, with a great soothing timbre, which he combines with a subtle contemporary touch in his style of singing. Whilst accompanying Izzy on the piano, I was deeply moved when his mellow voice convincingly testified of God's amazing grace.
>
> The experience, which made lasting impression for, I am

sure, all the members of the High Council of 2002, was the moment when the nominees for the office of General had to announce their decision whether they accepted or rejected their nomination. Now suppose Izzy would be chosen to become the General; that would really be history—the first black General in the history of The Salvation Army. Looking at the increasing variety of cultures that are represented at the High Councils of the last two decades, the day will definitely arrive for a nonwhite General to be chosen. It is even surprising that this hasn't happened yet. Modest as Izzy is and solely geared to serve the Lord through The Salvation Army, surely it must have been impossible to completely block out these thoughts. Was this a one–time opportunity for Izzy to send a giant message to the whole Army world—yes, even to many churches and organizations, that the Army leaders elect their world leader on the basis of quality, without prejudice to sex and race? Highly intelligent as Izzy is, these deliberations must have crossed his mind.

"Commissioner Israel Gaither, your response, please," the chairman asked. The next short moments of silence seemed endless. Izzy was emotional, which many shared with him. and I too felt my eyes fill with tears. Izzy explained that the Gaithers had only just been appointed as the territorial leaders in the USA Eastern Territory. He had committed himself to the officers, soldiers and friends of this territory and he felt that he would let them down if he accepted nomination for the office of General. In this crucial moment he chose for the commitment he had made to his appointment and to the people to whom he had given his heart. Without question, this must have been one of Izzy's most complicated dilemmas.

Some whom I came in close contact with during the 2002 High Council, I asked to write something personal in a little book I carried around. Maybe these few words which Izzy wrote in my book, say more about him than any biography could portray: *Dick, the 2002 High Council proceedings have left a remarkable impact*

"Meeting with Izzy at the 2002 High Council gave me the great honor to befriend one of the Army's pearls."

on my life. It's been a Kingdom experience! Meeting and inter-
acting with you has been especially significant. I have listened
with amazement at your gifted ability to make 'music.' I've been
profoundly moved. Thank you for allowing me to share your jour-
ney. It's good to be a fellow sojourner with you! Stand strong—
and you'll be blessed! Izzy Gaither (September 2002)

Meeting Izzy at the High Council of 2002 gave me the
great honor to befriend one of the Army's pearls. And, God,
am I proud to be his brother!

"A CHARISMATIC LEADER"

Commissioner Hasse Kjellgren, territorial leader of Sweden and Latvia, himself one of the three nominees, shares his reflection.

> From my first meeting of Commissioner Gaither, it was
> clear to me that this was a clear–thinking and open colleague.
> Although we had never met before, the willingness to gener-
> ously share from past and present experiences and concerns
> was immediate. I learnt to appreciate his way of making con-
> tact with an audience. The psychoanalytical definition of a
> charismatic leader and speaker is, "the ability to establish a
> connection to the listener also on an emotional level." Mark
> the word *also*! It doesn't say *only*! In a less sophisticated way of
> expressing it, we would probably say, "the ability to touch the
> hearts of the people." This capacity is undoubtedly one of
> Izzy's, and it is as God–given as any other of his gifts. Another
> characteristic that comes to my mind is his warmth. I've had
> the privilege of being on the receiving end of this on more
> than one occasion. Warmth is supportive, affirmative and re-
> leasing. This doesn't mean of course, that the Commissioner
> lacks the ability to set boundaries, an indispensable part of any
> leadership task. It is my impression though, that Izzy also is
> mature and humble enough to acknowledge his own bound-
> aries; i.e., he knows when to ask for help. In short, I like this
> man! And I respect him! And value and honor him! And I
> thank God for him!

Coming from Korea, Commissioner Kang, Sung–hwan felt an immediate
affinity with Gaither in meeting him at the 2002 High Council. "How comfortable and at ease Commissioner Israel Gaither made us all feel as he con-
versed with the group as a whole and when mingling among us. It was
obvious he burned with a passion for the Lord, stemming from his true heart

to be used in God's service. Although it was my first time ever to set eyes on him, I felt a kindred spirit and brotherlike rapport as we shook hands and as the proceedings of the High Council evolved. When nominated as a candidate for General, he did not readily accept nomination. This to me gave focus to his entirely unselfish attitude and great belief in God his Father." Retired Commissioner K. Brian Morgan from Australia discerned a spiritual authority in his colleague. "Israel Gaither has always impressed me as a leader of spiritual authority, endowed by the Holy Spirit and gifted for ministry. As chaplain to the 2002 High Council, my own spirit was encouraged and moved by the input of Izzy in open forums and times of worship. I will never forget his response when he declined nomination to stand for the high office of General, with sensitivity, his obedience to the will of God as he perceived it at that time, his commitment to the people of God for whom he was responsible in his current appointment."

A Shadow of Coming Events

Retired Commissioner Joshua Ntuk from Nigeria relates the perception of an African leader and employs a colorful metaphor for the future. "As the first Afro–American in such a role in South Africa, Israel was full of plans for the territory, and I enjoyed many conversations with him regarding territorial leadership. His grasp of the subject and responses to ideas caused me to recognize a man of depth and ability. When he declined nomination at the 2002 High Council, since he was among the few leaders I had in mind for the election, I quickly approached him in private wanting to know why he declined. He told me that he had prayed about it and could not accept it at that time. Since a golden fish cannot hide, God needed him for higher responsibility."

Indeed, "Coming events often cast their shadows before them." No doubt those present at this High Council saw an emerging presence on the horizon of the international Army.

chapter 25

A Shock of "Seismic Proportions"

"For I know the plans I have for you,"
declares the Lord ... "plans to give you hope
and a future."
Jeremiah 29:11

On the morning of Sept. 12, 2002, the new USA Eastern territorial commander was in conference with his executive cabinet at a hotel near headquarters. In that private session, the commissioner broke the jolting news to officers who so recently had welcomed him home with unbounded enthusiasm as their leader. He and Eva would all too soon be taking leave of them, for General John Larsson had asked Israel to take up the duty as the Army's Chief of the Staff at International Headquarters in London. The immediate reaction was shock!

Colonel James Knaggs, secretary for personnel at the time, describes the poignancy and power of those moments. "We had just recently returned from the Old Orchard Camp Meetings and were preparing for the welcome of cadets when the commissioner took us into his confidence. 'The General has asked that I serve as the Chief of the Staff of the worldwide Salvation Army, and Eva and I must salute and go as faithful soldiers.' It was a stunning moment, as we each knew that the hand of the Lord was in this new development and that the future of the global Salvation Army would be divinely impacted by this decision.

"As the Commissioner shared this announcement with his astonished Cabinet, the moment was emotional and powerful. As secretary for personnel, I moved to the podium and asked members to surround the Gaithers for a special prayer of relinquishment, anointing and empowerment. As I stood there in prayer, I was reminded of the spring of 1987 when Israel Gaither prayed for my wife and me. It was my charge to reciprocate in a holy way."

Within the hour, Commissioner Gaither asked for a meeting of all officers and employees at Territorial Headquarters. The cabinet members returned to THQ, a short drive from the conference hotel. All staff were interrupted at their desks to be summoned to gather in the chapel. They couldn't have imagined what they were about to hear. Upon arrival Gaither went straight to the platform, his serious demeanor signaling that a weighty matter was at hand.

With Eva at his side at the podium, they announced their new appointments and gave indication of the confirmation of the Holy Spirit in their decision to go forward. The room burst into an immediate standing ovation, each person filled with the strange, mixed emotion of pride that one of their own had been chosen for this high office, and sadness for the resultant immediate loss to the territory as their leaders responded faithfully in their calling. Celebration blended with disappointment at the Gaithers' impending departure to London. They had been home only a few short weeks, and now they were to leave.

The official bulletin from IHQ, released at that hour on Sept. 12, 2002, for posting to Army headquarters around the world read: "In my capacity as General–elect I am pleased to announce that, following consultation, I have called upon Commissioner Israel L. Gaither to be Chief of the Staff, and Commissioner Eva D. Gaither to be World Secretary for Women's Ministries and World President of Salvation Army Scouts, Guides and Guards, effective 13 November 2002."

The bulletin acknowledged that the Gaithers had entered into their appointments as territorial leaders of their home territory "as recently as six weeks ago—on 1 August of this year. The warmth of the welcome extended to them as they returned from service in the Southern Africa Territory is an indication of the regret that the territory will feel about their term being so brief—a regret which the commissioners share. But the global mission of the Army calls, and I know that God will wonderfully bless and use Commissioners Israel and Eva Gaither in the worldwide ministry that will shortly be theirs."

As The Salvation Army's 21st Chief of the Staff, Commissioner Israel L. Gaither would be second in command of the worldwide Salvation Army, and the first person of African descent to serve in that capacity.

THE SEISMIC SHOCK

Commissioner Gaither admitted that he and his wife had received the official request as "a shock of seismic proportions. We had no idea whatsoever that we were being considered for these significant responsibilities. It was the most difficult decision I have had to make as a Salvation Army officer." The General has the prerogative to appoint his Chief of Staff, with consent of five commissioners, but he had graciously asked him if he would be willing to serve in that capacity.

After that phone call, Israel and Eva shared several days of "spiritual exercises" together before their international appointments were formally announced. Gaither said, "God made it very clear to me that I had simply been a vessel of His message, a servant of the USA Eastern Territory for a short period of time. I do not own that vision, nor is the territory my personal property. I'm a steward."

> **"All we want is to be certain that we are doing His will, in His place, in His time."**

Reflecting on lessons they learned about submission to the will of God, he affirmed, "We are continually astounded at the way God mysteriously works in our lives. This was one of those occasions when He disrupted what we thought was best. But His Spirit reminded me that when my wife and I signed our officer covenants in 1964, we placed ourselves fully at His disposal. He has a right to do what He pleases. And all we want is to be certain that we are doing His will, in His place, in His time. We are His serving soldiers."

Commissioner Eva Gaither shared the personal feelings she and her husband have for the Eastern Territory. "This is home. The Eastern Territory is awesome! And we were thrilled and humbled to have the opportunity to return here from Southern Africa. We are so grateful for the wonderful love and support we have received from Salvationists and friends of the Army from every corner of the territory. And obviously, we are deeply saddened at having to leave so soon following our arrival. But we believe God is in full control."

To his territorial executive council and THQ staff, Israel spoke passionately and prophetically. "There is a 'promised land' for this territory. It's just over the horizon. I can see it in my mind's eye. I feel it in my heart. Someone else will lead you there. You will get there, but we can't go with you." Gaither affirmed the territory would be in good hands under its new leaders, Commissioners Lawrence and Nancy Moretz.

"A MOST DEFINING EXPERIENCE"

Israel Gaither described the background and context of this change and appointment as one of the defining experiences in his life.

We had been called back to serve as the territorial leaders in our home territory. It was a gift, something that we never dreamed would ever happen, and truthfully we had never purposely thought about. Throughout our entire years of officership, we never worried about the next assignment. We always gave ourselves to the present.

In a visit to South Africa by General John Gowans for a congress, we had an opportunity to have a private meal with him. During the meal John asked us if we would like to return home. We had mixed reactions because we really grew to love deeply the comrade Salvationists and colleagues in South Africa. But we also missed home and family. Eva had the experience during the South African tour of losing her father, and then near the completion of our time in Southern Africa, she lost her sister. So the chance to be home, nearer to two mothers who were aging, and of course to our children and only grandson at the time, was a joyful prospect.

But we had no idea that it would be so short–lived. We were confirmed in a Spirit–anointed way in the welcome meetings in Old Orchard in August 2002. It was a marvelous reception and the vision that God had given me that "Mission Matters Most" was specifically for that territory for that time. It was received with tremendous enthusiasm, as it followed naturally the creative leadership Joe and Doris Noland had given to the territory.

But to only be in those ministry assignments for 103 days confronted us with the most difficult decision we had ever faced in our officership. It placed us in a period of deep agony to ensure just as before, that this was in fact the leading of the Lord. We were aware that the Army world was awaiting the announcement of who the new Chief of the Staff would be, an added pressure point for us. But John and Freda were patient and allowed us time and space to pray—in fact, wrestle—in prayer, over the decision.

Eva arrived at comfort prior to me—just as she had when the South Africa question had come up. It admittedly took me longer, but on a Sunday morning prior to going to the meeting at the home corps for worship in Spring Valley, N.Y., after wrestling in prayer with God for several hours, and having deep conversation with Eva, I gave in and said "Yes." There has been no question that we have felt the hand of the Lord upon us in our ministries, both individually and collectively, and the privilege of serving with John and Freda Larsson will be a choice one.

We recognize that we are truly blessed to be in positions where we have been able to see the Army at work in the world, and it has richly added to the value and love we hold for the mission and ministry of the Army. We also understand that in the will of God, we could not engage in ministries of leadership on such a global basis had we not had the experience in Southern Africa. These are key points in our life that have served as defining moments in my personal and ministry development. And I can only thank God for His patient Spirit that has been with me through these experiences. I dread to think what might have been if I had not obeyed the direction of the Spirit. In fact that is the point to which Eva drew my attention when we struggled over the call of John Larsson to join him in London. Eva said to me, "We must do the will of God."

That is the primary thing that I want to accomplish in my life. I simply—just as I have throughout my officership—want even now and in the future to be found in and doing the will of God. I preach and believe for myself personally that it is not "about me." It is about the Kingdom of God and His call on me to participate in missioning His Kingdom in the world. I have been blessed beyond measure. I readily admit that without the anointing of God on my life, I am nothing, and all that I would ever do would amount in Kingdom terms to absolutely nothing.

I have no personal desires with respect to the future. I don't long for a position or a place. I simply want to minister in faithfulness to what God calls me to do because I have found that acceding to His will is the best thing. All will be well as long as I remain in His will."

A FOND FAREWELL

How was it to follow the Gaithers in an appointment? Commissioner William Francis, International Secretary at IHQ, who in 1977 had served concurrently with the Gaithers as a Divisional Youth Secretary, later followed them in three appointments, including that of Chief Secretary. Francis relates, "Since those early days we have grown to respect and admire the Gaithers for their commitment to each other, their family and their calling. Having followed them in three appointments we can testify first hand to Izzy and Eva as sterling examples of Christian discipleship, enthusiastic Salvationism, and their care of property and gracious manner in which they prepared for their successors. They were unequaled in this regard."

Disappointment within the territory for the sudden loss of the Gaithers was also mixed with deep pride at the recognition given to a "favorite son" in his appointment as Chief of the Staff.

On Nov. 8, 2002, officers and friends gathered at Centennial Memorial Temple in New York City to salute Commissioners Israel L. and Eva Gaither as outgoing territorial leaders but also as friends and spiritual leaders for 40 years.

General–elect John Larsson shared vicariously in the farewell salute by sending a message that was shown on large video screens. He spoke from the desk in his Chief of the Staff office, aware of the traumatic loss for the territory resulting from his decision.

> Dare I show my face here with you tonight? If you're wondering why I selected the Gaithers to take up these international roles, the answer is very simple. The reasons you are sorry to see them go are the very reasons why they are chosen to be leaders on the international scene. You know of their warmth and their sensitivity, their passion for the Lord, passion for mission. And it's these very qualities that will make such a difference to the Army's international scene.
>
> What an international team we're going to make! When you think of the Gaithers and their knowledge of the North American scene, and then for having been stationed in Southern Africa and their knowledge of the African continent, and then Freda and I with our knowledge of Europe, South America, Australasia—a good part of the world. These are some of the reasons why I have been led to choose the Gaithers. And I know you will be proud of them—you will be proud of Israel Gaither as second in command of The Salvation Army, supporting the General plotting the strategy of the Army.
>
> I know you will be proud of Commissioner Eva Gaither as she engages in world ministry of The Salvation Army. And they also will be proclaiming the Gospel and encouraging the soldiers in the 109 countries where we now work. So we want to say a very warm welcome here at the international scene and I know you will be supporting and praying for them.

The program, with the theme "Anointed by the Holy Spirit," was festooned with tributes to the Gaithers in words, drama, music, and video. Soldiers, officers, family and employees hailed the Gaithers as "servant leaders." On hand were Harlem Temple's New Sounds for Christ choir led by Ken Burton, OF, and the New York Staff Band which filled the hall with the strains of "Hail to the Chief."

Israel Gaither's message was taken from the words God delivered to Moses in Deut. 4:1–9: "Only be careful, and watch yourselves closely so that you do not forget the things your eyes have seen or let them slip from your heart as long as you live. Teach them to your children and to their children after them."

He challenged, "What have I been saying for 103 days? You and I are the mission. God needs you to think about the mission for tomorrow."

With those parting words, Israel and Eva Gaither would soon leave for their global responsibilities at the hub of the worldwide Salvation Army.

chapter **26**

Second in Command

*I can do everything through him who gives
me strength.*
Philippians 4:13

Only once in the 124–year history of The Salvation Army had an
American served as Chief of the Staff; Commissioner John J. Allan
had been appointed by General Albert Orsborn in 1946. Like Israel
Gaither, Allan also had come from a small corps in Pennsylvania—Hazleton.
Since those relatively halcyon days, the expansion and greatly increased com-
plexities of the Army had exponentially added to the administrative duties of
the Chief of Staff.

In London, the retirement service for General Gowans, 10 days before his
official leave–taking on Nov. 12, coincided with the public welcome of the
Larssons and Gaithers. Gowans presented Commissioner Israel Gaither as
Chief of the Staff–designate, saying, "The Gaithers are beautiful people, with
a strong conviction about mission who have proved themselves in battle."

Israel responded,
"We have been gifted
with a sacred privilege
in standing alongside
the Larssons in serv-
ing the global mis-
sion. Eva and I give
ourselves to this task.
I'm glad to be a
Salvation soldier."

He had earlier paid
tribute to the General
and Commissioner
Gowans at their USA
Farewell Salute: "You

The Chief of Staff at his IHQ desk

took the Army world by storm, and in your wake you leave a strong, resilient Army."

LIFE AT THE HUB

The Chief of the Staff and Commissioner Eva Gaither moved into their offices, but not initially at the Army's traditional address at 101 Queen Victoria Street. That site, originally purchased by William Booth in 1881, was being rebuilt and would not be available until November 2004. In the meantime, IHQ was housed in the temporary, and limited, facilities of the Army's William Booth College on the outskirts of London.

When they moved into the permanent edifice, the Gaithers were headquartered in a stunning facility, seen by some 10,000 passersby each day where it stands on a line from St. Paul's Cathedral to the Millennium Bridge spanning the River Thames. The new building, modern in design, frugal in operation and evangelical in purpose, conveys through its glazed exterior an openness and transparency. The Mercy Seat, the symbol of God's presence and a place of prayer, has its place in the heart of the building.

The Chief of the Staff has his own official flag, and his office in the five–story edifice is but a few steps from that of the General on the first floor, where their spouses and private secretaries are accommodated. The most dramatic space on this floor is the chapel—a centerpiece that hangs over part of the lower level and radiates a golden light at night.

Israel quickly discovered that "IHQ is a much different structure than a territory. Each day goes by amazingly fast. I must say that there are some areas that impress me. IHQ lives frugally for the sake of the mission, and rightfully so, since we live off the rest of the world. It is amazing to see how well every department does with the stewarding of their resources. It's also interesting to see how folks managed in the interim arrangement, crammed into small cubicles, sharing (face–to–face) an office with someone else! Although our offices are very small (I try not to think what I left behind in New York!), at least we have privacy!"

No two days in the life of the Chief of Staff are the same. Meetings—with international secretaries, overseas visitors, ad hoc committees and business personnel—engage a good part of the workday. An inviolate agenda for the Chief each day is a 9:30 to 11:00 a.m. meeting with the General, when, as Izzy put it, "we cover the world."

The Chief also held a daily meeting with Commissioner Raymond A. Houghton, international secretary to the Chief of Staff, who oversees these departments: Research, Spiritual Life Development and External Relations, Legal Matters, Doctrine Council, Moral and Social Issues, International Statistics, World Evangelism, Worship, and Creative Arts. Quite a weighty dossier on behalf of the Chief's office.

A weekly meeting took place between the Chief and the International Secretary for Business Administration. The Chief's Advisory Forum meets weekly, with the Chief receiving input before making a final decision. Ninety percent of its business relates to personnel, with the appointment of every divisional commander and other important appointments coming to this forum for review and approval.

At the office, the Chief kept his door closed until 8:00 a.m., when IHQ opens. When in conference, his door was closed, and he did not take phone calls. "I owed that person complete attention, with no interruption," he says.

Among the functions of IHQ is the handling of day–to–day business for the allocation of resources and strategic, long–range planning. IHQ acts as a resource center and a facilitator of ideas and policies for the worldwide Army. IHQ promotes the development of spiritual life within the Army and sets overall strategic leadership and international policies. A vital function is to strengthen the internationalism of the Army by preserving its unity, purposes, beliefs and spirit, and maintaining its standards. IHQ promotes the development, deployment and sharing of personnel and financial resources worldwide. The sharing of knowledge, expertise and experience, and encouraging the Army's external relationships, all come within its purview. Essentially, IHQ is the glue that binds the international Army together.

The Chief of the Staff carries a weighty portfolio as the chief executive for all these complex operations. Under his oversight come nine international secretaries, five of whom represent geographic zones, and four who relate to functions, with a close interplay between the two groups. Israel Gaither emphasized that IHQ must "not get too far removed from mission. We need to become less institutionalized and more mission–oriented, with a counseling and enabling role."

BEHIND THE SCENES

Major Jeanne van Hal, originally from the Netherlands, secretary to the Chief of Staff, describes her new boss as she came to know and work with him. "During the first day we had several informal discussions, and he told me how happy he was that I could stay on for some months before returning to The Netherlands. Our first working day started with prayer. Prayer was the basis of his and my work for His Kingdom. I tried to help him get into the IHQ routine. We were then temporarily housed at the training college while IHQ was being renovated. We lived and worked closely in a converted apartment, myself in what had been the main bedroom and Commissioner Eva next to that in a very small former bedroom. I arrived at the office around 7 a.m., when at that time I had already a desk full of papers, tapes etc. to be done, he having arrived at a very early hour. His daily meetings with the General were well–prepared. He worked hard—long hours, early morning and continued until late at night. Mrs. Gaither helped me to read his handwriting and to care for my boss, the Chief. (We liked to tease him together, and he once called us 'these two bossy women.') After just six months, I left for Holland. His farewell speech to me was full of compassion. It was a great privilege to serve him for such a short time."

Historically Israel had not always enjoyed such instant rapport with those who sought to serve as his secretary. In one divisional appointment, after trying out successive applicants over some weeks, he was teased by some of his colleagues about having a "secretary of the week." Thus, at the upper echelons of leadership, he was grateful to find those who served with high qualifications and were willing to adapt to his exacting standards of office procedure.

Martin Gilbert, the foremost writer and authority on Winston Churchill, in his book *In Search of Churchill,* devotes an entire chapter to "Private Secretaries," so vital did he consider them to the work of his subject. Indeed, great leaders' deeds could never be achieved without the diligent, devoted work of those who serve them behind the scenes. The people in those positions will see leaders in both their strongest and weakest moments. Efficiency, adaptability and loyalty are vital requisites. Such pertains to the office of the private secretary to the Chief of Staff, and the selection of that person would be one of the most important of Gaither's administration.

Major van Hal's departure left a void. "Jeanne was my key to becoming comfortable in the world of IHQ. Her service to me was invaluable." Through his International Secretary,[2] Commissioner Houghton, he requested Major Rob Garrad, undersecretary for administration at IHQ, to submit a short list of suitable people for the position. Among his criteria was that the person be a single man with prior IHQ experience, which narrowed the field considerably. Garrad, who had been at IHQ since 1977 except for five years in Russia, says "that requirement pretty well narrowed it down to me." He compiled a list of seven men, but none met all the combined requirements stipulated by Gaither. Garrad, knowing the position so well because he had previously served in it for six years, added a footnote saying that if he could help in any way, he would have no objection returning to the appointment. "When that offer came," said Commissioner Gaither, "I halted the search!"

Within 10 minutes of receiving the list, he phoned Rob Garrad to ask if he were serious in making the offer. Major Garrad replied that he was, but he had not expected to be taken seriously. The Chief said he was taking him very seriously and if he could carry the General's judgment on the rather unusual proposal, that was the way he wanted to go. The following morning he called Major Garrad again to say that the General was thrilled with the offer and thought it was just what the Chief needed.

[2]Secretary is a designation for a top leadership position, e.g., Secretary for Personnel, etc.

In his selection the Chief had tapped a man with an extraordinary background for the job. Rob Garrad had held IHQ appointments as under secretary for Europe, international auditor, director of Information Services and press officer, and as private secretary to three British commissioners. He had intimate knowledge of

The Chief with his private secretary, Major Garrad

the IHQ's workings and the global Army, and he had served as private secretary to three former Chiefs of the Staff (Ron Cox, Bramwell Tillsley, Earle Maxwell).

Never did a private secretary to the Chief come to that position with such a portfolio of assets and experience. Major Garrad was superbly qualified by both background and personal qualities. Israel Gaither had found the man who would work by his side for his entire tenure. Of Major Garrad, he says, "He was my right hand—he did it all—and fulfilled the closest and one of the most essential relationships to my office. He was in possession of all the requisite skills, fully engaged in the task, and never backed away from the demands of the desk. He understood the inner workings of IHQ. He also accompanied Eva and me on official engagements, usually within the United Kingdom. Rob had my confidence and trust. In short, I was blessed to have this resourceful, efficient and effective comrade officer at my side!"

Israel Gaither is known by his associates to lean toward a micro–management style, which can be demanding on his associates. Asked, "What was it like to be the personal secretary to Commissioner Gaither," Rob Garrad responds, "Exciting, demanding, stimulating, challenging, tiring, fulfilling. Some may view this appointment as losing your identity, simply taking instructions from someone else, with no life of your own. But, whilst there is a sense in which that may be true, by freeing the leader who is making a great impact on the Army world so he does not need to worry or give attention to the trivialities of life, you are in some small way contributing to the impact that he is having."

Major Garrad further shares, "No two days are alike. You never know what you are going to have to undertake in the course of a day." Sometimes the unusual can take a humorous twist, such as the time the Chief, as was his custom, came to the office before 5 a.m., and found that the night security guard had not yet opened the back gate in advance of his arrival so he could park his car in the garage. He had to park in back of the building and walk all the way round to Queen Victoria Street, only to find, when he came to the front door, that the night security guard was not on duty there either. Fortunately he had a front door key to let himself in. The guard had in fact fallen asleep on a sofa right outside the Chief's office! The Chief did not awaken him, and it fell to Major Garrad to pass on the word later in the morning of the security guard having been spotted "sleeping on the job." "Adaptability to the unexpected," observed the major "is one of the most important attributes for the private secretary!"

"One aspect of working with ILG [Israel L. Gaither]," says Rob Garrad, "is always his total thoroughness in preparing for a meeting, an interview or chairing a board. Nothing is left to chance. He insists on knowing absolutely every detail that is relevant to the situation. He does not like surprises. There is an intensity about his demeanor in the office. Woe betide anyone (apart from the General or EG [Eva Gaither]) who dares to enter his office when the door is closed. There can be a good deal of laughter when he is dealing with his peers in the office. It seems clear that the Chief 'comes to life' far more, and is more within his comfort zone, on the platform than in the office. He is a gifted communicator, and that becomes abundantly evident the moment he is on his feet in a meeting. Here again, his preparation for public engagements is thorough and detailed." It was not unusual for the Private Secretary to have to call forth at times his own resources of diplomacy in ensuring data is available when people may be pressed for it at the last minute.

Eva Gaither had quickly established her own relationships and appreciation from those who related with her. Colonel Joy Cooper had served as personal assistant to two wives of former Chiefs, "And now the Army wheels had turned yet again as I was waiting to meet Commissioner Eva Gaither. Naturally I was a little apprehensive, but there was no need to worry; they were a breath of fresh air. The commissioners were a pleasure to work for; the Chief always with a good word, always caring, even though so often he was under great pressure. He was the perfect gentleman—courteous, well–mannered. His love for the Lord shone in his face and in all his actions."

When it came time for Joy Cooper's retirement, it was arranged for Major Marlene Hagar to come to that position from South Africa, where she previously had served as Gaither's secretary. She brought her proven skills and added to the international composition of IHQ. The major had earlier made known her interest in serving outside her homeland and in particular for serving at IHQ in a support role.

GLOBAL CONCERNS

As Chief of the Staff, Israel Gaither's global concerns for the Army both widened and came into a sharper focus. Recurring world tragedies, to which the Army responds, are always a priority on the Chief's agenda.

On Dec. 26, 2004, when a massive earthquake trembled the earth's crust setting off a tsunami disaster unlike any other in living memory, it left titanic destruction and a staggering death toll in its wake. Salvation Army personnel, already part of the infrastructure of the affected areas, immediately swung into action to provide for immediate needs and to restore hope in ravaged South Asia. The Chief, discerning the monumental and unparalleled response needed by the Army, moved decisively. He called and chaired a historic IHQ summit meeting, bringing together leaders of territories and commands affected by the catastrophic disaster and leaders of donor territories. He called for the Army not to just provide immediate need, but also to maintain a permanent presence of aid in the affected areas, which had been visited and assessed by members of IHQ's Program Resources Department just days before the meeting took place. Recognized as a major priority was the need to write project proposals to obtain further funding from governments and other agencies. From the Chief's chairing came also ground rules for future program management and policy to assure substantive relief efforts that would be immediate and sustaining. Major projects were designed and resources released. In Sri Lanka, where 53,000 people in one district had been left homeless, the government allocated two pieces of empty land totaling 344 acres for the Army to use to provide 1,000 homes.

A multiracial composition in the vertical mobility of Army leadership remained a major concern for the Chief. In a July 2005 article published in the *Salvationist*, he spoke out on this concern. "This is the 21st century, and for the Army not to have officer leaders of color in top leadership roles clearly signals the urgent need to give attention to the early identification and developing of not just officer leaders but also nonwhite leaders. It must be not mere 'window dressing.' That has not ever been, nor is it now, acceptable. On the global scale we have made significant progress. I am proud and grateful to be standing next to the General, who has appointed a truly multiracial team of highly committed and qualified international secretaries who are superb to partner with in giving collective leadership to the international mission. The General and I talked about this soon after my arrival at IHQ. This was our dream, and we consider ourselves blessed to see it become reality."

Israel strongly holds to the unique birthright and God's calling of the Army in the context of the universal Church. "I believe we are gifted as a unique branch of the Church of Christ. I understand the conventional church because it is part of my heritage. Being the Army is to move away from insular thinking and the 'clubhouse' mentality. We are a mission movement, not just an ordinary denomination. We like being with ourselves, talking to ourselves, looking like each other. We need to get out and away from ourselves and engage the world. Thankfully, in our travels in so many places, we see this happening. What emerges is a stronger, bigger Salvation Army.

"In terms of evangelism, we were amazed to see people kneeling at the drum and accepting Christ at open–air meetings in South Africa. I had not seen this for years. This is not going to happen everywhere. But we need an aggressive, in–your–face Salvation Army that is out to transform the world."

He gave strong support to the recent initiatives for strengthening the international bonding of the Army. "The General and I believe in the importance of moving leaders beyond their known environment, taking officers out of their context, giving them opportunity to serve in a place other than the familiar and then return home. This helps build mutual global understanding of the value of mission. Also the Partners in Mission program (linking territories in partnership with each other) is something many of us have wanted for decades. As territories team together, and as Salvationists support each other, we begin to more highly value one another."

As Chief of Staff he emphasized the importance of IHQ's leadership role for the global Army. As chair of the International Finance Board he took steps to address the financing of the international administration and operations that had been described in the past as "acting as beggars when it came to the contribution by territories for IHQ's administration cost." An IHQ colleague, Commissioner Thorleif Gulliksen, shares, "Under the leadership of Commissioner Gaither, this thinking changed. He took the initiative for open discussion with the financially independent territories for support of IHQ, with now a level of fiscal support that makes it possible for the General to have some freedom in his dispositions, with the territories agreeing and supporting this policy. The result is that financing to serve the Army's global mission is stronger than ever before."

Not all the initiatives set in motion during the Larsson/Gaither administration will be fully realized. Some will remain seedlings, yet to grow and bloom. Elton Trueblood, Christian author and statesman, once said, "A man has made at least a start on discovering the meaning of human life when he plants shade trees under which he knows full well he will never sit." Many in days to come, when engaged in the heat of the battle, will have cause for gratitude for the clear vision and creative plantings of the Larsson/Gaither team.

A FIRST–RATE LEADER TEAM

Colonel Joy Cooper describes Eva Gaither from both a personal and official standpoint during Eva's time at International Headquarters with Israel as Chief of Staff. "Commissioner Eva was not only my boss but my friend. I discovered she was 'cool,' as my grandsons would say! She was a breath of fresh air. I had been a little anxious before she came, wondering what this lady from the USA would expect, but I needn't have worried. She was gracious, capable and experienced.

"We had many things in common, both having worked in Africa, where a bit of our heart would always remain, and both of us being mothers and grandmothers, with all the joys and anxieties this brings. I especially enjoyed working with Eva in her capacity as World President of Salvation Army Scouts, Guards and Guides. She and I shared a real love for these and other similar youth sections around the world.

"We shared many precious moments together. Her office often became an altar where we prayed for others around the world whose need had been brought to our notice, as we read the marvelous reports that came to her desk, as well as bringing our own families to the Lord in prayer. She also had a good sense of humor and there was much laughter in her office and the Chief's corridor! I count myself truly blessed to have had the Chief and Commissioner Eva to be the last officers I would serve. I thank God that they came my way—what a wonderful benediction on my 40 years of active service!"

And a great company around the world whose lives have also been richly blessed by Eva, echo that sentiment.

When the long day's work is done, Israel finds at home a place to refresh body and soul, to renew his vision and gain strength for the next battle. Family has always been a top priority for him. Insulated from the press of life, his soul is nurtured and he draws sustenance from those who love and believe in him. Eva, over the years has grown into an Army leader of substance, skill and quality. Israel manifests a wholehearted love for and commitment to Eva, who provides him with spiritual support, good counsel, and the comfort and love of a secure home life. Together they make a first–rate leader team.

In an article, "Building Loving Relationships," in the Army's United Kingdom publication, *Salvationist* (Feb. 12, 2005), several Salvationist leaders were cited with cameos on their marriage relationship. Captain Dean Pallant, the editor, concluded his article: "Finally, I believe this last joint response sent to me says it all: 'In our experience a loving relationship deserves intentional cultivation. In our relationship, we know that our union is of the Lord, but we also accept that it is our responsibility to nurture and develop it. So we desire an enduring relationship through marriage.' And the result? The Gaithers have been happily married for 38 years."

When Eva is asked, "Who has made the foremost contribution to your spiritual life and development?" Without hesitation she replies, "Izzy. I know the man, and what he preaches is true and backed up by his life. He has had the primary impact on my spiritual life."

Israel reciprocates her affirmation. "Eva is a wonderful soul mate. She is deeply significant in my ministry and, of course, in my personal life."

The romance of their lives has not diminished but only blossomed more deeply through the years.

REFLECTIONS ON THE CHIEF

Israel fully subscribes, theologically and experientially, to the Army's doctrine of "entire sanctification," based on 1 Thessalonians 5:23, "And the very God of peace sanctify you wholly; and I pray God your whole spirit and soul and body be preserved blameless unto the coming of our Lord Jesus Christ" (KJV). He perceives personal holiness as "being completely absorbed in Christ, with every fiber of my being cleansed and possessed by the Holy Spirit. For me it has been a continued growing experience. I've seen holiness modeled by those who have had a powerful effect upon others by their Christlike lives. Eva and I strive for that in our lives."

Commissioner Keith Banks of Scotland shares his insights from a close working relationship with the Chief of Staff.

> The Gaithers epitomize the concept of diversity within unity! By that I mean they maintain their own uniqueness and individuality within the context of a strong, rock solid partnership. Their strongly held views—often quite different from each other's—can be expressed forcefully in the presence of each other without tension or fear. Israel Gaither is a totally committed man. His commitment to God and to the Army is beyond question. It is stamped over everything he says and does. A weakness is that he sometimes gives the impression that total commitment is best seen in weary eyes and an exhausted body.
>
> In terms of spiritual leadership, he is a giant. His passion for the Kingdom dominates all he says and does. He has a superb business mind, an ability to think logically, to think creatively, to see the big picture, and to think outside the box. I became very aware of this in his discussions with me pertaining to the newly created International Personnel Department I had been appointed to lead, and its place within a well established, deeply entrenched IHQ system. After all, IHQ had existed for almost its entire life without a personnel department as such, and to suddenly impose one onto a time–honored operating structure needed a lot of courage. He encouraged me to persevere, and indeed, he took the initiative to change a number of procedures so that the new department could fulfill a meaningful role.
>
> As a board chairman, he leaves no stone unturned. Just occasionally I feel he was too "picky" in this role, with a tendency to micro manage. But this only demonstrates his passion for everything to be done according to procedure.

Eva is a fine Salvation Army officer in her own right. The support she gives to Izzy is first class and I would risk my neck to say that he would not be able to accomplish what he does without her. She is her own person, with definite thoughts and ideas and expresses them with clarity, conviction and force.

The way ILG approaches his task as Chief of the Staff is both impressive and humbling. He has an ability to encompass a variety of global needs mentally, to stand the grueling pace physically, to maintain balance emotionally, and enrich spiritually. These 'total personality' qualities impact the Army world powerfully. They enable him to meet each day's challenge with confidence and courage. I suspect there are times when he would prefer to close his eyes and let some things go away, but he never does.

Israel Gaither is not exceptionally tall, yet he is of immense spiritual stature. He is anointed for his task, truly a man of God.

Robert Booth, great–grandson of the Army Founder and grandson of Herbert Booth, is a prominent restaurateur in Connecticut. A warm and supportive friend of the Army, he says, "I have a great deal of respect for the Army and what it stands for and what our great–grandfather started." To Gaither, he wrote, "We marvel at the size of your undertaking. To be second in command! I know what it involves just in my household!" Bob Booth wrote of the Gaithers, "They are The Salvation Army at its very best in all respects." Such was the tribute from a now vintage child of the regiment.

Some international leaders who have had associations with Gaithers at IHQ share their recollections.

Commissioner Raymond Houghton, International Secretary to the Chief of Staff, reflects:

> When the Gaithers were appointed to IHQ, we found them instantly to be warmhearted people, with a genuine interest in others. Izzy's letters of appreciation are a model in not only expressing gratitude but giving encouragement and value to the person. He makes you feel good about yourself and your part in mission.
>
> He is well known for his early mornings, for being the first to arrive at IHQ, and that before most have even risen from their beds! His preparation is meticulous—be that for his preaching or for a routine board meeting. So often in boards we realize that he has not only read the papers in advance, but delved into the background and considered every nuance.

Needless to say, he expects others to be similarly well–informed!

His chairmanship style is perhaps best described as cool and efficient. He is straight to the point, does not encourage unnecessary discussion, and comes quickly to a decision. Some find this a little intimidating, especially if they are lacking in confidence or unsure of their ground.

"Mission" is his keyword. The mission is the driving force and the focus of everything. We have heard, as never before, phrases such as "missioners together," "a partner in mission," "mission effectiveness," "mission impact." "Mission" comes through constantly. As a consequence of this, mission has become increasingly the focus of others too. His enthusiasm for mission has caught on.

Commissioner Makoto Yoshida, international secretary for the South Pacific and East Asia, observes an important attribute of Gaither in his interpersonal relations: "He is a listener in normal conversation as well as in the boards and councils. Because he is a listener, he is always prepared to change courses if necessary and appropriate."

Commissioner Mohan Masih, India West Territorial Commander, writes of his progressive impressions of Commissioner Gaither.

During the two High Councils, in talking with Commissioner Israel Gaither and hearing his presentation as the nominee for General, I observed him as a visionary man, a leader with passion for souls and evangelism. Talking with other leaders, I found that Commissioner Israel is a hero and beloved leader among the people where he served and the territory from which he has come. His practical, skillful and humble life is like a magnet which attracts people. While the IHQ was functioning at the training college for the General's Consultative Council meeting, I was sitting with some officers at a dining table when the Commissioner came behind and put his arms around my shoulders, the way only an intimate friend will do. He asked, "How are you, Mohan? How is Swarni, the family and the work going?" I was very much surprised that the Chief of the Staff should come to the corner table where I was sitting and greet me in such an intimate way. When he had gone, the other officers sitting at the table told me that he is a wonderful leader. He came to the dining room to greet and meet everyone, even the least. I admired him in my heart, saying, "O God, what an extraordinary leader." He is a busy leader with heavy responsibilities in the position of second in

command as the Chief of the Staff, but he carries the spirit of
a friendly, caring and servant leader.

Majors James and Helen Bryden of IHQ, who had served in Africa, write:
"Every now and then God sets aside a man or woman for his great purpose.
Israel Gaither is such a man. Often with a twinkle in his eye, Izzy, as he is af-
fectionately known, displays a real sense of humor and can laugh easily at
himself as well as with others. Eva, a gifted woman, is also a wonderful
homemaker. Recently our daughter and son–in–law met Izzy and Eva in
their home. Later on in the evening Danny remarked, 'God is in that place.'"

Commissioner Thorleif Gulliksen, as international secretary for Europe,
had a close, working relationship with Gaither. He writes, "As the Chief of
the Staff he is effective and sensitive in the way he leads the different committees and business meetings and will always let the people involved be
heard and aim to come to clear conclusions. In difficult discussions he man-
ages to keep a good spirit among the colleagues with his humor and anec-
dotes. He is a warm and caring person. And most important—the
commissioner will always set the mission first!"

Pakistan's territorial commander, Commissioner Gulzar Patras, relates, "I
have found him to possess a very fine and sharp mind and am always impressed by the strength he exudes. He is a man of strong convictions, and his
belief in himself and his vision is easy to see and feel. He is a great motiva-
tor, and in his presence, you always feel encouraged. He is a spiritual man in
the true sense of the word, someone who has come to know and love the
Lord in a personal way. All this in a person who is extremely friendly, jolly
and kindhearted. I have found him to be humorous and witty and always
ready to share a laugh or an amusing incident. I have always felt comfortable
and welcome in his presence."

Japan's territorial commander, Commissioner Nozomi Harita, sees
Gaither through Asian eyes. "Commissioner Gaither is calm and gentle, yet
it seems that he is not afraid of speaking out his mind, and his opinions are
sound and dependable. He listens to people very well, and his gentleness invites those around him to be included in the circle. I remember being in the
same discussion group with him once, and he would show great interest in
what I would say about the Japan Territory. Later, he would make reference
to my comments so that the situation could be taken into account on the
particular topic. His thoughtfulness and empathy made an impression on
me."

Retired Commissioner Tadeous Shipe recalls the visit of the Gaithers to
his home territory in Zimbabwe. "The Commissioners conducted three different interdivisional congresses; visited our schools, hospital, home for the
aged; and reached places that had never received an international leader.
Many new souls were won for Christ, and on one of these visits, a remarkable sign of the working of the Holy Spirit was experienced through

Commissioner Gaither's moving messages. One woman possessed of the evil spirit paved her way through, strongly gripped the hand of Commissioner Gaither, cried out for help, and many officers and Christians were drawn to her attention. She received Salvation through this visit. Commissioner Gaither is a man of God, a Spirit–filled leader with a heart for the people. We glorify God for this servant."

Commissioner Amos Makina, International Secretary for Africa, says, "We found the Gaithers to be devoted Christian leaders who lead with love. They are humble and yet professional. Commissioner Eva is a wonderful supporter to her husband, a good example in women's ministries, and many women admire and love her for that. Commissioner Gaither is not an ordinary man; when he is on the platform, the devil has no chance. We thank God for giving us such a man to be second in command of our international Army."

" When he is on the platform the devil has no chance."

AT THE INTERNATIONAL CONFERENCE

The triennial International Conference of Leaders convened April 29 to May 7, 2004, in New Jersey, with the theme "Renewal." Presided over by the General, the agenda was designed to "look at the big issues." These included how to keep The Salvation Army focused on its mission, world evangelism, opportunities in Africa, Asia and Latin America, reaching and holding children and youth for Christ, new trends in reaching women, combating social evils, training and development of officers, and the challenge of financial resources.

Humans are both spiritual and temporal beings, and God has called the Army to a holistic ministry that addresses this duality. Emphasis on the Army's core values addressed this duality, requiring a balance between its evangelism and social work.

As Chief of the Staff, Commissioner Gaither had a significant role in the planning of this highly choreographed gathering, assuring that it would be productive for the Army at the crossroads of a world in dynamic change. One hundred twenty–six international, territorial and command leaders met for eight intense days of listening, discussing and worshiping. At the conclusion they signed their names to a declaration for Salvationists worldwide, de-signed to embody the passions and heart concerns of the conference dele-gates. Entitled, *Towards 2010, A Declaration of Renewal,* it was based on Isaiah 43:19, "See, I am doing a new thing!"

In a plenary session, he spoke passionately and powerfully on "Mission First!" His words resonated deeply with the Army's international leaders, upon whom would rest the task to steer the Army's ship through the changing tides and troubled waters of the future. The Chief left no doubt that the mission of the Army would need to be the rudder to help stay the course. His declaration of "Mission First!" became a watchword of the historic conference.

Commissioner Kang, Sung–hwan of Korea remembers this powerful metaphor. "His preaching remains vividly alive in my memory even now. I believe that if all territorial leaders were able to catch some of his prophetic thinking and world vision for saving of the lost, we would be a much mightier Army indeed. That which I remember ever so clearly was his metaphoric use of a mighty wind. We, The Salvation Army, with defiance, must fight the wind of the world by evoking the wind of the Holy Spirit to rouse us to battle for Him."

Commissioner K. Ross Kendrew of New Zealand shares his remembrance from that conference of an eloquence expressed in tears. "My wife June and I had opportunity for warm conversation with Israel and Eva. On one occasion Eva was in tears in speaking of the paucity of the resources of the Southern Africa territory when compared to the lavishness of the resources available at the conference. One saw in those tears something of the heart of Eva and Israel."

Commissioner Jean B. Ludiazo, territorial commander of the Congo and Angola Territory, said, "Some will never forget his leadership in the 2004 Conference; how he electrified the audience by his words and prayer in the welcome meeting, identifying himself as a good team leader and partner with the General."

Commissioner Lawrence Moretz, who has closely observed Israel since his earliest days in the Army, remarks about his friend, "It was obvious that, having been through the struggles of Africa and now in his world leadership as Chief of Staff, he had captured the picture of the global Salvation Army. He spoke with authority and presented a dynamic vision. And he left a legacy of that vision for me as I succeeded him in our home territory."

Commissioner Raymond Houghton, who as International Secretary to the Chief of Staff, closely observed Israel Gaither's leadership qualities. "The example and leadership that he has given as Chief of the Staff have been of the very highest order. As one who has worked so very closely with him I have increasingly come to value the depth of his spirituality and devotion to the Lord through the Army. I have learned of those deep convictions which have driven him to mission, I have seen his pastor's heart of compassion, I have witnessed his integrity and strong sense of responsibility. There has never been any attempt to shy away from a problem, but rather a determination to face it squarely, discover the facts accurately, and deal with it justly and compassionately. I have come to realize that Izzy seeks only to fulfill

God's divine purposes for him. He seeks nothing for himself. In life and in leadership he has lifted up Jesus."

LEAVING A LEGACY

Significant changes occurred in the Army during the stewardship of General Larsson and Commissioner Gaither. International Headquarters became more ethnically diverse with the representation of Asian and African officers at the High Council and support level. An exponential growth worldwide of members known as adherents (persons who become church members without subscribing to the full covenant of a Salvation Army soldier) assumed greater status as it was redefined and now includes a faith statement. The *2005 Year for Children and Youth,* declared by the conference, sparked renewal among a new generation, and the Army's mission of world evangelization moved forward with a new energy.

It is obvious that the office of the Chief is multidimensional in its oversight and duties, all that in addition to the expenditure of energies in world travels and an ongoing and demanding platform ministry. The prayer of Phillips Brooks seems apt: "Lord, we do not pray for tasks equal to our power, but for power equal to our tasks."

chapter 27

A Magnificent Obsession

But seek first his kingdom and his righteousness.
Matthew 6:33

A great leader is said to have the ability to see where the organization needs to go, and to articulate that direction in a way that inspires people. Israel L. Gaither has been a leader with such vision, powerfully articulated with his motto, "Mission Matters Most," a cornerstone of his preaching and platform.

Mission Calling!

His conviction and commitment to the mission of The Sal-

"I hear mission calling."

vation Army were immutable. His clarion call of "Mission Matters Most" had been once again clearly sounded in his farewell message to the USA Eastern Territory on Oct. 9, 2002.

> I hear the mission calling. It's a clear and urgent call to engage the Good News of the Gospel for the transforming of our sector of the mission field. It's a call to press the Kingdom into our secular environment. And we must get on with it passionately and quickly.

I hear the mission calling. My wife and I believe in the purpose, place, and power of the mission. Our world needs a Salvation Army, an Army of Holy–Spirit–filled, Spirit–led missioners, mission teams who are agents of Christ boldly infiltrating the world, making way for the kingdom. Every center of Salvation Army activity must serve as a mission station, and every single Salvationist must see herself or himself as a valuable member of the mission team. It just can't be any other way.

Our success will be measured in the transformed people who have become empowered by Christ to transform their circumstances. We win when corps take on more Salvationists, we win when corps fellowships multiply with new congregations in new places. We win when beneficiaries in our institutions experience compassionate care and then feel differently about who they are and what they can become. These are the signs of a mission that is winning.

I'm grateful for every Salvationist who is firmly committed to Christ in this great mission. We need you. We need every soldier unleashed for Christ and missioning in your world. And I'm calling for more creative, flexible and relevant action. It must happen. We have no choice.

The world beyond our walls in every city and town is waiting for you collectively to show up. I'm calling you to ensure that every ministry, every activity, every dream in your place of service be linked to the center, of mission.

Remember this—a corps hall, a service, an activity—none of these are the mission of the Army. They are means to mission, pathways to missioning for the sake of the Kingdom. And we fail God's intention if these things become the end rather than the means of mission objective—of getting people saved, growing saints, serving the suffering. All result from saturating our world with the Gospel of liberating news.

There is much more to do and a higher level is required of every Salvationist, to live a life of practical holiness because there are still too many places where Jesus does not yet reign. I'm convinced we haven't seen the best yet.

I hear mission calling, calling us to center our purposes in Kingdom–building ideas and action. I hear mission calling—calling us to be obedient to our God–given mandate. I hear the sound of mission calling, calling us to be faithful.

Keep on missioning. It must always matter most. And God will bless every good and faithful effort.

RENEWING THE MISSION

When Israel Gaither moved to IHQ, mission still mattered most to him, and his vision took on a global emphasis. His article, "Renewing the Mission," was published in the Army's 2004 Year Book, and on the IHQ Web site. The following are excerpts.

" The spiritual compass that once guided behavior is broken."

It's time to keep an eye on the future! Twenty-first century ministry requires a mission–centered Salvation Army in continuous renewal. And at the center of this mission endeavor is the passion to call the people of the world to Christ.

The administering of mission, no matter the context, requires Spirit–driven action. It's time for more bold initiatives pushing us beyond our comfortable patterns of behavior. It's mission renewal time!

War wreaking havoc on nations has given rise to a new definition of "disaster relief."

As waves of refugees are lapping at the shores of many nations of the world, new challenges and significant opportunities arise for creative and innovative "home missionary" strategies.

Liberal thought and behavior are exerting significant challenges to orthodox, biblical belief and moral behavior.

What does it mean to be a missioning Salvation Army gifted to a dangerous world that's uncomfortable with itself? What will it take to fulfill the Great Commission and the Great Commandments in today's world? The challenges facing our world are the proofs that continuous mission renewal is desperately required.

Anywhere in the world where The Salvation Army is found, a signal of hope is still alive! The Army is in the neighborhood, and no one needs to give up! We are the "special forces unit" of Christ's Church on earth. We're more than a conventional church and much more than a mere social–serving agent. The call to mission renewal sounds the urgency of renewed understanding about "who" we are and "why" we exist.

Renewing the mission implies renewing of covenant. We're the keepers of a covenant that can only be sustained by continuous renewal.

It's getting dark in the world. The spiritual compass that once guided behavior is broken. We're losing our way. And those engaged in this mission must be an unerring guide for others who search for hope and belief.

We are burning lights! That's our passion—to burn with God's dream for his world. And caught in the flames of renewal—we'll keep the promises!

The Army's mission is Israel Gaither's core agenda. He espouses mission as an article of faith. His ardor for mission is expressed, not only in his platform and preaching, but also throughout his officership, from his earliest days as a corps officer. He exemplifies the Army's mission in his lifestyle and ministry. Mission, for Israel Gaither, was his compelling vision, his magnificent obsession.

On the march in Norway

Preaching with a translator in Norway

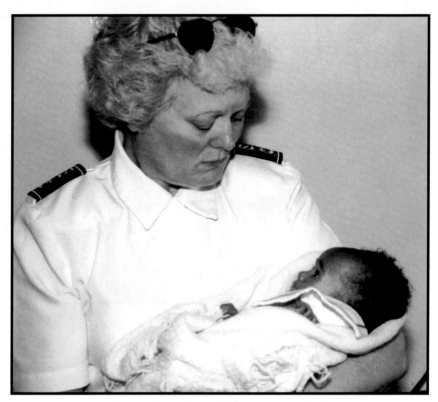

Eva Gaither coddles a baby stricken with AIDS

The Gaithers with Commissioners Noland and officers of Southern Africa

Israel Gaither leads a prayer meeting in Korea

With Tanzania Command leaders Lt. Colonels Forster, saluting the 2005 cadets

A colorful welcome in India

The Gaithers with the Southern Africa Staff Band

General John Larsson, Commissioner Freda Larsson,
Commissioners Eva and Israel Gaither [2005]

Israel and Eva Gaither during their time in South Africa

chapter **28**

All Around the World

In journeyings often ...
2 Cor. 11:26

Augustine wrote: "The world is a book, and those who do not travel read only a page." In that regard, the travels of the Gaithers make up quite a volume, encompassing the diversity as well as the unity of the Army on all seven continents.

The sun never sets on the Army's tricolors. It is a restless banner, hoisted and proclaiming its trinitarian message of the Gospel in 111 countries and territories of the world. The flag's emblazoned "Blood and Fire" signifies the Salvationist's immutable doctrine of the atoning work of Christ and the cleansing and empowering work of the Holy Spirit. A miniature Salvation Army flag once even traveled to the moon, carried by an American astronaut, and today reposes in a showcase at the Army's headquarters in Philadelphia. As Chief of the Staff, Gaither took the world as his parish, and its far–flung frontiers beckoned him and Eva on an odyssey of the spirit to more than 50 countries and territories of the Army world.

"MOBILE BUT NOT ROOTLESS"

A reporter in Sweden wrote of their visit there, "Israel and Eva Gaither personify the concept that often permeates their preaching—they are 'mobile but definitely not rootless.' In all their travels their messages and interactions sprang from the deep roots of their lives and ministry." Travel around the Army world confirmed for them the theological truth that the oneness of humanity transcends accidental differences of geography, color and race.

The international Salvation Army is a family of nations and of God's people, with a unity in its diversity that should make the United Nations blush with envy. When Salvationists meet, an instant rapport results, without the shadow of a barrier between. The Chief of the Staff and his wife, in their world travels, are always warmly received as representing the General in leadership of the global family of Salvationists.

A traveler's experience depends on what one brings to places visited. If, for example, in attending an opera, one is familiar with the music, it enhances the listening. What would the scene of the Battle of Waterloo mean to someone who knew nothing about Napoleon? The Gaithers did their homework before each international visit, bringing with them knowledge, not only of the history and data of the Army in that country, but also of the nation's history, culture, economics, politics, issues and its people.

The Western mind knows the world better than it knows man, but the Eastern world knows man better than it knows the world. The Western world, more an extrovert, produces a technological civilization; the Eastern world, more an introvert, seeks to develop wisdom through contemplation. Both of these worlds had an impact upon the Gaithers in their visits and deepened their understanding of what it means to be a servant of Christ in a pluralistic world. As they saw the extreme depths of suffering and destitution of people from the ravages of war and abject poverty, they perceived that hunger is not only an economic problem; it is a moral and spiritual problem.

The words *travel* and *travail* have a practical as well as a linguistic kinship. The frequent global travels of the Gaithers imposed their own heavy draft on the leaders' physical and emotional resources and energy. But they proved resilient enough to keep up with the demands of meeting airline schedules and check–ins, recovering from lost baggage in transit, adjusting to major time changes, and being at their best upon arrival for meeting sometimes thousands of people. And of course, there is then the major responsibility of being in tune spiritually as they minister both to individuals and to the large gatherings. Indeed, world travel and ministry exacts one of the heaviest tolls on the time and energy of the Chief and his travel partner.

To prepare the way for their global journeys, A *Memorandum of Guidance For International Visits* of both the General and Chief of Staff is sent in advance to territories the leaders visit. The guidelines spell out the purpose of visits, the balance and time limits for supporting speakers in meetings conducted, and translation arrangements. Protocol for the Gaithers' accommodation and meals stipulate, "The commissioners prefer no meat with meals. They enjoy fresh fruits and vegetables. For health reasons the Chief must avoid spicy foods of all kinds and coffee and tea." The Chief's office requests information about events and programs six months before a visit, and eleven copies of a "brief" of detailed information three weeks prior. The brief includes schedule and events, addresses and phone numbers, list of leading officers, transport details, current exchange rate, time differential, climate information, uniform details including whether the territory requires headwear for women, and biographies for interviews with special guests. Thus the foundations and preparations for visits, well–formulated in advance, smooth the way and enhance the effectiveness of the visits.

The Chief's journeyings opened new and revealing windows on the worldwide Salvation Army, and gave opportunity for a more sensitive and adequate response for linking resources with dire needs. The late General Arnold Brown capsulated the Army's worldwide mission, "The front lines of The Salvation Army run through the tragedies of our world." As the Gaithers visited those front lines, they brought the love and presence of Christ amid the slums, the hovels, the emptiness of stomachs, the destitute and dying. The One Who said, "I was hungry and you gave me to eat" journeys with all who go in his name.

A Most Extensive Wardrobe

In her role, Eva Gaither had an extensive wardrobe of Salvation Army uniforms—of navy blue, white, and gray, for the various countries she visited. African territories have multiple uniform styles, and when she went to Zimbabwe for the 2005 All Africa Congress, she had to pack four different style hats. On occasion she has "modeled" the varied uniforms, wearing a different national style in a series of meetings, illustrating both the diversity and internationalism of The Salvation Army.

Eva, as world secretary for the Army's Women Ministries, gathered and shared reports on the exciting results in that field. In 2005 she reported on 15,659 women who sought salvation and 6,033 who were enrolled as new Salvationists. One of her favorite programs to describe was Junior Miss, which, on the African continent gives instruction to girls and young women 9 years old and up. She relates, "We taught them about themselves, about sex, AIDS, and encouraged parents to participate in a Christian ceremony in place of horrible rites that otherwise may mutilate and damage them for life [female circumcision]." Eva tends to get choked up a bit when she talks about babies with AIDS, some having been left on the doorstep of, or brought by police to an Army shelter. She says, "I knew the next time I would visit that shelter, the baby I held would not be there."

On a personal level she made it a point to walk the floors at IHQ regularly, greeting the staff and occasionally sitting and chatting. "It was important to know our IHQ family," she said, and the members of that family testify that they were grateful for the interest and encouragement she radiated.

Commissioner Eva, in her secondary role as World President for Salvation Army Scouts, Guides and Guards, received a warm welcome at the Finland and Estonia Territory's Scout Camp. Accompanied by Colonels Carl and Gudrun Lydholm and Major Kelly Pontsler. she met with 93 scouts and leaders from five countries who had gathered for a week of adventure, fellowship and skill–building. As the delegates joined together for worship on the side of a hill overlooking the sea, the scouts and leaders sang in three languages as the sun set. Commissioner Gaither, having herself been a General's

Guard when she was a girl, spoke about Jesus as the light of the world. Her message crossed the barriers of language, and many young girls' raised their hands in commitment to the light of God.

AROUND THE ARMY WORLD

A review of the Gaithers' schedule while at IHQ shows them traveling somewhere in the world on the average of twice monthly. In each visit they met with Salvationist leaders and the rank and file, toured Army ministries, and sought to encourage the troops. The Chief would always issue his call that "mission matters most." The following is but a sampling of their visits.

At the Berlin Wall

The Gaithers were guest speakers in November 2004 at **Germany**'s national officers' councils and undertook a three–day tour of Berlin, visiting social service centers and sharing a meal with active and retired officers. They experienced moving moments in the "death zone" at the Berlin Wall. Peering through a hole in a remnant of the wall, they looked upon "the slaughtering fields" where people had given their lives in pursuit of freedom. "We left, not with a dry eye," says Israel. On that visit to Germany, Gaither preached at a divisional rally, declaring, "God can bring down the walls built by man!"

Speaking from the robust Salvation Army in **Korea**, its territorial commander, Commissioner Kang, Sung–hwan, shares his recall of the Gaithers' visit in October 2004 for the 96th Anniversary Celebrations and Congress meetings. "The Commissioner's messages were well–received by the congregations here, leaving a wonderful impression upon his hearers and enthusing officers and soldiers alike for greater ministry. The Chief thoroughly relied upon the Holy Spirit as he preached. His rich humor and warm love, interest in even a small child, his conversations with lay Salvationists, and all his interaction with the people, bore testimony to Commissioner Gaither not as the Chief of the Staff but, first and foremost, as a humble servant of the Lord.

Commissioner Chun, Kwang–Pyo, then chief secretary in Korea, adds: "I was greatly impressed by his zeal and compassion for officers. Through his messages, he gave a great hope yet earnest challenge to all his listeners. This was easily conveyed to the congregation even through the need for translation. Something he said that will remain forever in my heart is that 'We are all one family. Even though we have different cultures, different languages, different skin colors, yet we are one family in the Lord and in The Salvation Army!' I was so moved when I heard those words! During the time of the visit, I was the Chief Secretary, having taken up this appointment some four months prior. My wife and I were scheduled to meet with the Chief in his hotel room. Imagine how nervous we both were, realizing we were to spend time in the company of one of our world leaders, and in his private hotel room at that. Yet he made us feel so comfortable. How he encouraged us both with his fervent prayer! It was at that time when the Lord granted me firm confidence to be able to take up my new tasks this year for the sake of the territory. How grateful I am to the Chief for his God–given words and encouragement to me. While the Chief and Commissioner Eva Gaither were here, it was beautiful to see the loving, caring support they gave to each other as a married couple. Wherever they were, it was not unusual to see them holding hands or sharing advice and comments with each other about the day's schedule and the program to be undertaken."

"God has something new for The Salvation Army's mission in **Moldova** that has never been seen before," declared the Chief of Staff during a July 2004 visit to Eastern Europe Command, where he and Commissioner Eva led a congress celebrating a decade of work in Moldova. "You are celebrating what God has done. You have power and possibilities in Christ, so celebrate that. Dance! Praise him!" He commissioned 18 cadets, encouraged them individually and challenged his hearers, "Things in Moldova aren't the way they should be, but you can be an agent of change if you give yourself to God."

In an August 2004 visit to Eva's home division in the **USA**, the camp meeting tent was transformed into a tabernacle as people moved forward in submission to God. The weekend program was complemented with a Bible study, "Sharing God's Glory in Our Marriage," led by Colonels James and Carolyn Knaggs. From the Gaither's May 2004 visit to Chicago the territory's newsletter gave a unique report. "As he looked out on the more than 900 Salvationists gathered for the closing session, Commissioner Israel Gaither saw a reflection of the world—young and old, African–Americans and Caucasians, Hispanics, Laotians, Russians, Swedes, Koreans, Jamaicans, and more—the diversity that is the Metropolitan Division. His powerful message prompted a standing ovation. In speaking to the cadets about his world travels, he took a lesson from the different uniforms he wears. "I hate to brag, but I really look good in a white uniform," he quipped. "But the problem with a white uniform is keeping it clean. We may be making a good appearance, but are there any edges of our life in need of cleansing? We must get rid of those things that keep us from being what we should be."

UNIQUE ENCOUNTERS

The Army's Oslo Temple's capacity crowd greeted the Gaithers in July 2003 for the congress of the **Norway, Iceland and The Faeroes** Territory. "Do not let the annual congress, so rich in tradition, become just a yearly pilgrimage and an opportunity to meet friends," exhorted the Chief. "Let it be a spiritual experience, to meet Christ and to be in Him." A unique encounter for the Chief on his visit to Norway was with the Salvation Riders, founded in 2001, and initiated by a man who had been a part of the notorious "Hell's Angels" motorcycle gang, internationally known for crime and violence. The man had found Christ as his Savior and started The Salvation Riders as a way of sharing the faith with other bikers.

Israel Gaither on a Salvation Riders motorcycle in Norway, with leader Anne Nordboe

A traditional welcome with spears and colorful costumes greeted the Gaithers on their arrival in **Zambia** in April 2004. The Chief spoke of the importance of the continent of Africa in the context of the Christian Church and The Salvation Army. He referred to the fact that 2004 saw the 40th anniversary of Zambia's independence and that freedom of worship had been written into the nation's constitution. The challenge to be identified as free Christians brought many seekers to the mercy seat. Gaithers also visited the Army's famed Chikankata Mission, with its long tradition of dynamic and multidimensional ministry.

In **Indonesia**, in June 2003, the Gaithers dedicated a new building and laid the first stone for Jakarta 1 Corps at the training college complex. The international guests were welcomed by a ceremonial dance accompanied by traditional music. In his message the Chief used Bahasa Indonesian to introduce each of his points. Forty–eight cadets—the largest number in the territory's history—marched to the platform to receive their summer appointments. During the altar call some parents of the new captains moved forward and sought Christ. The territorial commander leaned over to Israel and said, "That woman cadet is praying with her father, who is a Muslim." Israel, in his preaching in another country would later say, "I watched that young woman cadet lead her Muslim father to Christ. I believe in miracles!"

Colonel Olin O. Hogan, territorial commander of the **Mexico** Territory, reported, "At the meeting of the leaders of Mexico, Latin America North, South America East and West, and Caribbean Territories, Commissioner Gaither presented the truth in a powerful way. We are blessed to have him as the Chief of the Staff."

Almost 4,000 people attended and more than 1,500 rededicated themselves in **Ghana** in February 2005 during the first–ever visit to that nation by a Chief of the Staff. Commissioner Eva Gaither was welcomed to the women's celebration by a traditional dancing group. In her Bible message she spoke about the prayer life of women, and when the invitation to the mercy seat was given, more than 500 women responded. The Gaithers toured the Army's Vocational Training Centre, where 400 girls receive training. An overflow crowd had to follow the Saturday "Festival of Joy" on closed–circuit TV. The mercy seat was lined with hundreds of Salvationists following the Chief's preaching on the ability of Christ to transform lives.

Chief receives *hongi* greeting in New Zealand

The official report stated that the Gaithers in January 2003 "touched the hearts of listeners during their visit to the **New Zealand, Fiji and Tonga** Territory. They took the Lord's message to two large public meetings as well as [to] events with officers, cadets, employees and recovering addicts." The people greeted the Gaithers with the traditional *hongi* greeting—the gentle pressing together of nose and forehead. In Auckland some 400 Salvationists packed the Army hall to witness the Army's highest honor, the Order of the Founder, bestowed by the Chief on Lt. Colonels Lance and Faye Rive for 36 years of sacrificial ser-vice of far–reaching influence.

Lt. Colonel Dick Krommenhoek shares a unique encounter when the Gaithers visited **Denmark** in October 2004. "Commissioner Gaither spoke to some 60 teenagers during their late–night program. He started out by making so much fun with these youngsters that he had them crawling over the floor with laughter. None of the jokes was at the expense of someone else, and it was marvelous to see that he was not afraid to exercise a large dose of self–irony in which he readily involved Eva, who jokingly added to the fun by telling Izzy to behave. Seconds later, though, Izzy managed to turn the moments of fun into a period of deep devotion, where all youngsters were challenged to focus their life on Jesus and on Him only. The spiritual intensity of these moments was so deep and sincere that for some of these youngsters, this became a life–defining experience."

The mystique of **India** weaves a spell upon its visitors, but the India Central Territory confronted the Gaithers with the reality of poverty and hunger. A crowd of Salvationists greeted them at three in the morning upon their arrival in March 2004. The Gaithers visited and conducted meetings at several of the Army's schools, the William Booth Junior College, and the Evangeline Booth Hospital, where they learned of that institution's involvement in an HIV/AIDS Awareness program. In Eluru the 2,500 capacity *pandal* used for the holiness meeting was soon full, and people had to find vantage points outside. In his Bible message that day, the Chief spoke of the Spirit of Jesus as more powerful than the huge power of the tsunami, which had not long ago struck that part of the world.

In Russia, Nina Davidovich is admitted to the Order of the Founder.

In **Russia** in March 2005 the Chief shared in the Elevation Ceremony Congress, a historic event held in Moscow to mark the change in status of the Eastern Europe Command to that of a territory.[3] Delegates welcomed pioneers from the early days of the Army in Eastern Europe, and Salvationists representing the five countries of the territory—Georgia, Moldova, Romania, Russia and Ukraine—presented songs of praise, dramatic sketches, and dance numbers. A highlight was the admission to the Order of the Founder of Nina Davidovich, "for compassionate Christ–inspired ministry that reaches and embraces the needs of the poor, the ill and the homeless in Russia, through which she has displayed personal courage and sacrifice, perseverance and faith despite opposition, suffering and loss." Nina thanked all who had prayed for her over the years, especially during the months she was held hostage in Chechnya.

---

[3]"Command" is a smaller type of territory, directed by an officer commanding; "Territory" is a country, part of a country, or several countries combined, under a territorial commander

At Home in the UK

While living in London, the Gaithers made themselves available to respond to invitations to participate in many events in the United Kingdom Territory. The UK *Salvationist* of July 24, 2004 headline read, "*Gaither is positive under fire in Jersey.*" It reported his challenge, "The new building will mean nothing until it is crowned with the sacrificial offering of souls for God," as the Chief officiated at the reopening of St. Helier Corps hall, which had undergone extensive refurbishment. The Chief's message was a climactic conclusion to the corps' 125th-anniversary celebrations. The opening ceremony, in front of a large crowd, included an unexpected water bomb attack aimed at the Chief. Two youths threw them from an adjacent multistory car park, just missing the commissioner, who continued unperturbed and reflected on early–day Salvationists who faced similar resistance. He urged the corps not to "stand still and look back, but move forward and extend the ministry on the island."

As the Gaithers conducted campaigns in the South and Mid Wales Division in March 2003, Israel urged the congregation to "choose life." His passionate messages resonated throughout the weekend as he and Commissioner Eva fulfilled a number of engagements. The Chief delivered a fiery message, reminding listeners that those who have chosen Christ are winners, for they have chosen life. The many responses at the altar left no doubt that the Salvationists of South and Mid Wales were intent on choosing life for themselves, their corps and their communities.

In May 2003, the Chief conducted the dedication of the Winton Corps' refurbished buildings. This long established corps, with one of the largest properties in Great Britain, has a band and songster brigade of exceptional quality and offers a galaxy of services in its expanded facility. It houses a thrift store, a restaurant that seats 100, a large community hall, extended health–care programs, a ministry for stroke victims, a corps team that does meal runs for the homeless, and even an ongoing assistance program in the Ukraine. The corps newsletter reported, "In his inspirational message the Chief of the Staff stated he saw the "W" of Winton as the initial of its qualities. The corps is wonderfully warm, wonderfully working, it's not going to be found wanting!' These two servants of God, each possessing the priceless gift of communication, presented the eternal truths they had been given for us, through their personalities. The Word became flesh through them, and we were the better for it, as many responded in commitment to the mission of the corps."

" The Word became flesh through them, and we were the better for it."

The Chief of the Staff and the General traveled together to some events, where they presented a dynamic duo of Salvationist leadership and Gospel preaching. Such was the London Celebration in November 2003 when 2,000 Salvationists gathered in Royal Festival Hall. The international news reported that "the day's close revealed the answer to the question posed powerfully in the morning meeting by Chief of the Staff, 'Are you listening?'" Later in the month Commissioners Gaither joined the General and Commissioner Larsson for celebrations at York.

"The Chief of the Staff helps shape the future of the UK Territory's Central North Division" was the headline of the news report on the Gaithers' June 2005 visit for the divisional congress, which had a galaxy of creative and visionary facets, including a vibrant variety of music and witness. The weekend climaxed with "many people moving forward to stand with the Chief in their commitment to be true soldiers of Christ." The closing sentence of the report stated, "Perhaps the clearest expression of all that had been achieved was seen in the action of three teenage girls who asked to be allowed to meet with the Gaithers as they were about to leave for the journey back to London. They just wanted to say thanks and to tell the Chief that their lives would never be the same again."

THE GLOBAL VILLAGE

Salvationists of the 15 countries that comprise the Army's **Caribbean** Territory came together in June 2005 to Kingston, Jamaica, under the leadership of the Gaithers for the commissioning of cadets. Jubilant expressions of praise and worship, climaxed a report of "wave after wave of seekers."

July 2005 found Gaithers in war–torn **Liberia**, where the Chief commented, "Youth of the country knew only war or the aftermath of war." One of the most common sights on the streets was men with machine guns. There, the Army has persevered through the years and grown despite much suffering and political unrest. "We shall never forget," Israel recalls with deep emotion, "hearing our Salvationists there sing, 'God cannot fail,' and then singing, 'I cannot fail.' We've seen ordinary people do extraordinary things through the power of God."

In August 2005 more than 12,000 came to the All Africa Congress in **Zimbabwe**, with General Larsson, Commissioner Larson and the Gaithers. Africa now occupies a dominant position in the worldwide Army, with four out of ten Salvationists being Africans. The vice president of Zimbabwe, Her Excellency Joyce T. Mujuru, a Salvationist, was among the dignitaries who welcomed the international leaders. During the five days of the congress the National Stadium became as a "Salvation Army City," with Salvationists in colorful uniforms milling throughout the seminars and many events. As the thousands in serried ranks marched past the reviewing stand, Israel's right hand held up in salute tired from the long march. He noted that the General, similarly finding it hard to keep his hand raised, uplifted his left hand. Israel shared, "Then I uplifted my left hand to be consistent with the General!" Many recommitted themselves following the Chief's preaching at the Men's Rally. Gaither led the final meeting of 12,000 on Sunday morning. After General Larsson preached, thousands came forward to pray at "the largest mercy seat in the world," the soccer field where the meeting took place.

As the band played an African melody welcoming Commissioners Gaither in native fashion to the **Congo and Angola Territories**, they responded by dancing in rhythm to the melody. The October 2005 Congress yielded "mega–statistics." More than 2,700 attended the opening meeting, with 175 moving to the mercy seat. At the territory's first men's rally, more than 500 heard the Chief's challenge, with 170 responding at the altar. Commissioner Eva Gaither gave the Bible message to more than 5,000 at the women's rally, with nearly 800 responding in acts of rededication. Some 5,700, gathered for the soldiers' rally, with more than 400 responding to the Chief's altar call. A 90–minute march featured more than 5,000, led by the national band. And almost 9,000 people in the holiness meeting witnessed the Chief enrolling 270 senior soldiers and 147 junior soldiers, with more than 900 dedicating themselves to God and more than 700 seekers at the concert of praise that followed. "An unforgettable Congress, with the Spirit of God powerfully present," summarized the Chief.

In their November 2005 visit to **Australia**, the Gaithers joined with territorial leaders and many of the 1,500–member congregation in signing a "Declaration of War," affirming on the Army's 125th anniversary in Adelaide the continued battle against sin. November 2005 also found the Gaithers leading in a spiritual mountaintop experience in **Tanzania**, the southwest Africa country that rests at the base of the 19,000–foot, snow–covered Mount Kilimanjaro. In a colorful program festooned with Army tricolors, the Chief commissioned cadets of the 2005 Visionaries session.

FULFILLING THE COMMISSION

Some four decades earlier, God had spoken to a 17–year–old high school senior through a postscript on the back of an envelope, "Go into all the world and preach the Gospel." As with Abraham of old, Israel Gaither, with faith and obedience, started on a journey to an unknown destination. And now that call had led him to a worldwide ministry of which he could never have dreamed.

Indeed, the Gaithers had become mobile, with official and in–depth visits to the global outposts of the Army world. But at the same time, as the Swedish journalist had earlier observed, "They were mobile but not rootless." Wherever they went, they remained true to their roots, and from those roots sprung abundant fruit for the Kingdom of God.

chapter **29**

A Passion for Preaching

*Preach the Word; be prepared in season
and out of season.*

2 Tim. 4:2

Israel L. Gaither, in his leadership and ministry, is above all a preacher. When people speak of him or describe him, invariably it is his preaching that comes to the fore. His reputation depends less upon his printed notes than upon the effect they produce upon his hearers. His powerful pulpit proclamations have become his signature, The Salvation Army's "gold standard" for preachment of the Gospel.

His preaching is, first, fueled by his devotional exercise. He spends time very early in the morning in prayer, focused on family, the Army and its leadership, friends, circumstances. "I always end presenting myself to the Lord." He doesn't claim to hear audible words from God but has received strong impressions that, at times, have been pivotal moments in his spiritual jour-

Reprinted with permission of the
UK *Manchester Evening News*

ney. These epiphanies spring from an intimate and ongoing relationship with God that keeps him on "good speaking terms" with his Lord. He takes seriously the inspiration of the Spirit for his selection of material.

"The Lord is the first person to whom I speak each day," says Israel. He prays over what may pass through his desk during the day. If he will be chairing a board meeting, he prays over the agenda, and matters that come by way of letters. As Chief of the Staff, he routinely prayed for John and Freda Larsson. His standard devotional reading is the Bible only; he does not bring other reading into that time.

The powerful impact and results from his preaching do not come without the hard work of prayer and preparation. His sermons are organically linked to Bible texts. His preaching never deals with the marginal, but always on matters undeniably deep, deftly applying a biblical text to the need of his hearers. He preaches for a verdict; no listener escapes without a challenge or an inspiration of what God wants for their life.

He prepares his notes using a computer, and uses a fairly copious text, highlighting some sections, while at the same time preaching with a freedom from notes.

He acknowledges, "The most important thing I do, above all important things, is to preach the Word. I will do whatever necessary to assure I have time carved out for preparation. I will not be in the office during that time. My first principle is the need to be alone and have time. My second principle is that my most productive time is early morning." He guards this "prime time" from secondary pursuits.

Although he excels in the craft of homiletics, Israel realizes that all power in preaching comes ultimately from the Holy Spirit. He deeply believes in the need for the anointing of the Spirit upon his preaching and ministry. "I honestly seek to be empowered by the Spirit. Before we leave a hotel room, while someone is outside waiting for us, Eva and I pray together, seeking the Holy Spirit's anointing. I learned long ago that it cannot be about me; it must be about God." The highest accolade that continues to be expressed of his preaching is that it is "anointed."

Spiritual leadership can be precarious, hanging by the silver thread of people's trust in the preacher. First of all the preacher must be his message, an incarnation of the truth he presents. As Francis reminds us, "Unless you preach everywhere you go, there is no use to go anywhere to preach." Gaither's preaching power also derives from the authority of his integrity, his pastoral compassion, his genuine goodness. Prayer and character and pastoral mission are indissolubly wedded to his pulpit.

His preaching style is active. He aims at the very start to "make a connection" with his hearers. That connection may be through a personal word that relates to them, reference to the event or persons present, an expression of courtesies—all in some way to have his congregation "with" him at the start. Humor and even laughter on his part at times may season his sermon. And always after mirth comes "the still small voice." His messages although deep in convicting truths, are clearly understandable. He takes as his model the One of whom it was said "the common people hear Him gladly."

He moves energetically and purposefully around the platform as he preaches. An "Amen?" with a lilt at the end will elicit an affirming echo from his hearers. He is animated without being theatrical, expressive without affectation. Hearers sense he is authentic and preaches in the power of the Spirit. The sermon derives its potency from the freedom, the verve, the passion and the cadences of his delivery.

Repetition of a key word or sentence reinforces what he wants to get across: "I believe Jesus one day shall fully reign. I believe it! I believe it! I believe it!" He draws illustrations from observations and experiences. Colorful and humorous expressions fall naturally from his preachment. "I know when I'm on the good side of Eva; she calls me 'honey,' 'dear.' But when she addresses me as 'Mr. Gaither,' I know I'm on the bad side." He describes in eloquent terms the transparent architecture of IHQ, and then says, "Everyone can look in on us as they stream across the Millennium Bridge, and see us at work—or some sleeping at their desk!" In unequivocal terms he preaches, "As Salvationists we don't go to church." (Pause) "We don't go to church, we are the church! We are not huddled behind stained–glass windows; we are in the world, in warfare for Christ, and making the devil uncomfortable!"

A special passion resonates when he draws examples from his South Africa experience. At an American camp meeting series he preached: "Western Christians need not feel sorry for Christians in Africa. South Africa is a stunningly beautiful country with some of the most beautiful people. Its people have gone through deep suffering, but they intensely prayed, and today South Africa is free because of the prayer and power of the Church, the transforming power in the name of Jesus. Christ reigns in South Africa." He drives home his point, "Why not in America, in your town, to be his people in unity of purpose, and a transforming influence for Christ?" He throws out the challenge: "Let me remind you, the church is not a building; we are the church!"

He often enters into a dialogue with his hearers. In his farewell meeting in South Africa he preached on the subject of Moses' obedience to God's command and related how he has submitted to God's leading, which was often in contrast to what he himself would have chosen. "Eva and I," he said, "have never desired any appointment, any right. We have never refused any ministry, any responsibility. We are soldiers under orders." Then he walked to one side of the platform, bent over and spoke directly to the cadets sitting in the front, "Do you understand that, cadets? You are under orders."

A theme common to his preaching is that of the unity of believers, of all nations and races. "I have seen all around the world," he declares, "the beauty of the Church with its unity in its diversity. Many don't look like us, are a different color, speak a different language, but we're family in Christ." (He adds the humorous aside, "It means I can borrow money from you!") The ultimate gathering of believers around the throne of God, as portrayed in the Book of Revelation, is often the capstone of his preaching on the universality of the church. This unity–in–diversity, witnessed in his world travels, resonates in his psyche, which was forged in the crucible of his own journey toward acceptance and unity in the body of believers.

He does not speak in a monotone; his voice is euphonic, clear, resonant and strong, with a good range. His inflections enhance meaning, just as a music composer inserts dynamics in his composition. Gaither preaches in cadences that echo in his hearers' hearts.

Those who come to hear him will never be fed 'Pablum' (baby food). Martial expressions salt and pepper his sermons. He makes it clear that we are engaged in a spiritual warfare, but climaxes by saying, "We will win!" He does not tend to use boilerplate paragraphs, but like most preachers, he has his favorite words and sentences. To get his point across he is given to coining verbs such as *missionize, missioning, remissionize, visionize.*

His sermons are not the echo of any teacher or author but are forged on the anvil of his own thought and experience. They are presented with action words and style, clearly understood by the most simple among his hearers. No obtuse words or abstruse constructions will fall on the ears of his congregation. He crafts and presents his message to the level of the people, taking to heart the biblical injunction, "Feed my lambs," and does not mistranslate it to, "Feed my giraffes." Although his words are simple, the concepts and interpretations of the text are often fresh and complex.

When preaching overseas he will rehearse his gestures with the translator and expect the translator to imitate him as he uses his arms and movement in the course of the sermon.

THE IMPACT

The Salvation Army's premier international photographer, Robin Bryant, upon retirement after a 28–year ministry with the Army's global publications, selected what he considered his best photos, primarily "ones reflecting what I believe and have witnessed." Among the nine published in the

A photo selected by Robin Bryant as one of his best

June 4, 2005, *Salvationist* was one of Commissioner Gaither preaching. Of that photo Bryant wrote, "Commissioner Israel Gaither, preaching with the

> **"I remember thinking that it is never a burden to be led by a leader who weeps for his people."**

passion that he does, reminds me of my own need to embrace others with the Gospel."

Major Mark Tillsley, School for Officer Training principal in USA East, remarks, "Following one of the Gaithers' visits to The School for Officer Training, my own sons, Michael and Paul, indicated that they could listen to the Colonel every Sunday. I remember thanking God for his wonderful gift of preaching, which not only blessed the officer staff and cadets but also reached the hearts of my teenage sons. His careful choice of words, meticulous preparation and presentation continue to motivate me to aim high in my preaching ministry. The Gaithers came to the New Jersey Labor Day camp meetings while serving as territorial leaders of the South African Territory. As they shared the hardships their people lived under, I remember them being overwhelmed with emotion and quietly weeping for a few moments. My own spirit was tremendously moved, and I remember thinking that it is never a burden to be led by a leader who weeps for his people."

John R. W. Stott, an eminent theologian, in his book on preaching, *Between Two Worlds*, writes, "Authentic Christian evangelists, bearing the good news of salvation, have never been far from tears." He cites, besides the Apostle Paul, such renowned pulpit worthies as D. L. Moody and George Whitefield, of whom his biographer records, "He could seldom manage a sermon without weeping." Stott reflects, "I constantly find myself wishing that we twentieth–century preachers could learn to weep again." This combination of mind and heart, the rational and the emotional, are compatibly wedded in Israel Gaither's preaching.

Commissioner Ken Baillie, territorial commander in the USA Central Territory, writes from observing Israel over the decades: "Izzy was the son of a Baptist preacher. He loved and admired his dad, who I suspect was his most influential role model. That influence always showed in his preaching style, back then as now. His style really hasn't changed very much through all the years. Passionate, winsome, and biblical, with the cadences and intensity of Black Gospel. I love it."

Daniel Diakanwa, a first–generation immigrant from Africa, writes: "Commissioner Gaither has been my model preacher. He is undeniably one of the few charismatic preachers the Eastern Territory has ever known."

Lt. Colonels William and Joan Bamford, now retired, add their comment: "The predominant strength of the commissioner is his preaching ability. His

Spirit–filled messages never fail to challenge his listeners. While we were stationed in the Swoneky Division, the commissioner visited us on several occasions. One that stands out in our memories was during an officers' retreat when the commissioner spoke on being anointed by the Holy Spirit. After introducing and singing the chorus, 'Anointed,' officers were on their knees praying for a fresh anointing by the Holy Spirit. We will never forget that experience."

In Manchester, Conn., when dedicating an expanded corps building, Israel challenged, "Now that you have this place, what are you building for the future? What can we now expect from The Salvation Army 'Up on Main Street'?" The Gaithers had a special connection to Manchester, having soldiered there during their four–year tenure as divisional leaders in Southern New England. The corps, Eva said, had provided a strong foundation for the Gaither children, Michele and Mark. Gaither cautioned, "Don't let this become a fortress. You must see people who enter these doors for what they can become, not for what they are. This is not a private meeting place, and it's not your clubhouse. It should be a hospice for souls and broken hearts. This building must always remind you what you have been called to do."

Retired National Commander Commissioner Andrew S. Miller, one whom Israel cites as a model, observes: "I've watched and seen both Commissioner and Mrs. Gaither continue to grow in God's grace and in the Spirit, with each appointment adding to their leadership growth. We were together once as an evangelistic team leading a revival series in Providence, R.I. I was the preacher and Captain Gaither the song leader and soloist. I suggested that perhaps at least one evening the Captain would preach. He humbly said he would be honored but was concerned only that I might be suggesting that I would do the singing!"

Colonel James Knaggs, chief secretary in the USA Eastern Territory, had often been exposed to the power of Israel Gaither's preaching. He writes: "We made it a point to attend whenever the Commissioner was giving a message. His exposition of the Word was always masterful, penetrating and God–inspired."

Commissioner B. Donald Ødegaard, territorial commander in the Norway, Iceland and the Faeroes Territory, adds a caveat: "Izzy is very mission–focused, warm and friendly. They visited this territory in 2003 as leaders of our annual congress, and people were inspired by their ministry. But the translator had a hard time following him around on the platform!"

Commissioner Keith Banks, Scotland, observes: "Israel Gaither is an anointed preacher and a gifted communicator. Wrap these twin giftings up in his Baptist heritage, and you have a preacher who demands your ears and your heart every time. Following an Easter celebration meeting at a Scottish corps, the Commissioner's challenging message to a mature congregation captured the imagination of an 8–year–old girl to the extent that she could not stop talking about it with her father on the 20–mile journey home."

THE SECRET

Commissioner Makoto Yoshida, international secretary for South Pacific and East Asia, writes: "His preaching is powerful and inspiring. I could see that he must put a lot of energy in preparing his sermon. I do believe that the Holy Spirit works to give words to speak to preachers as they preach, but I believe more that the Holy Spirit works in the preparation even to the greater extent. The secret of his powerful preaching should be found in his preparation and prayer."

One day there came to the desk of the Chief of Staff the following somewhat unusual letter.

> Hello Commissioner Gaither, my name is Matthew Lang and I am the son of Commissioner Ivan Lang, currently serving as the TC of the Australian Southern Territory. My father has recommended you as somebody who is a superb communicator. I love the process of communication and the dynamics that are at work with effective communicators. Over many years of watching people speak, I have noticed that some people are brilliant at getting their message across the edge of the platform out to the congregation. What I am trying to do is to capture the essence of what makes those speakers powerful and effective.
>
> My heart is to see every Officer/Pastor be effective in how they present the Gospel of Jesus from their pulpit. The reason I am writing to you is because I believe you are a great communicator of the Gospel. With this in mind I am hoping that you might share with me, the three most important ingredients that you see as critical to a great sermon or presentation. These three aspects or ingredients would be the three things that you do every time you speak.
>
> I am talking about things like, preparation, voice projection, passion, humor, strong content, eye contact with your congregation, clear pronunciation, visuals, expressive gestures etc., whatever it is that makes you effective in your communication.
>
> What would I like you to do? Simply reply to this e-mail with your three key ingredients that make you an effective speaker/preacher. Make sure you also include the three critical skills that need improving or developing in the Officers/Preachers of today. If you want to add further comment on communicating, preaching or presenting in general I would love for you to do that.
>
> Thank you so much for your valuable time in completing this research project. Your contribution will contribute

strongly to producing more skillful, passionate and effective preachers, speakers and presenters in the Kingdom.

Blessings! Matthew Lang

The Chief of the Staff graciously responded, revealing some of the secrets of his preaching prowess, as in the following excerpts.

By the way, your father is a superb communicator as well! And you'll no doubt have received some good tips from "the old man"!

A few key principles in the *preparation* of my Bible messages/presentations are—seeking the Holy Spirit's anointing. I spend time in worship before the Lord before I begin preparing a sermon/presentation. Regarding the priority of preparation, I commence preparations early in the morning—with a clear mind. It is the most creatively effective time of the day for me to get a good start in my thinking and preparation. My preparation always occurs in my home study. Never in the office. And I take as much time to prepare as I require. In fact, I include in my diary time for preparation to ensure its priority. My belief is that as important as all of that which I ever do in ministry is—nothing is more important than preparing to stand before a congregation to deliver the Word of God.

Research, inclusion of relevant illustrations and appropriate humor are included in my material. I tend to use personal illustrations—that which I have seen, heard and/or experienced. Only occasionally do I use quotes, stories or incidents from the experience of others.

I remind myself during the course of the preparation that my purpose is not to deliver my opinions

"The Salvation Army is a sent movement," states Israel Gaither in Australia.

but to offer the truth of His Word. I state "what I believe," but it is fixed in "Truth."

I've found—every time—that preparing to preach is "hard work"!

I never engage the preparation of sermon material after dealing with other office "mission business." It creates distraction.

As far as possible (in my current ministry circumstance), I try to become informed of the congregation and the context in which I will be speaking.

I'm aware of whom I am—and very often the end result contributes to my spiritual formation. I figure, after all, if the presentation does not challenge or bless me—it won't do a thing for anyone else.

I like to be aware of the timing available for both the message and the opportunity for congregational response. The Word and the response to it is the heart of worship. So I preach for a purpose.

Principles I acknowledge with respect to *presentation* include the anointing of the Spirit. I need to be sensitive to His leading during delivery. His Word is powerful and prophetic. And I say what He tells me.

I must "be myself." I'm not out to imitate anyone.

The message is paramount. I'm just the messenger.

I'm always conscious that it's not a production—it's the presentation of the sacred Word. Connecting with the congregation/audience is critical. I always like to see the venue before making the presentation. Amplification and lighting are vital for me. I must have the ability to move freely during the course of the presentation—and I like to be able to look into the faces of the audience without distracting artificial lighting.

Prior to the actual presentation of the message and during the course of worship, I very often will look for the faces of the receptive. They are the people who serve to inspire me in the course of the delivery.

At the conclusion of the preachment, I always give the result to God, with thanksgiving. Delivering His Word clearly, with a clean heart, is my gift offering to the Lord.

I'm not certain I've given you what you are looking for, but what I've done is provided a bit of insight into how I approach both the *preparation* and *presentation* of the Word. In the course of writing this response I've realized that I've never before been asked to comment on the manner in which I approach these sacred tasks. So you're the first recipient of a bit of personal insight into what I regard as the most beloved aspect of my calling.

By the way, my father—a wonderful Baptist pastor now re-
siding in the presence of the Lord—was the one who has had
the most significant impact on my approach to and delivery of
the Word.

Thanks for the inquiry. And I hope it is helpful. Stand
strong Matthew, and stay blessed!

Israel L. Gaither, Chief of the Staff

A "Doorkeeper in God's House"

In The Salvation Army, often the prayer meeting that follows the sermon becomes the culminating and pivotal part of the meeting. An invitation is given
to come to the mercy seat to pray for salvation, renewal, or whatever need the
Lord reveals. The leader of the prayer meeting in those moments stands in
that fateful intersection between God and the people to whom God speaks, a
sacred place "where angels fear to tread." Eternal destinies are at stake.

Wedded to Israel's preaching is his leadership of a prayer meeting. His gift
in this area was discovered early as he led the prayer meetings following the
evening's sermon in the large weekly gathering at New York City's Friday
Evening at the Temple. There he had observed Major Bramwell Tillsley, at
the time the Training School Principal in New York, effectively leading the
prayer meetings. Israel says he learned by observing "his intensity, his compelling invitation." Israel's friend, Major William Groff observes, "Gaither
can follow a poor sermon with a good prayer meeting."

In large public gatherings, the USA Eastern territorial leaders at the end
of their sermon would often turn the prayer meeting over to Gaither "who

Waves of seekers respond during a prayer meeting in India.

had a unique ability to appeal to people's heart and lead them to decision making." During a territorial congress in the United States, General Paul Rader called on Israel to lead prayer meetings following his preachment.

Commissioner David A. Baxendale, now retired, recalls: "When I returned to the Greater New York area as the training school principal, the Gaithers were in a leadership position in the division and had responsibility for the Friday Evening at the Temple, one of the Army's largest and longest continuous evangelistic series. We noticed how his spirit and leadership had greatly matured and his spiritual sensitivity deepened. But the best skill that I saw sharpened was his deft ability to 'invite men and women to the Savior,' what we in the Army refer to as 'the altar call,' the invitation for people with need to come and kneel at the 'mercy seat.' Over the years God led him to be filled with the Spirit in such a way that he knew the words, the songs, the feelings, the emotions that would touch the hearts of those to whom God spoke, leading them to rise from their seats and come and pray. Here was a young officer able to reach out to a broad spectrum of society, both churched and unchurched alike, to invite them to accept Christ's forgiveness and His redeeming love and grace, and for this we praised God!"

Commissioner M. Christine MacMillan, territorial commander for Canada and Bermuda, writes, "I was with the Gaithers over a Congress weekend in Bermuda when they were our guests. At that congress Commissioner Israel Gaither preached the word with an impassioned plea of both conviction and hope. His ability to engage from the platform brought the congregation to its knees with a greater resolve to follow Christ."

A hallmark of Israel Gaither's ministry has been to serve in this way as "a doorkeeper in the house of the Lord," inviting hearers to enter to meet the Savior. "Is something crippling you this morning in your spiritual life? Christ can heal, can make you whole. Someone here has to say yes to Jesus," he urges. "Be authentic." His perfect pitch enables him to start a prayer chorus with the piano then joining in. The chorus "All that I am," or "To be like Jesus," sung prayerfully, invites his hearers to a deeper spiritual experience. He often calls for hearers to raise their hands for prayer, and then for some of them to stand, then "come forward to pray." Sometimes he invites "prayer warriors" to join him on his right and left, or prayer circles to form, and as prayers are raised from all over the venue, he exclaims, "When we come into the presence of God, we expect God to do something! What a wonderful sight! And something is going to happen! God is going to work miracles!"

A countless number, now from around the world, look back to such a moment of coming forward to the altar as a life–changing encounter, one that led to salvation or to a closer walk with their Lord, as Israel Gaither stood as a "doorkeeper in the house of the Lord," and graciously invited them to enter in.

chapter **30**

Dr. Israel Lee Gaither

*The greatest use of a life is to spend it on that
which outlasts it.*

William James

On November 17, 2004, a letter, one of the most auspicious he had ever received, came to Israel Gaither. It read: "Dear Chief: It is my joy to inform you that in recognition of your outstanding leadership gifts and service to the cause of Christ, the Board of Trustees of Asbury College has approved the conferring of an honorary doctorate on you during our commencement exercises here on Asbury's campus on Sunday, 8 May 2005. In addition, I would like to invite you to be our preacher for the Baccalaureate service on that same Sunday morning. Kay and I join in sending our congratulations and warmest greetings." The letter was signed: Paul A. Rader, President, Asbury College, Wilmore, Kentucky.

The Chief's reply the next day revealed

Israel Gaither receives an honorary doctorate
from President Rader

his being taken aback and humbled at such an invitation. As always, he re-flexively resists any vaunting of self–honor, but ascribes the praise to his Lord: "Dear Dr. Rader, Your letter of 17 November has arrived containing a marvelous blessing and sacred privilege! Eva and I were moved to tears. I could never imagine that I would be considered to be the recipient of such a wonderful honor from Asbury, an institution that is held in high regard in the Gaither home.

"Thank you for the signal that is sent conveying your belief and trust in me, and the great mission of The Salvation Army. I am truly humbled to ac-cept, with thanksgiving, this very special honor, and it is with pleasure that I also accept your invitation to serve as the speaker for the baccalaureate ser-vice. In accepting the honor I must acknowledge that whatever good has emerged as a result of my ministry—it is all because of Him. And I gladly confess that it is our Lord who is to be praised."

AN HONORARY DEGREE

The commissioner was cited for his position as second in command of the worldwide Salvation Army. He was acknowledged as becoming the first African–American to attain the rank of commissioner, become territorial commander, and to be selected Chief of the Staff, "putting fresh heart into persons of color within the Army across America and around the world." He was also recognized for having been twice a nominee for General of The Salvation Army, and having created "A Bridge of Hope" when territorial commander in South Africa—linking substantive resources from the USA with constructive proj-ects for the people of South Africa.

" He has put fresh heart into persons of color within the Army across America and around the world."

As President Rader officiated in the hooding of the Commis-sioner, he read the citation, which concluded with the statement: "In recognition of his long and distinguished career in advancing the Kingdom of God; his com-mitment of bringing the hope of Christ to needy and suffering people; his dedicated and un-selfish service through The Salvation Army around the world; and upon recommendation of the Board of Trustees, Asbury College confers upon Commissioner Israel L. Gaither the honorary degree of Doctor of Humane Letters (L.H.D.) with all the rights, honors and privileges appertaining thereto."

Following the events, Paul Rader commented, "It was our great joy and privilege to honor the Chief of the Staff, Commissioner Israel L. Gaither. In so doing Asbury College was itself honored in recognizing his outstanding leadership, administrative acumen, unique giftedness in proclaiming the Word of God, and his contribution to the cause of Christ around the world."

"The receiving of the honor conferred by Asbury College was a humbling experience," Commissioner Gaither reflected, "and one that I never dreamed would ever be part of my life or ministry experience. It is a sacred privilege to be associated with Asbury College in this way, and I want to be a faithful representative of this fine academic institution. I have accepted the honorary degree—but have presented it back to God for His blessing and use in bringing glory and honor to Him through the mission of The Salvation Army. I am keenly aware that were it not for the privilege of my officership, the honor would never have been bestowed upon me."

Before a capacity congregation that Sunday morning baccalaureate service, Gaither preached passionately to the graduating students. He moved with ease from the poignant to the humorous, calling them to respond to the immense challenges and rich opportunities awaiting them.

The event took place on May 8, Mother's Day. Dr. Rader remarked, "I wish I could personally introduce all mothers here today, but since I cannot, I would like to recognize one mother in particular." He invited Mrs. Lillian Gaither, the commissioner's mother, to stand and receive the recognition and applause of the large congregation, described by Gaither's daughter, Michele, as "a very cool moment."

Asbury College has a long history of close association with The Salvation Army. Following his retirement as the Army's international leader, General Paul A. Rader was invited to serve as its president. The college through the years has hosted one of the largest Army Student Fellowships and as of 2005 had six Salvationists on its faculty. A $1 million "Friends of Andy Miller" (Commissioner) scholarship fund has been established for Salvationist students. Following the commencement, Israel and Eva Gaither visited with Salvationist graduates and their families at the Salvation Army Student Center that adjoins the college campus.

The Gaithers' son, Mark, and daughter, Michele, are both Asbury graduates. Michele was a member of Asbury's first Master's degree graduating class, and had taught at the college. She reminisced, "Once again I was proud to be Izzy Gaither's daughter as my Dad spoke prophetically and powerfully. For my grandmother, it was one of the highlights of her life. She told me she wished my grandfather could have been there. She was moved to tears over and over again throughout the weekend. Education has always been an important part of the Gaither family. My dad receiving a doctoral degree was another extension of that. It was a phenomenal weekend of family time. We laughed together, cried together and prayed together."

"DON'T KEEP US WAITING!"

Israel Gaither's sermon for the baccalaureate service was "Don't Keep Us Waiting." He affirmed his affinity with Asbury College, saying, "My wife Eva and I have a love for this institution that we have embraced deeply through our children—Mark and Michele—as well as through our affiliation in the ministry of The Salvation Army." Then he directly challenged the graduates.

Men and women, you have been tutored, mentored, challenged, stretched, even threatened, by world-class instructors who believe in the transforming power of your presence in the world. They understand why the church in the world needs you. And they've done their best to get you ready—to join us in advancing the cause of Christ. The Kingdom is urgently calling you to take your place in the world. Don't keep us waiting.

The emerging generation of believers who will influence and lead the Church are not interested in "doing church." They want "to be" the Church—engaged in transforming a harsh world. They want to be part of the unfolding redemptive drama. They want the Church to use its divinely ordained power to fight against evil that takes form in injustice, poverty, war, sickness and unnecessary death. They want the Church to do something about children

Gaither family members, with the Raders, at the Asbury College program

in slavery to war and sexual exploitation. They don't care about making themselves corporately comfortable.

That's the message I'm getting from the emerging generation of believers. And by the way, graduates, I guess that includes you!

Thank you for understanding that the Church is not brick and mortar, or a mud or bamboo hut. The church is not a place of worship in a stained–glass cathedral or a rented theater, or a borrowed garage, or a tree under a high blue African sky. The Church is flesh and blood. And the universal church of Christ is poor—but powerful, dominated by powerful believers in the poor places of the world. Believers in unloving places who are filling it with the presence of redemptive love.

And so, members of the class of 2005, we're proud of you. But don't keep us waiting. We need you in the world. And we need you to join us—quickly. The Kingdom calls. Don't keep us waiting.

And grads, you're getting back into the world at just the right time. And I'm already feeling more confident about the future of the global mission of the church—because of you. Just don't keep us waiting.

But why the urgency, you ask? "Let us take a little time off and enjoy life. Give us a break!" But you've been prepared to be global–thinking, ready and responsive believers, burning–heart Christians. While you have lived in the safety of Wilmore, out in the world, belief and faith is at risk. In some sectors humanism and secularism are beginning to dominate the values of societies. Opponents would have us believe that Christianity is just one more system of belief.

Don't keep us waiting. We live in a time of unprecedented spiritual and moral untidiness, and there are evidences of a clear and present danger to Christian belief and values.

Don't keep us waiting. Because in some parts of the world we kill unborn children and argue the legal "right" to do it. We play God and perform so–called mercy killings on the infirm and the aged and mistakenly hold the view that it is morally correct. It is a dangerous time.

Resolve to stand strong in Christlike values. Don't keep us waiting!

"Most Powerful Baccalaureate Sermon"

At the afternoon commencement, when Commissioner Gaither was introduced, with reference to his morning sermon, the more than 2,000 in attendance erupted with applause. The chair of the Asbury College Board. C. E. Crouse, referred to it as the most powerful baccalaureate sermon he had heard in a long time. "The Spirit used him to be a blessing to us all," summarized President Paul Rader.

The noted psychologist, William James, said, "The greatest use of a life is to spend it on that which outlasts it." Israel Gaither personified the wisdom of that statement, as he was honored by Asbury College for investing his life in the eternal mission of God.

chapter **31**

On the Personal Side

*A good name is more desirable than great
riches; to be esteemed is better than silver
or gold.*

Proverbs 22:1

I t has been said that the face is a window to the soul. A feature of Israel
Gaither that quickly stands out is his smile and the warmth of his counte-
nance. An innate friendliness, his signature way of meeting people, is quickly
disarming and reveals his genuine interest and warmth in relationships.

IDIOSYNCRASIES

There are two kinds of people in the world—the "diurnals" and the "noc-
turnals," the "roosters" and the "owls," the "larks" and the "nightingales"—
and often they marry one another! Eva likes to see the daylight when she
arises, whereas Israel starts his day well before sunrise. Among his associates
he became legendary for his early morning arrival at the office and getting a
jump start on his day's work.

The logistics of his early–hour starts often have not been convenient for
his life partner. Israel rises quietly and dresses in the guest bedroom, so as
not to disturb Eva, and breaks his night fast in solitude.

When he was working at Pittsburgh Divisional Headquarters, Eva was
known for driving Israel to the office in the early mornings while still in her
pajamas and curlers, then returning home and traveling later to the office
herself! In South Africa, a compromise was reached, with Israel going to the
office a bit later.

The before–dawn regimen has been a lifetime habit for Israel. He always
begins his day with meditation and prayer. "The day is wrong if I fail to start
that way," he says. Because he leaves home before Eva's day has commenced,
he tries not to bring a lot of work home so he and Eva can spend evenings

together. He had promised to Eva long ago, "You allow me the early morning, so I commit the evening to you."

Israel is known to be fastidious in his personal habits, meticulous about his appearance, fussy with his clothes. Wherever he goes, he takes with him as part of his equipment a bag containing pills, bandages, ointments and medicines. Some have humorously referred to his "traveling apothecary." He is not dependent on these medicines, but he is predisposed to be prepared for any exigency that may arise.

He wants meetings, visits, discussions, and work to proceed in an orderly fashion, with clear evidence of advance planning and attention to detail. A strong perfectionist streak runs through his personality. This can be irksome to some people. One of his colleagues, when someone mentioned this trait to him said, "I could only reply by saying just imagine what that perfectionist streak would be like if it wasn't sanctified!"

Although not strict vegetarians, Israel and Eva rarely eat beef, opting occasionally for chicken or turkey. This regimen started some years ago when their children became vegetarians. Israel says, "They really got on our case. They pronounced the edict: 'Dad and Mom, you are getting older and you eat too much meat.' So we were threatened, and now for many years this has been our practice. We don't miss meat, and we save a bit of money!"

Israel has been captive to the paradox of education: The more you know, the more you realize how much you don't know, and the more you want to learn. His thirst for knowledge, intellectual growth and sharpening of his ministry skills led him to take part–time studies at Pittsburgh Theological Seminary, Gordon College in Massachusetts, and church growth courses at Fuller Theological Seminary in California. In January 1987 he was appointed to attend the International College for Officers in London, England, for a two–month study of the foundations and internationalism of the Army.

"A MAN FOR ALL SEASONS"

USA retired Commissioner George Nelting, who has observed Israel from his fledgling officer days, writes: "Izzy moved from one level of responsibility to another with quiet confidence. We also saw Eva grow from a reserved young person to a very capable leader. While others seemed sometimes to despair—moaning about the Army's problems—Izzy always believed in the Army's mission and future. Where others saw problems, he saw possibilities. He reminded Salvationists, young and old, of what God had called us to be by the power of the Holy Spirit. Izzy was known for his spiritual sensitivity, impassioned preaching, beautiful singing and his ability to communicate with people at a very personal level. One of his solos was 'Fill My Cup Lord,' and as he sang, hearts were melted and moved by the

Holy Spirit. When he witnessed or preached, we could sense the influence of his preacher father. The Gaithers seem to be an example of what Paul wrote about in Romans 15:13, 'overflowing with hope by the power of the Holy Spirit.'"

Lt. Colonel Thomas Adams, who associated closely with Gaither in headquarters appointments, sums up what he saw of the qualities of his associate: "I know of no one in our Army who is so talented in so many areas and who has completely committed that talent to God. He can sing (I almost said he was a musician but then I remember a time when we played in a quartet together in front of a Times Square Theater). He is a preacher (one of the finest we have), who combines personal passion with Bible knowledge and meaningful illustrations. He is a business administrator who could teach all of us the proper way to do the business of the Army. He is a family man beloved by his children. He knows his people by name, is both warm and firm, has a great smile, a strong handshake and a hearty laugh. He is intensely related to God and at the same time easily accessible by man. He is The Salvation Army's man for all seasons."

Majors William and Lorraine Bamford relate his ability to touch the lives of people of all ages. "The integrity and commitment of Commissioners Gaither have been an inspiration to us in our own life and ministry. Commissioner Israel has the ability to weave the serious necessity of introspection with the humor of our everyday lives. His gifted method of preaching causes congregations of all ages to be drawn to the message. We witnessed this when Colonels Gaither came as guests to our Youth Councils. On the Saturday evening they opted to join in the late–night roller–skating offered to the teenage delegates. The Gospel message on Sunday was conveyed more effectively because of their presence on that hardwood floor the night before. Their commitment to their marriage and family is a shining example to others of a Christian couple. We see the Gaithers as paramount role models of Christlike living, embodying the essence of Salvationism as seen in their respect for the Army and its mission, servanthood as exemplified in their daily ministry and their willingness to go where God leads. In so doing they touch the lives of many of us."

ON THE DISTAFF SIDE

As a counterpart to the relationship between General John Larsson and the Chief, Commissioners Eva Gaither and Freda Larsson also became bonded in both friendship and faith. Eva said, during her time as World Secretary of Women's Ministries, "Freda is a caring, quiet and lovely person to work with, and when opportunity permits we enjoy doing things together." The two world leaders shared a secretary and related to a network of Salvationist women around the world.

Freda Larsson, before her retirement, reciprocated Eva's sentiment, "Commissioner Eva Gaither and I enjoy a close working relationship, and I believe we make a good team as we are very much on the same wavelength on all matters related to Women's Ministries. We both find our global link with women leaders to be inspiring, exhilarating and very fulfilling." The two women leaders also enjoyed shared ministry with their husbands and often had stimulating "foursome" discussions.

Freda added, "I have found Commissioner Eva to be a person of strong convictions, particularly when it comes to the Army's mission and core values, and she is not afraid to make her opinion known. Alongside that is a great tenderness for people, particularly the underprivileged, and a desire to encourage sensitivity to their needs. She is an enthusiastic and avid supporter of Women's Ministries as an effective and exciting evangelical tool.

"I have observed in the Gaithers a very happy and loving relationship. They clearly know each other well and have a great respect for each other's point of view and individual space. They are also very loving parents and grandparents, and I know it has been costly for them to live so far away from their family. At times it has been great to share their excitement when visits have been planned or photographs have arrived. We do not have a lot of time to meet socially but it has been most enjoyable when we have—even enjoying the opportunity of going to the gym together."

"PART OF ALL WE HAVE MET"

Poet John Donne reminds us, "No man is an island." We are a part of all who have impacted our lives through the years. Israel Gaither deeply values

The General and his Chief in daily conference

the many who have contributed to their lives, through their friendship, encouragement and modeling of leadership and ministry. He acknowledges, "The kind of man I am today is due to all those who have played a significant role throughout my life. There are men with whom I have become acquainted in very recent years who are contributing to my continued development."

During his time as Chief, Israel's loyalty and support for the General was without qualification. When one was out of the country and they were apart, they kept in regular contact by computer, often making decisions in that way. Before John Larsson's retirement, Israel said, "To work alongside and in support of General Larsson is another sacred gift. On Army matters, the General knows 100 percent of my mind, and I know 95 percent of his mind. Ours is a real friendship. We are together for God's purpose at this time." General John Larsson, in the selection of his Chief of Staff, and working in partnership with him, became the seventh person used of God in the major development and ministry of Israel L. Gaither.

When asked about the foremost contribution to his spiritual life and development, Israel answers that it has been what he has learned from others, from their faith and trust. "I have found myself standing next to men and women who love the Lord, particularly those in South Africa who triumphed in their suffering, men and women among whom I was dwarfed in their presence.

"Relationships have always been important to me, and I guard carefully as much as possible the friendships that have been developed over the years. It's remarkable that Eva and I have been able to maintain such close relationships with others, even though we have spent a number of years away from our friends, living and serving in other lands. I treasure the gift of friendships."

As Israel and Eva served away from their homeland, their congenial spirits resulted in many new relationships. Of these Israel says, "We are more than associates; we are actually friends." But a unique feature of these new relationships, as characterized by Israel, is "they don't have history."

In London the Gaithers attended the Bromley Corps, one with a rich tradition of leadership, music, membership and quality worship. Israel observes, "Bromley is a warm, family corps where we are spiritually fed with superb music, preaching and fellowship."

Israel's foremost hero, his first champion, is John Waldron. "Other than my father, he had the greatest impact on my life. His integrity, his depth, his mind, his preaching, his many gifts, impacted me. I consider him one who embraced what it meant to be an apostolic leader—one with spiritual authority, anointing, integrity, and focused on his mission for Christ."

Of all the people Israel Gaither has met around the world, the one who most impressed him is Nelson Mandela. He calls him "a giant among us in his courage, his ability to forgive." After visiting Robben Island, where Mandela was imprisoned for 27 years, Israel said, "To see him come out of that and be a symbol for healing and lead his country from the evils of apartheid to democracy and freedom makes him one of the greatest symbols of healing. When I met him, he seemed larger than life."

Foremost among Israel's closest friends has been Commissioner Lawrence (Larry) Moretz; a friendship that began in their time together as cadets. Moretz says of their bonding, "Israel became to me the brother I never had and has remained a strong brother for these many years. We were both Pennsylvania boys, and a natural gravitation evolved over our cadet days. Through the years our appointments took parallel paths—we were young corps officers together in Greater New York with similar challenges. Our children were the same ages; and we benefited from each other's gifts and skills. A trust in each other surfaced and has grown through the years. We were known as "the lads" on the Board of Trustees when together we were appointed to THQ. We each went on overseas appointments at the same time, as Ron Irwin provided opportunity to enlarge our global vision."

One late night Larry Moretz received a call from his territorial commander indicating that his promotion to lieutenant colonel would be announced the next day. He responded, "I don't want to be a lieutenant colonel if Izzy is not a lieutenant colonel." Then he learned that his and Israel's promotions had already been processed to be concurrent. They were also promoted to the rank of commissioner in the same "batch."

Commissioner Nancy Moretz adds, "Eva's great love for Izzy has contributed to their beautiful partnership and family life. Their standards for marriage and home and family are very high. She also has an amazing love for people, as shown in her compassion for babies with AIDS in South Africa. She is a fine example of a culturally adaptive person." Nancy poignantly reflects, "And we have shared deeply with each other in our family crises."

Nancy often accompanied Israel on the piano in their cadet days and has done so at times since. She says, "When he would sang, you would get goose bumps, which is a sign of giftedness and anointing." Israel sang at their wedding, as he has done at many others.

She tells a humorous story of their visit to South Africa when Israel arranged for them to go on a safari. Israel secured the tickets and the four of them clambered into an open jeep that took off into the African wilds. They rode past a water buffalo and fleeting gazelles, then stopped to observe a pride of 14 lions lying down. Their driver and guide advised them to stay huddled close together, to sit still as one unit and not make any big motion, as lions don't see well and won't attack anything bigger than themselves. The driver turned off the engine for his guests to quietly observe the lions. At this time several observations began to cause Nancy some apprehension. She had noticed that the driver seemed quite young. She wondered, "What if the car won't start up again?" Also, the guide had said that the lions were fed once a week, every Sunday. "This is Saturday," thought Nancy, "and we may look like four Swedish meatballs!" She also noted that there was no weapon in the jeep. Her fears were not helped by Izzy, Eva and Larry laughing and gesturing wildly, amused over her concern. She said, "I think we should move out of here, and Larry, you can read all about lions in a book!" The finishing touch to Nancy's experience came when at the end of the safari, Israel confessed, "What I didn't tell you was that when I bought the tickets, I had to sign a release for all of us for the park not to be held responsible."

The oceans apart did not prevent them from keeping in touch with family and friends. The marvel of e–mail enables Israel and Eva to keep in regular contact. "We have treasured friends," says Israel, "that stretch back to the beginning, and since we have been out of the country, some communicate on a very regular basis via e–mail." And the phenomenon of a three–cents a minute phone rate further facilitated regular family conversations.

Like Ulysses in Tennyson's poem, Israel acknowledges, "I am a part of all that I have met."

AUTHENTIC IN AN ARTIFICIAL WORLD

Izzy Gaither himself is uncontrived, but he has no illusions about the artificial world in which he lives. He calls Christians to be authentic in each phase of their life. His philosophy on this subject was published in an anthology by Commissioner John Waldron called *The Salvationist Pulpit*, first printed in 1991 and reprinted in the July 4, 1992, issue of the USA *War Cry*. Following are excerpts from the article, titled, "Authentic Christians in an Artificial World."

> Americans, generally, are growing discontented with the artificial. We recognize the potential damage to health from ingredients that are unnatural and impure. We are growing tired of living with second–rate, deceptive products. We want authenticity!
>
> We seek the truth. We want to be real. We want our lives to count for something. We need to be authentic Christians in an artificial world.
>
> I remind you that we share in a faith that is rooted and grounded in Jesus Christ! We have a faith that has stood the test of trial and time.
>
> Free from the penalty of sin! Free from the power of sin! Free from the chains of habit! Free to know Christ is to be possessed by Him through the indwelling of his Holy Spirit. To know Him is to have every impulse, every act, every thought, every emotion come under his divine influence. To know Him is to be His—without reservation.
>
> He lives with you! You have an authentic relationship! The desperate circumstances of people all about us require that we possess, for them, a real, living and vital relationship to Christ.

The commission to every believer is to be a witness! To win the lost.

You have an authentic relationship if Christ dwells within you.

There is no time for artificiality. God's people must be authentic. It will make a difference in our motives, in relationships, in deeds, in attitudes and in the way we affect others around us.

Do you know the indwelling of the Holy Spirit in your life? Are you under the wonderful, liberating control of the Spirit of God? When you allow the Holy Spirit to have full possession, you then will know your complete freedom. And that's what God wants for His children. So take full possession of this part of the inheritance that God has for you.

The story in this book is the life story of an authentic man of God living out his life and ministering faithfully in an artificial world.

By the anointing of the Spirit and his effective leadership, Gaither did not merely fill a chair or a niche in the Army's hierarchy, but he made a difference in each appointment, from his early days as corps officer up to positions of high leadership.

By the anointing of the Spirit and his effective leadership, Gaither made a difference in each appointment.

The life story of Israel L. Gaither is about far more than the important precedents that he set. It makes a statement of what it means to be anointed by the Holy Spirit, to be unalterably focused on God's mission for the Army, to be a faithful pastor to the flock, to engage in a passionate and prophetic preaching, to exercise the disciplines of the spiritual life, to model a work ethic and commitment to excellence, to exemplify the priorities of life to family and friends.

In all these facets of his life and ministry, Israel Gaither has surmounted with grace the both subtle and overt challenges of racism and has made an inestimable contribution to the great company of lives he touched and to the movement to which he has given his life.

The Greek philosopher Heraclitus observed that no man can step into the same stream twice because the stream is always changing and so is the man. This account bridges the stream of one millennium and the start of another that continues to grow into an ever–broadening river and in some ways a tor-rent of change. Israel Gaither has crossed and recrossed the river, at each stage being broadened in his vision and goals and helping his beloved Army navigate safely through ever–changing tides and torrents.

Indeed, as Israel Gaither is the first to acknowledge, this story of his life is the story of *What God Hath Wrought!*

PART FIVE

Looking Forward

2006

chapter **32**

The 2006 High Council

Then they prayed, "Lord, you know everyone's heart. Show us who you have chosen to take over this apostolic ministry."
Acts 2:24–25

A ll active commissioners and territorial commanders received from Commissioner Israel Gaither, Chief of Staff, in November 2005 their summons to attend the 2006 High Council, to convene once again in Sunbury Court Conference Centre outside London. The council was called to elect the successor to General John Larsson, who would retire on April 1. It was the largest High Council to date, with a membership of 102—86 commissioners and 16 colonels, and 100 of the number in attendance.

The new international leader would be charged with guiding a now venerable and conservative movement through a modern and ever–changing world or, as Gaither had described it, a world that "has lost its compass." New issues made some old issues the Army had faced seem quaint by comparison. This new era flaunts its challenge of macro–ethics—wide–scale poverty and hunger, pollution of planet earth, bioethical issues, exploitation and slavery of children and young women, end–of–life care, the silent holocaust of abortion and euthanasia, the emergence of Islam, religious pluralism, increasing terrorism and the threat of mass annihilation.

Neither Christian leadership nor a Christian movement can isolate itself in pietistic platitudes, away from the real world and its grave dangers. To be relevant and effective, the new leader of God's global Army must lead the troops in the forefront of the battle, out where the air is blowing, the issues are real, and where people are hurting. These challenges would require a leader theologically astute, affirming that the foundations of faith remain immutable, yet interpreted in light of a postmodern world.

The Salvation Army has been acclaimed for its enduring mission, a solid pillar in a rapidly changing world. But defenders of its traditions and promoters of progress sometimes contend for the soul of the movement. Its music, worship style, married–officer covenant, legal impingements, fiscal policies, and other issues present their challenge. The times called for a leader of extraordinary faith and spiritual vision. The High Council members would be praying and assessing candidates for preeminent credentials of leadership.

On January 21 London's historic Westminster Central Hall hosted the only public event relating to the High Council—a kaleidoscope of the Army's internationalism in a welcome to the High Council, a celebration in worship, and the farewell salute to General John Larsson and Commissioner Freda Larsson. Live viewers far exceeded the capacious Hall that evening as the eyes of the Army world were literally on the event via the Army's web site.

Commissioners Gaither presented a joint tribute to the Larssons in a sparkling dialogue, with esteem and affection on behalf of the international Army. The Chief narrated, "For years to come this mission shall reap the benefits of their legacy of service. When John and Freda Larsson became our world leaders, The Salvation Army was placed in the hands of anointed leaders. We have felt safe as with a calm assurance they have, under the guidance of the Spirit, led this massive global movement in these early years of the new century." A touch of humor graced the dialogue when Eva said, "As our eight–year old grandson says of the General, 'He's really cool!'" Israel concluded, "Eva and I publicly declare our gratitude to God for having had the privilege of standing at your side. Having run the race and kept the faith, may God bless you, in abundance, with new ministry opportunities." The Chief then called the congregation to rise for a prayer of dedication.

Israel Gaither leads a pre–High Council session.

"FOR SUCH A TIME AS THIS"

The Chief of Staff as convener of the High Council presides over its opening, conducts the initial devotions and arranges for the election of a President and a Vice President. When that has been accomplished, he takes his place as a member of the council.

Israel Gaither knew his leadership at the start would be "delicate" in that he consciously wanted to maintain a low profile while at the same time giving the leadership merited for the moment in its most sacred task.

In his opening devotional message Israel drew on a well–known text from the Book of Esther, stating that the Army requires leadership equipped by God to face the challenges of "such a time as this." He emphasized that the story of Esther is a reminder to believers that God has his place, and time, and purpose for those whom He has called.

"What are the implications," he asked, "of our serving in key leadership roles 'for such a time as this'? The question is answered within the context of our varied places of leadership. In some regions of the world it is a dangerous time with rising religious militancy. So the times call for courageous, consecrated leadership. In other sectors of the mission it is the time to stand strong as Christian values clash with deepening secular ideologies. So the times call for clear–headed and clean–heart leadership. And yet, this mission, no matter the time zone, is in the hands of our able God. The times beg us to do our task well."

He then juxtaposed the Esther text with that in Acts where the 11 disciples chose Matthias as replacement for the twelfth of their number. The disciples, he said, had "a fully surrendered life. They gave themselves to prayer for they understood the task was too great to accomplish on their own. They were obedient to the leading of the Spirit. Finally they were of one mind." He then invited the Council, "Let us now move into a season of prayer, that shall be led by the Spirit to receive our anointing from the Spirit."

One member said, "All present in the opening session of the High Council led by the Chief sensed that we were standing on holy ground. We experienced the presence of God and it was as though the Lord brought us to this place for 'such a time as this.'"

Following the establishing of procedures, preparing questions for the candidates, and above all a time of devotion and prayer, the High Council settled down to its main business—election of the next international leader, the 18th General of The Salvation Army. From its elite membership, candidates would be nominated for the awesome task of leading the movement, now in 111 countries and territories of the world.

A Time of Spiritual Intensity

For Israel Gaither, the time leading up to the 2006 High Council was fraught with inner struggle and intense prayer. Many friends and colleagues had expressed their confidence and hope that he would be elected to the Army's highest office. He especially carried the hopes among non–Anglo Salvationists—Africans, Hispanics and Asians, who now constituted three–fourths of the Army's world membership. The World Council of Churches places Christianity's demographic center of gravity in Africa, with some theologians calling this "the African century of Christianity." Salvationists in Africa were approaching the 50 percent mark of Army

The High Council delegates from the Americas

membership. For many it seemed the time had come for such a moment in the Army's 141–year history.

Expectations were high on behalf of Israel Gaither. One Army leader at IHQ wrote before the High Council: "I believe that Israel Gaither is a man 'set apart' and has not just the necessary qualifications but has the spirit of one who is a 'leader under God.' The next General will have to face many issues and Israel Gaither could do it." But other good and qualified candidates would emerge, and the High Council, representing the worldwide Army, was bathed in prayer as they sought God's will for their selection.

Israel did not aspire to the office of the General. His personal predisposition was one of reluctance. There were the personal issues. He and Eva had been away from their homeland, a combined seven years in South Africa and England, except for the 103 days as USA East territorial leaders. Closely bonded with family, they had been painfully apart from aged parents and fast–growing grandchildren.

Deeper than all the personal feelings, Israel had a commitment to the Lord's will, and once more on his spiritual odyssey he was led to pray, "Not my will, but thy will be done." He knew he could be nominated. He could not know the outcome, but he was led to stand as a nominee, in deference to those who would nominate and vote for him. He would be at peace, whatever the outcome. To a friend he wrote, "We come into this setting with no personal desires or expectations. We just want to be in sync with God's intention for us. He has, and we believe continues to have, a place where we can serve Him best."

Commissioner W. Todd Bassett, who served as President of the High Council shares the following observation on Gaither's leadership role at the High Council.

> As would be expected, the strong positive leadership of Commissioner Israel L. Gaither was demonstrated in the pre–High Council meetings, especially as he took leadership of the opening dinner meeting. Throughout the two–and–a–half days of the pre–High Council and, even moving into the formal setting of the High Council, Commissioner Gaither maintained an appropriate and discreet projection of himself, realizing that once the High Council was convened, in the process he would take his place as a member among peers.
>
> In the early stages of the High Council, during the general discussion a momentary reflection was made in a generic sense about the impact of the selection of a Chief of the Staff. Certainly, one would have to project that the exposure gained in this position would lend itself to this person being a forerunner in the process of seeking and selecting the next international leader. Thus, the importance of the present Chief of the Staff to be discreet in the projection of himself both in the dialogue and discussions of the council as well as in personal interaction. Both Israel and Eva Gaither handled this with care and discretion. Their interactions with other members of the council were as equal participants in the process.

Commissioner Garth McKenzie, Territorial Commander for the New Zealand, Fiji and Tonga Territory, shares his perception of Israel Gaither at the High Council.

> Commissioner Gaither's leadership of the 2006 pre–High Council programs was excellent in every way and set a very high tone for the 16th High Council. All matters were attended to in a thoroughly appropriate manner with the administrative backup. When Commissioner Gaither was nominated for the office of General his answer to the questions and his speech confirmed his capacity for the highest leadership position in The Salvation Army should he be elected. His responses in every way were entirely appropriate, clear minded, focused, Spirit–led and articulate. His international insights and spiritual perception brought helpful and illuminating comments from time to time. His presence throughout, along with Commissioner Eva Gaither, was significant, yet in no way

did they seek to be overbearing, but rather acted in an entirely appropriate, encouraging and supportive manner.

Israel Gaither, as Chief of Staff, had become well known around the Army world. Both his leadership and spirit had deeply commended him to those whom he had met. It was obvious he would be a primary candidate for the international leadership of The Salvation Army.

Commissioner Ivan Lang of Australia reflects:

> From the first occasion we met Izzy Gaither, we felt a warmth of spirit and a genuine desire to know us personally. His ability to make a connection was apparent that here was a man with a heart for people, a leader who would be transparent and caring. In his role as Chief of the Staff he demonstrated an ability to be incisive in his thinking and decisive with his decision making. Mission was the priority. His ability to acknowledge past tradition was evident and yet the present and future was well in focus on his radar screen. There was no question in our minds that Israel Gaither would be nominated as a candidate for General at the 2006 High Council. It would be true to say that not only a large percentage of the Council members, but indeed a great number of Salvationists from around the Army world, had their eyes fixed on Israel Gaither as the next General to lead our international Salvation Army. We thank God for Izzy and Eva Gaither, both anointed leaders who at all times proclaim biblical truths with passion and deep conviction. Our Army world has been intoxicated by the Holy Spirit as He has revealed himself through two of God's special people.

Colonel Michael Marvell (Denmark) relates his impression of Israel Gaither:

> During the High Council procedures, Gaither put on no special airs. Despite having to shoulder the pressures and emotions as a candidate for the office of the General, he seemed at ease with himself; content to be 'Izzy,' especially when he had Eva at his side. Those who were with him at the High Council will remember him, not just as a man with the gifts of preaching and administration, but also as a man with the gift of listening. In one–on–one conversations and in moments of informal fellowship, as well as in formal sessions, he was keen to hear what others had to say about the issues that engaged their hearts and minds. For me, an even more lasting memory will be the sound of his laughter. Rich and resonant, coming from somewhere deep in the heart of Afro–America, it was never very far away. No

need to search to find him in a crowd—just listen for the sound of his laughter. The weight of responsibility and expectations obviously did not spoil his enjoyment of good company and the good humor that it generates. And that, I think, was one more testimony to the quality of his commitment and leadership.

"Pressing Forward!"

Israel Gaither never felt a greater burden for the preparation and delivery of a message than as a nominee for office of the General, in addressing the Army's international leadership at this High Council. It was a moment to share the deep burdens of his heart and his vision for the mission of the Army. He would draw deep from the well of his convictions, choosing the topic, "Pressing Forward!"

There would resonate his core belief that the Army is called to press forward into the future, guided by its sacred heritage, and that a mission with a lost heritage places itself in peril. He would call for the modeling of the Kingdom of God in the face of post–modernism.

He does not believe the Army needs to reinvent itself, but rather to be what God has called the Army to be, marked by personal and corporate holiness. He emphasizes that Salvationists "don't do the mission," but rather they embody the mission of Christ. Gaither advocates a greater releasing of the gifts of married women leaders, and more power to soldiers in ministry. He says, "The war against evil will not be won at a headquarters," and views headquarters as the support team for those in the front line. He underscores that "evil is defeated at ground zero, by engaged foot soldiers, who face the raging battle every day."

Gaither calls its worldwide members to make true brotherhood in Christ the exclamation mark of Salvationists as a people of God. He urges a commitment to growth, not acceptance of a lack of church growth as a "sign of the time."

While recognizing the vital role of women in the Army, he appeals for a stronger focus on taking the gospel into the lives and circumstances of men. He urges and prays for a powerful "Men in Mission" movement to sweep the Army world.

He also invokes a re–positioning of the Army's dialogue on the sacraments, to "transition from a negative defensive position to a positive offensive posture." He calls on Army constituents to exemplify a vital non–sacramental community of believers who have direct access by grace to communion with God.

Overseas experience intensified his awareness of the issue of demand and supply for financial and human resources within the global movement. He sees the need to address disasters and distress that afflict the poor, the trafficking of women and children, and breakdown of the family.

This was to be a moment to speak out on the confrontation with syncretism that erodes biblical principles and practice. He challenges those in the ranks "to confront the world as saved, sanctified and serving Salvationist believers."

For Israel Gaither, pressing forward means replacing a controlling leadership with a shared and consultative leadership. He does not perceive the role of shepherding to be limited to a congregationally based appointment, and readily acknowledges that his "first calling is to be a shepherd. No matter what I do or where I may be deployed—I know I must be a faithful shepherd."

As a nominee at the High Council, Israel Gaither would lay down and affirm his credo of the Army *Pressing Forward!* to its new frontiers of challenge and mission for the Kingdom of God.

THE NOMINEES AND THE BALLOT

Seven candidates had been nominated, each by at least the required three members. Two declined to stand. Five stood for election: Commissioners Carl Lydholm (Norway), Hasse Kjellgren (Sweden), Christine MacMillan (Canada), Israel Gaither (USA), and Shaw Clifton (UK). Each candidate brought high credentials of leadership ability and experience.

He brought to the Council a portfolio of impeccable credentials—his record of outstanding leadership and service as Chief of Staff, second in command of the international movement, his extraordinary relational and administrative skills, and his powerful preaching and pulpit ministry.

The five 2006 High Council candidates: Commissioners Lydholm, Kjellgren, MacMillan, Gaither, and Clifton

Shaw Clifton brought the most outstanding portfolio of credentials of any candidate in the history of the High Council. Holding a law degree, he had earlier served at IHQ as the Army's Legal and Parliamentary Secretary. One of the Army's premier writers, he had authored several books. He had served on five continents including early service as corps officer and educator in Africa, and as leader of the Army in Pakistan during which a record growth and development took place in that Muslim country. Clifton, like Gaither, had also been a nominee at the 1999 and 2002 High Councils, having stood at each of them.

Candidates made their response to the prepared questions and gave their nomination speech. When the Council had opportunity to reflect on the answers to questions, including those by the spouses, and speeches by candidates, the President made the following declaration: "As we, the members of the High Council, approach the momentous task of electing the next General of The Salvation Army, we do with one accord render glory to the Triune God, Father, Son and Holy Spirit, and, in the name of Jesus Christ our Savior, invoke the guidance and aid of the Holy Spirit in the discharge of our solemn responsibility, desiring only that the will of God shall be done." Promises of prayer came via Internet from around the world, including from Junior Soldiers, some who sent crayon drawings with handwritten greetings.

The balloting procedure was ably piloted by the Council's president, Commissioner Todd Bassett. In the hush of the council chamber each member entered the voting room to place a check opposite one of the names on the ballot, as other members engaged in prayer. The voting completed, tellers tallied the votes. In the first three ballots, to be elected a candidate must receive more than two–thirds of the votes, and from the fourth ballot onwards only receive a majority vote. The candidate with fewest votes in each ballot is dropped until only two candidates remain. The President announces the number of votes each candidate has received in each ballot. This Council made the decision not to publish the actual number of votes, nor some details of the proceedings, until a lapse of 10 years.

Finally on the fourth ballot there stood Clifton and Gaither, each with a strong support which had precluded a two–thirds majority in the first three rounds of voting.

The fourth ballot completed, the council chamber doors were thrown open, and towards the waiting cameras strode the next General of The Salvation Army, viewed on the Internet in the first such live web cast by thousands of Salvationists around the world. The General in office, John Larsson, who up to this point was absent from the High Council, headed the group of well wishers to his successor. The president of the Council now announced and presented the General–elect, Commissioner Shaw Clifton.

None of the candidates viewed the election as a contest, but rather as a searching for the will of God. To Israel Gaither, who had left the church where his father pastored in response to God's call to serve in The Salvation Army, was accorded this lofty honor within its ranks—to have stood as a nominee on the final ballot with the now–elected General. Council members, who had prayed intensely to know the will of God, unanimously acknowledged and expressed unqualified support to their newly–elected leader.

AFTER THE BALLOT

Commissioner Nancy Moretz in her published reflections on the High Council, shared the following. "I was so proud that The Salvation Army values and includes women in leadership and in making decisions. Proud of the women for whom English is not their first language." She added, "The selection and election of a General is not a competition, it's not a political effort, it's not loud and boisterous; rather, it's focused, prayerful and earnest. When our General was finally chosen we did not engage in a type of celebration. Rather, there was a holy hush as we went immediately to prayer for the Cliftons, the nominees, and for our Army. Every delegate had opportunity to affirm, support, embrace, greet, and pray for our new leaders. As I embraced them, I could feel that they were shaken in submission to the authority of the One who called them and set them apart for His purposes."

In farewell words to his territory Clifton shared, "The High Council, under God, has caused a unique trust to be bestowed upon me. They knew, because I told them, that I felt reluctant. Our strong commitment to our home territory was a big part of that reluctance. Long before any outcome was known or could even be guessed at, the 100 present came strongly under the hand of God the Holy Spirit. We poured out our hearts in many languages at the throne of grace."

As General–elect, in February 2006, Commissioner Shaw Clifton responded to the author's invitation with his reflection of high esteem for Israel Gaither, who stood with him in seeking God's will in the final ballot.

> I was almost 50 years of age when I first met Izzy Gaither. Helen and I had been appointed to lead the Massachusetts Division in the USA Eastern Territory. Izzy was the Territorial Secretary for Personnel, so we had frequent contact. My impressions? Favorable, very favorable.
>
> Here was someone who was not going to be pushed around. He was his own man. He had a determination about him. He was passionate about the gospel. As time went on I discovered him to be an encourager. He was secure enough in himself to pay compliments. And when he spoke, he was articulate. Add to that a natural courtesy and sense of fun to soften

the strong–mindedness, and you get a man worth knowing. He once told me he liked my style. I remembered that, and still do. I also remember replying that I liked his style too. Helen and I noted his deep commitment to Eva and to his family, as well as his proper pride in his pastor Dad who received not infrequent mentions from the platform.

Before we left Massachusetts for Pakistan in 1997 Izzy had become the Chief Secretary. He teamed up well with Commissioner Ron Irwin. I had come to know Ron and to value his leadership. If he trusted you, it was a mark worthy of note. Ron trusted Izzy, and rightly so. I thought they were an excellent team.

It was Izzy and Eva who honoured us by conducting our Farewell Meeting in the Boston Central Hall and who sent us off with their blessings for service in Pakistan. That meeting lives in our memories. It was handled with grace, sensitivity and warmth. We felt encouraged and valued.

Two years later we met again at Sunbury Court near London for the 1999 High Council. Can we ever forget the High Council pausing to allow Helen and Eva to fly in? Izzy and I had both accepted nomination as 'mere Colonels.' Our wives were not eligible to attend a High Council, but the nominations meant that they would unexpectedly be invited. It was something of a bonding experience and Izzy's inspired words of encouragement to me, spoken in private, are with me still. When the High Council convened again in 2002 he was equally encouraging.

Soon thereafter the world learned that General John Larsson had appointed Israel L. Gaither to be the Chief of the Staff. I wrote to the General to say what pleasing news this was, and I took the liberty of adding that had it fallen to me to find a new Chief, I would have done exactly the same. In the years that followed Izzy proved eloquent in public ministry. In private he was unswervingly supportive of me as a Territorial Commander in both New Zealand and the United Kingdom.

He and Eva are ideal role models for their demanding and high profile tasks. Helen and I know we are truly blessed to be partnering with them across the miles in these momentous days for God's great Army of Salvation.

Shaw Clifton invited Gaither to lead his welcome meeting and dedication as General on April 8 in the Kensington City Hall, London. Israel and Eva were pleased to respond, interrupting the transitional time with family to make the quick round trip to participate. Israel's opening words in the meeting were, "Tomorrow has come. We enter into a new era of Salvation Army history." Following his prayer of dedication for the new leaders, he led the capacity attendance in a standing ovation and tribute to the new international leaders of The Salvation Army. Clifton expressed his gratitude to the Gaithers for coming and stated that he would soon reciprocate by conducting their installation as national leaders in the States. Once again, Salvationists in attendance and around the world via live Web site video witnessed the bonded spirit of Salvationist leaders, transcending the world's human rivalries and ambitions.

> **" Israel Gaither's life is a dance of gospel inspiration."**

Commissioner M. Christine MacMillan, Territorial Commander for Canada and Bermuda and one of the candidates on the ballot, adds her word of appreciation for Gaither. "The response to Israel Gaither at the High Council as Chief was graced with an intent to follow a process depicting an international leadership team mobilized by God. One picked up the passion of mission Israel expressed through his journey of childhood, influenced by his own mentor–preacher father. The spirit of Israel Gaither captures a man of unmovable conviction rooted in gospel imperatives. His return home will penetrate the USA Salvation Army with a global perspective. As Israel weeps with the world's poverty he rejoices in our potential to let freedom reign through the joy spirit of our brothers and sisters less encumbered with material gain. Israel Gaither's life is a dance of gospel inspiration."

Commissioner P.D. Krupa Das, Territorial Commander of India Western Territory, viewed Gaither as a "champion." He writes, "He knew the pulse of the Army both in developed and developing countries and the way forward for the Army. He championed the dignity of receiving territories while acknowledging the humility of supporting territories as Partners in Mission. The close result in the voting for the office of the General revealed the highest esteem in which he was held. He maintained poise and serenity in accepting the ultimate will of God. That's greatness in him."

ISRAEL'S SOUL MATE

Eva, Israel's soul mate, had always been an integral part of his life journey, his odyssey of the spirit. She has made her own inestimable contribution to the Lord and the Army. Her gracious spirit has touched the lives of countless around the world who rise up and call her blessed.

As she and Israel in their last month were preparing to leave their London appointment and return to the States as national leaders, Commissioner Helen Clifton shared her reflection on Eva and her personal touch and ministry.

Commissioner Eva D. Gaither is one of those people who light up the room when they walk in. I met her first in New York when Shaw and I had been in the USA only one week, taking up our appointments as divisional leaders in Boston. During one of the intervals between sessions at the Conference of Executive Leaders, Eva, Nancy Moretz and I sampled the chocolates while our husbands were not looking! It was delightfully conspiratorial and fun, belying the highly professional attitudes we were exhibiting in conference! Seriously, the warm fellowship of these sisters in Christ was deeply appreciated and has not changed through the years.

Eva and her husband went to South Africa as territorial leaders not long after Shaw and I went to Pakistan. We knew this would be a profound experience for them and we kept our friendship across the miles during these years.

In 1999, our daughter Jenny, and her husband Marcus, took up positions as youth pastors in the small corps of Sidney, Ohio. Mentioning this to Eva one day, I found that Sidney was her home corps and that her mother was the retired Home League Secretary. I subsequently met Mrs Shue on a visit and saw how proud she was of her daughter and son–in–law, her grandchildren and great–grandchildren. The second time we went, Mrs Shue was not there—she had traveled to California for Christmas! At the age of nearly ninety, this was quite something! Eva can rightly be proud of her.

I was very happy when the Gaithers visited New Zealand during our time as leaders there, and especially when Eva and I were guests at the coffee and dessert event for women leaders in Wellington. As always, Eva made the evening special, speaking from the heart and communicating her transparent enthusiasm for women ministering to women in the name of Christ. I respect her greatly for her giftedness, her unfailing warmth and friendship and her unrestrained commitment to the Gospel and to those she loves.

Entering a New Era

Israel and Eva Gaither were now ready to enter a new era of their lives, which would return them home and to the highest posts of Salvation Army leadership in their homeland. *Salvationist*, The Salvation Army's United Kingdom periodical that also reports on major international news, in its February 11, 2006 edition, published the following report under the headline: "First African–American US National Commander."

After outstanding international ministry as Chief of the Staff and World Secretary for Women's Ministries, Commissioners Israel and Eva Gaither are returning to the USA to take up appointments as National Commander and National President of Women's Ministries. They will farewell from International Headquarters on 1 April and, following leave, will take up their new appointments on 1 May.

Commissioner Gaither will be the first African–American appointed National Commander. Commenting on the news, General–elect Commissioner Shaw Clifton said: "Leading the Army in the land of their birth, the Gaithers will serve with grace and effectiveness. We are proud of them both and salute their special ministry to the international Army and the United Kingdom Territory in recent years."

The Chief and Commissioner Moretz, lifelong friends at the High Council

The Chief of the Staff responded, "Eva and I have been gifted with three amazing years of leadership on the international scene. The privileges of ministry among Salvationists worldwide, including the United Kingdom Territory, have deepened our commitment to God, fixed our belief in the power of a Salvationist and flourished our love for this grand mission!

We now look forward, with great joy, to the turning of the page and the commencement of another chapter in our officer service. Needless to say we are thrilled to be returning to our homeland to engage Army mission in a sector of the world that is making enormous advances for the sake of the Kingdom. It's another privilege of leadership for which we give thanks to God."

"THINGS REMEMBERED"

At the Gaithers IHQ farewell program on March 23, conducted by General Larsson, Israel and Eva shared a dialogue on "Things Remembered, and Not Forgotten," from which the following is excerpted.

Eva and I thank you for things remembered, and things not forgotten. General and Commissioner Larsson, Eva and I count the privilege of serving with you as a sacred gift. We are leaving two people whom we love and deeply respect. You are more than just colleagues and leaders. You are friends.

We believe, with passion, in the reason for a Salvation Army. After having served for three and one–half years with you we really know why there must be a Salvation Army in the world.

We are proud to say that we have served at the heart of the of the Army world. It is from this place that the call is sounded to move beyond the comfort of the known into risks unknown.

Eva and I take our leave assuring you of our key desire to serve the call of the Kingdom. You have helped us become better believers. From you, we have learned more mission lessons. We have something more to "go and talk about" when we return to our homeland. Thank you for believing in us, for trusting us, for loving us, for opening your hearts and letting us in.

We shall be forever grateful that our journey has taken us to 101 Queen Victoria Street. We promise you we shall cherish and remain true to "things remembered, and not forgotten," all of which has given us incredible joy in following Jesus.

chapter **33**

USA National Commander

"Well done, good and faithful servant! You have been faithful with a few things; I will put you in charge of many things."

Matthew 25:21

National *War Cry* cover, April 29, 2006

L ife is lived in chapters. We have followed Israel Gaither through the chapters of his life—his roots and early days, the formative years and beginning his life journey, choosing his life partner, overcoming the racial barriers, as corps officer, headquarters officer, as shepherd, pastor and preacher, the soul's journey in South Africa, at the High Councils, second in command of the international Salvation Army, a doctorate at Asbury College, and around the world travels. We now come to the penultimate chapter of Israel Gaither's epic life journey, as National Commander of The Salvation Army in the United States, an exclamation point to all that has gone before.

Although news articles highlighted the fact of his being the first black man in the appointment, Israel Gaither downplays any racial aspect in his choice as national commander. "I'm not here because of my color, and I wouldn't be here if I thought I was. I want to serve all men and women. I am aware I can serve as a model to African–Americans, as well as to whites and Hispanics."

USA NATIONAL LEADERS

His parish as national leader embraces the vast reaches of the nation's boundaries, from Alaska to Hawaii, from Maine to Puerto Rico, and all in between. It includes the largest and most complex conglomeration of Salvation Army personnel, finance, programs and services in the Army world. National statistics list 427,027 members, of whom 113,525 are ecclesiastical members known as "soldiers." A secular journalist described the Army in the States as "an extraordinary charity empire with 60,642 employees, 3.5 million volunteers and an annual expenditure of $2.6 billion for its social services."

Commissioner W. Todd Bassett, in his final weeks of office as National Commander of The Salvation Army stated his anticipation relative to his successor.

> As I reflect on the gifts and skills that now will be brought to the office of National Commander and National President of Women's Ministries, one realizes the impact potential that comes with the Gaithers. A large portion of the national leader's portfolio rests with representing The Salvation Army to the American public as well as coordinating and facilitating the work among the territories. Commissioner Gaither's skill in conducting board meetings, and his worldwide experiences, will only serve to enhance and strengthen the impact of the donor process of The Salvation Army in the United States to the worldwide mission. The SAWSO (Salvation Army World Services Organization) Board of Directors will be enriched by his overseas experience. The public platform that is given to his position will be well served by the articulate and forthright manner in which he has earned a reputation as an outstanding speaker and preacher. The appointment of Commissioners Israel L. and Eva D. Gaither as national leaders will serve to enhance and strengthen the work of The Salvation Army in the United States.

After serving outside the USA for seven and a half years, Israel was quoted in the Army's *War Cry* as saying, "We are thrilled to be returning to the

USA. We look forward to renewing friendships, making new friends, and of course being closer to our families. We have missed some very important events in the life of our children and grandsons." (Only a few weeks later, Eva and Israel shared in the joy of the arrival on May 25 of their granddaughter, Virginia Marie Gaither, and Eva was providentially able to be at her mother's side when she went to be with the Lord, at age 91, on June 16, 2006.)

Eva echoed the sentiment, "We have been blessed with an incredible gift of service overseas that has exposed us to this worldwide mission in a way that has forever changed us." Of her new position as President of Women's Ministries, she said, "I receive it as a sacred responsibility. I strongly believe in the powerful role we have in the ministry of and to women, and our incredibly positive impact for the Kingdom of God."

Israel views the large picture of the Army in the States. "We are aware of the high regard in which the public holds the Army's ministries of service. We honor Salvationists, volunteers and friends of the Army for their outstanding work. We pledge to do our best in representing the front line of ministry. Eva and I look forward to engaging with the National Advisory Board. The Army in this country is gifted with the trust, expertise and profound support of men and women who are willing to stand with us to ensure that we do well what we have been born to be and do. We are also proud to be in partnership with territorial leaders in this country who share the same passion for mission as we do. We deeply respect them, want to support their leadership and be a source of encouragement for them.

"We are looking forward to ministry opportunities throughout the country and we're pleased with the invitations that have already arrived. One of the key ways we believe we can support the vision and leadership of the territorial leaders will be evidenced through visits to corps, institutions, divisions and territories.

"The Army in the USA is vital to a strong universal Salvation Army. We are so proud of the way in which the individual and collective support mission units in this country makes mission effectively happen in other places in the world."

Asked of his aspirations for the future direction of The Salvation Army in the U.S., he replied: "We believe that all we do is for the mission. That implies Salvationists must truly seek to be a people of God. We want to see Salvationists become 'soldiers'—actively engaged in transformational ministries. Every soldier can do something to contribute to the Kingdom."

Israel emphasizes that the Army of today needs to keep in touch with its roots and core values of the past. He sees the Army's heritage serving as a compass to chart its course amid the fierce winds of change that surround it. "For me, the most important thing is to know the purpose for God raising up the Army. This also means we must guard against losing our heritage. We have a rich history that informs the present as the means for the shaping of

God's plan for the future. We won't understand the 'who' or the 'why' if we lose our past. In it all the most important voice is the Spirit of God."

"Keepers of the Dream"

On May 1, 2006, the journey of Israel L. Gaither that had its start in New Castle, Pa., now led to Alexandria, Va., in the office of the National Commander of The Salvation Army in the United States. From his terms of territorial leadership in South Africa and as second in command at IHQ in London, he brought a global perspective to this high office. And having gone through the ranks from a corps officer to territorial commander in the States, he brought an intimate understanding of the Army in its vast and varied facets in his homeland. Both at home and abroad the Army was confronting issues that could redefine its purpose and program. Never in its history did it need so much to be reminded that "Mission matters most."

On his first day in office, the officer and employee staff of National Headquarters gathered in the NHQ chapel for a welcome program, followed by a reception. Who represented the NHQ officers with words of welcome? None other than the National Editor in Chief and Literary Secretary, Major Ed Forster, whom we met earlier in Israel's life story. He shared how as a lad of 17, Cadet Gaither's ministry in his home corps had been used of God to turn his life in the direction of full time ministry as a Salvation Army officer, and how their paths had intersected through the years including their time in London together. "God works in wonderful and mysterious ways," observed the major.

Eva Gaither in her remarks said that they "would not change the past seven years of overseas service for anything," but expressed her joy "that the Lord has now brought us home and we will be present for the first time later this month with the birth of a grandchild." [Eva and Israel were able to be present for the advent of their new granddaughter, Virginia Marie, born to son Mark and his wife Amy, in Pittsburgh on May 25, 2006. In an e–mail Israel wrote, "Eva is ecstatic!"]

Speaking not far from where one of the nation's most electrifying speeches was delivered, Martin Luther King Jr.'s "I have a dream," Gaither's first message as National Commander in his headquarters to all his staff, was an invitation and challenge to be "Keepers of the Dream." He laid down the gauntlet for his leadership: "Together we are dream–keepers of the Army's mission in America." He quoted a famous line from African–American poet Langston Hughes, "Hold fast to dreams. For if dreams die, life is a broken winged butterfly.

"We must hold fast to God's dream for this mission. It was given a long time ago—and the intention has not changed. The Salvation Army is not William Booth's idea. He did not invent it. He was the instrument of God in which the dream was contained. And like the subject of Langston Hughes poetic reflection—this butterfly, this beautifully delicate mission moves gracefully with two wings on one body—the wing of our ecclesiastical ministry and the wing of our helping ministries. There must be no restriction or breaking of either wing of this mission. Because a broken wing cripples the dream.

"The posture I have for our journey together is in three words—'for the mission.' Any other reason is a distraction. If any one of us forgets the 'why' of what we do, the dream just might be deferred. And a dream deferred means that a person, a place, a situation gets left behind.

"We believe that we are joining a journey with dream–keepers who are intent on ensuring that the dream is never misplaced or replaced, delayed or deferred. We are those who must remain determined that nothing shall cripple the purpose or deny God's best work in us and through us.

"Let those who are working for this mission, scattered across America, know that 'dream–keepers' are at work at 615 Slater's Lane in Alexandria—for the mission.

"Just imagine what God can do through our Salvation Army. This is not about day–dreaming. Hold fast to God's dream for this mission. This dream was given a long time ago and has not changed. The Salvation Army is not the mission, it is a vehicle. We are stewards of the dream. Eva and I are here because we choose to be here. On this day one we start writing the next chapter of fulfilling God's dream for The Salvation Army in America."

THE HOMECOMING AND INSTALLATION

On May 12, 2006 Army leaders, family and friends gathered at the Army's venerated West 14th Street center in New York City for a reception and welcome dinner preceding the main event of the evening. To the avalanche of accolades in these initial days, Israel's standard response was, "This is not about me, it is about God, and the mission."

A near capacity crowd filled the 1,500–seat auditorium, the largest of its kind in the Army world, the Centennial Memorial Temple in New York City, for the installation of Israel Gaither as USA National Commander. The program, led by National Chief Secretary Lt. Colonel Larry Bosh, was supported by the four territorial commanders and Salvationists from across the country. They came to be a part of history for the 26th national leader installed in the 127–year history of The Salvation Army in the States. The Eastern Territory's premier musical and media arts forces enhanced the program. Robert J. Pace, as vice chairman, brought greetings on behalf of the Army's National Advisory Board.

"This is a historic event," declared General Shaw Clifton, as he conducted the installation of Commissioners Israel L. Gaither and Eva D. Gaither as national commander and national president of Women's Ministries, respectively. "Commissioner Gaither is a model of spiritual leadership," said the General. "His experience in South Africa and London gives him a world view of the challenges facing the Army today, while retaining the historical mission of the Army rooted in biblical truth and values."

General Clifton said of the Gaithers, "They are part and parcel of the fabric of our lives, because of Jesus Christ. We have a love and respect for these two special godly leaders, and that's what brought us across the Atlantic for this meeting. They are held in highest regard at International Headquarters, and they now come from a distinguished global leadership."

The General confided to his listeners that after the High Council, in discussion with the Gaithers, "It became very clear they wanted to be home. They are here for you, for America. They are here because of deep, genuine, authentic, pure and godly reasons.

"God wants the Gaithers," declared the General, "to lead an Army in America that is Christ–centered. God wants the Gaithers to lead an Army in the power of the risen Savior——not in the power of our own skills, not by the power of our massive know–how, not by the power of our mightily impressive professionalism, not even by the power of those who stand alongside us as our beloved and affirming friends. But He wants the Gaithers to lead an Army by the power of God the Holy Spirit, a Christ–centered and a Calvary–conscious Salvation Army.

"God wants the Gaithers to lead a Salvation Army in America that is an Army coherent in doctrine, able to give an answer for the hope that is in us. God wants the Gaithers to lead the Army in the United States of America with a compassionate heart. You in America are known the world over for your compassion.

"God wants the Gaithers to lead an Army poised, under God, in the power of Jesus Christ, true to the precious distinctives which make salvationism what God intended it to be. They understand what it means when we talk about the sanctified life, the blessing of a clean heart. They understand the

" They are the right people in the right place at the right time."

distinctives of our theological stances—living a holy life without reliance on external sacramental rituals.

"I know their hearts, their mind. We thank God for the Holy Spirit present in Israel and Eva Gaither. They are the right people in the right place at the right time."

Addressing the Gaithers, Clifton said, "We love you. We're proud of you. We offer you our respect, our admiration, our esteem, our support in prayer,

General Shaw Clifton installs the Gaithers as USA national leaders

and above all else our Christian love. We're going to be praying you on, in London and wherever we are. We're going to be talking to God about you, God, go on using them, empowering them, enabling them, make them fruitful for your holy kingdom."

General Clifton invited his hearers, "What would you ask for if you were advertising for a National Commander?" Then he shared the requisites he would include. "I would be looking for someone who is close to God, for people have a passion for the gospel, and a passion for souls, for people with a pastor's heart, who love people more than their position, people who will be orderly in kingdom business. I would ask for people deeply and passionately concerned about Salvationism, people who have a good family life, who have a sound marriage. The Gaithers model all these qualities."

Prior to the formal installation of the Gaithers by the General, Commissioner Keitha Needham sang, appropriately a composition by Stanley Ditmer who was Israel's first mentor in the Army when he was a teenager at Camp Allegheny. Selected by Israel, the words of the first verse expressed the Gaithers' testimony at this junction of their life:

> Long ago the Savior laid his hands on me,
> And I promised I would serve him faithfully.
> The days have come and gone, and still I'm pressing on,
> As today I do his bidding joyfully!

What a joy to follow ev'ry day!
Follow Jesus on life's pilgrim way.
Daily working where His will appoints;
Knowing with His Spirit He anoints.
What a joy to serve where He would choose,
Conscious that He would my service use.
Satan cannot daunt me if I will my Lord obey.
What a joy to follow ev'ry day!
What a joy to follow ev'ry day!

The installation ceremony culminated with the General accompanying Israel and Eva to the altar, where the two knelt as the General prayed over them. Upon return to the platform, the General pronounced the words of official installation. He then presented the Gaithers to the congregation as national leaders, who were greeted with a standing ovation of unrestrained enthusiasm.

PROMISES TO KEEP

Once again, as always, Israel Gaither's message did not consist of boilerplate utterances, or pious platitudes. His preaching resonated with affirmations on his topic, "I Promise," based on the Bible text of Galatians 6:10: "Therefore, as we have opportunity, let us do good to all people, especially to those who belong to the family of believers."

Musicians, leaders and participants behind him on the platform, and those seated in the far away balcony, did not escape his occasional looking towards them and words aimed in their direction. All present became linked with the challenge of his message, from which the following is excerpted.

> Re-engaging our mission in America is a sacred gift. Our seven and a half years away, minus 103 days, is a long time of separation from things familiar. But it has been worth it. We've seen and experienced this amazing Army in ways that few do. We are not the same as we were when we took our leave from this platform in November of 1998.
>
> America is not the same either. It's a disturbing time in America. We are at the crossroads, in spiritual and moral transition.
>
> We have been humbled by the respect for the Army by church, business, civic and governmental leaders in this nation. In our first four days in office, high profile Christian leaders and well-placed business executives have said to me—"We need The Army. Tell us what you think about this or that,

Commissioner Gaither. The Army has a voice and a presence that we want alongside our cause—will you speak with us? Will you walk with us? Will you help us?" It is what Nelson Mandela said to me in a private meeting in Johannesburg several years ago, "South Africa needs The Salvation Army."

And so does South Los Angeles, and South Florida, and the Southside of Chicago and South Jersey, and every place where the Army banner flies in this great nation.

In an early morning hour last week, I was moved to tears in private prayer. I said to God, "Alright, you know the impact of this mission. Now what more do you want us to do? What else is possible?"

America needs The Salvation Army. America is in a culture war. There is a battle for the heart and mind of those on the margins—those to whom we have been called are those at greatest risk. The world attempts to mute the voice of the church and sideline the influence of the believer. So someone must talk about the transforming love of the risen Lord with a clear and consistent voice. Someone must say "no" to wrong and "yes" to right—even in the face of being misunderstood or misinterpreted. Someone has got to do it. [At this point Israel strode away from the pulpit, and with great force of expression, threw out his challenge.] So why not us? We're here for a purpose. Why not The Salvation Army? Why not us?

This is our time. This is the time for a sanctified Army of men and women to make good on promises some of us made a long time ago to God, and to this mission.

In fact—it's time for some of us to discover commitments made that now become our promises to keep. I believe it's time for all Salvationists to become Soldiers.

I believe God is calling a revived Army of battle–ready soldiers to stand up. The reasons for the battle look and feel different, but spring from the same cause that has spoiled the intention of God since the beginning of time. The underlying cause and effect is sin. And it must be identified and brought under the blood of Jesus Christ.

Since our return home I have had to make some promises to God before stepping into this role at 615 Slaters Lane in Alexandria, Virginia. I had to say to God again, "I promise."

I gladly confess, I'm more blessed than I ought to be. And I had to promise again, that as never before, I am His. I promise!

Despite the raging culture war, sweeping natural disasters, or attempts to re–cast God's intention for family, or the sickening ugliness of wrong that is being re–shaped to make it look and feel like it is right—in the face of it all this is a great time to be a Salvationist missioner in America. I'm proud to be a soldier.

If we really accept that our ultimate purpose is to get people ready for the reign of Christ—if we really believe it—then Salvationists of America get ready to engage spiritual warfare as never before.

Voices of the post–modern age ask us to lessen our grip on biblical values. To ease off living on purpose for Jesus—it's not politically correct to think, feel or speak like Christ. We are urged to believe what you want to believe, and live any way you desire to live, and be tolerant no matter the violation of biblical or moral or ethical values.

In the face of it all, salvation soldiers say, "I promise. I promise to live to "do the most good. No matter where the battle lines may fall; no matter what it requires of me; no matter what sacrifice is demanded—I promise."

I contend that being precedes doing. As good as we are, we can be better. In fact, this season in America requires, no it demands, the best of a unified, single purpose Salvation Army.

I think John Wesley was speaking to all of us when he said, "Do all the good you can, in all the ways you can, to all the people you can, as long as you can."

Evangeline Booth intended that when she wrote of the great "romance" between The Salvation Army and the public following the Great War. You have been reminded of her words: "There is no reward equal to that of doing the most good to the most people in the most need."

But John Wesley and Evangeline Booth were not the first to talk about doing good. In a letter from the Apostle Paul to the churches in Galatia he urged the believers to "not become weary in doing good," (and in fact do more) "do good to everyone."

This is not the time for an Army to retreat. Women still cry because of abuse, isolation, and disregard. Children are still aborted and abandoned, lost, emotionally scarred, misused. This is not the time for the Army to disappear into the sanctuary of a citadel.

This evening is promise making time–about being and doing better. Tonight we say, "I promise."

Colin Powell on the eve of his retirement from a brilliant military career was asked what are you going to do now. He replied, to the point of his calling to service, saying, "I'm a soldier."

That's what we are being called to truly become—soldiers. And I invite every person in this congregation and those who are viewing this service by video, to make three promises with me.

Here's the first one. **I promise to live for Jesus.**

We must be those who seek to be perfectly filled with the Spirit. We are would–be seekers of the indwelling, sanctifying presence, of the Holy Spirit. Let holiness forever be the mark of one who has said, "I promise."

This is about being before doing and I remind you that as believers, our good works are the fruit of our faith.

Would you promise to be a seeker of the holiness of God? As I stand before you in the presence of God I say to you, I promise.

Let's make a second promise. **I promise to serve like Jesus.**

This is a movement known for its ability to serve. We've made a promise to God and this nation. We'll be good and do the most good—every time. We'll serve with excellence.

Serving in the style of Jesus is transformative. That is why I insist that all we do and are is summed in three words. "For the mission." You will hear it continually from me. Serving the purposes of the Kingdom is not about who I am, or what I do, or how I'm seen. It's all "for the mission." It's not for me—or you. It's about Jesus.

Mission ought to consume us. The Salvation Army in and of itself is not the mission. The mission is to seed the Kingdom, transforming lives of people, giving new belief and new hope.

I promise to serve in the spirit of our Lord—for the mission. Will you make that promise with me?

That suggests a third promise. Let's say, **I promise to stand for Jesus.**

Doing God's good purpose in the world will have us moving in places and among people where we will be uncomfortable. But it must be done.

This is a disciplined Army of soldiers who live their lives within spiritual and moral and ethical boundaries. This is an Army of soldiers sustained by grace who refuse to lose! This is an Army of winners. No element of this mission anywhere in

America needs to lose. Reject losing. Every mission center in
this land was formed to win. If you lose—it's your mistake, not
God's. Winning is in our DNA.

This is promise–keeping time. I'll stand strong, by grace, for
Christ! I promise.

Following his sermon, the prayer meeting led by Israel, with scores
coming to the altar in dedication, evoked for many a memory of the
young captain who years earlier had been called on to lead the weekly
prayer meetings in the Friday Evening at the Temple series. Now as national leader of the Army in the States, he once again called for dedication
from the same platform, to the same altar, and once more many responded
to his invitation.

But this occasion hosted a new dimension to his prayer meeting leadership. Not only did he address those in the far reaches of the balcony, "Don't
get lost up there, come tonight and make your promise," but he addressed
an even wider group of listeners. Facing directly into the video camera, he
spoke to those who were among the viewers on the Web site or in the future
would be viewing a DVD. Indeed, as Commissioner Lawrence Moretz fore-
cast at the beginning of the meeting, "Glory crowned the mercy seat," not
only the one in the auditorium that night, but also in unique and far flung
places where the power of the message went forth by means of the marvel of
electronic communications.

Following a concluding and rousing song of praise, there came to the pulpit to pray the benediction, one who as a young teenager had his life turned
around by words spoken to him by the young Captain Gaither as a corps officer. His exemplary service through the years earned him the Army's highest honor—Order of the Founder. Now he, Ken Burton, brought the
historic meeting to a close with his prayer of benediction.

The Heavy Mantle

In his new position Commissioner Israel Gaither became the national
spokesperson for The Salvation Army, articulating its mission, speaking on
key issues, and abetting the Army's advance in the States. Gaither considers
this opportunity to preach and minister across the country as a special gift
and sacred trust. A major role includes support of the leadership in the four
U.S. Territories, while at the same time garnering support for the critical
needs of the Army's overseas mission where vital resources are not available.
Primary leadership roles include his chairmanship of the Commissioners'
Conference, chairman of the National Corporation and SAWSO (Salvation
Army World Services Organization) Board of Trustees, and relating to the
prestigious and actively involved National Advisory Board.

Israel and Eva Gaither, in the office of the National Commander

"America loves The Salvation Army," said Gaither. "There is a strong confidence in who we are and what we do. But there's more to be done. This position is an honor and I intend to lead with total dependence on God and in partnership with territorial leaders to effectively impact those on the margins of American society."

At the time of his taking office, a unique opportunity for The USA Salvation Army opened to forward its mission with building of community centers in line with the $1.5 billion gift from the estate of Joan Kroc (McDonald's). It also coincides with continuing the $363 million community recovery services for Hurricane Katrina survivors, while preparing emergency response plans for potential new disasters.

The Army, with a history of operating in the United States since 1879, has been nationally recognized for its stewardship of using 83 cents of every dollar raised for support of its humanitarian services. Its vast array of services range from providing food for the hungry, relief for disaster victims, assistance for the disabled, outreach to the elderly and ill, clothing and shelter to the homeless, counseling and social services to those in need.

As National President of Women's Ministries, Commissioner Eva Gaither supports the service of the Territorial Presidents for Women's Ministries, and is chair of their triennial conferences. She will partner with leaders from the four USA territories of the Army to address common issues that affect women throughout America.

Serving in close harmony with the Gaithers would be his newly appointed National Chief Secretary, Lt. Colonel Barry Swanson, and Lt. Colonel E. Sue Swanson, both with an outstanding record of pastoral and administrative leadership.

MAN WITH A MISSION

This retrospection has permitted us a clairvoyance to see how God led a young lad from New Castle, Pa., to a global ministry and the high offices of spiritual leadership, where now this story ends. But every ending precedes another beginning, and Israel Gaither will not soon recede into the proverbial mist of the years.

As this part of his life story now comes to a close, he will stay the course as further chapters of God's will and work unfold. His ultimate legacy under God's leading and yet to be defined, will redound with enduring enrichment to countless lives across America and throughout the world.

Indeed, as we have seen throughout these chapters, and as the subtitle of our book states, Israel L. Gaither is a "Man With a Mission." The future remains bright with promise, for as the psalmist reminds us, "The steps of a good man are ordered by the Lord" (Psalm 37:23).

Who Am I?
A Daughter's Reflection

My father has always known me.

Maybe he knew I was going to have his personality, mixed with my mother's looks. Or maybe he knew that he and I would share an affinity for seafood, collard greens and sweet potato pie. Or maybe he just knew that I would always be his "baby girl."

Yes, my father *has* always known me and has always reminded me who I was and was to become.

From our teenage years, my brother, Mark, and I were constantly told, "Remember who you are." There was a lot wrapped up in that and I think my father had it right years before the "WWJD" movement became so large.

Each time we wore the Salvation Army uniform, we were told to remember who we were. At 18 and 12 years old, Mark and I didn't have much time for it. We normally would roll our eyes and quickly say, "Yes, Dad, we remember who we are." Eighteen years later, I know what my father meant.

He meant we were a Gaither and there was a large Christian heritage to that name. My grandfather was a pastor and preacher, who daily upheld the Bible as his support and guidance. Mark and I had a lot to live up to.

The Gaither family was very respected and loved in the town of New Castle, Pa., and this was never more evident than at the funeral of my grandfather. Crammed into my grandfather's one–room–with–a–cellar church, people from across the community gathered to honor a man whose life was lived fully for Christ. As I looked around the room and saw people weeping over the loss of this man, I realized the full impact of the Gaither name.

My dad has followed in his father's footsteps. He remembers daily who he is and the legacy his father left him. Every time I enter a Salvation Army gathering, I am told about the impact my father has had on someone's life. Whether it was when they were a child or just last week, my father has helped bring hundreds of men and women around the globe to the feet of Jesus.

I do remember who I am.

I am a follower of Christ who has a lineage of preaching the Gospel Truth.

Mark and I were also told to remember who we were as we were running out the door to meet up with friends to go to a basketball game or to a movie. Once again, we would recite back, "Yes, Dad, we know who we are."

We were children of God.

My father always has had a gift of making us feel special. He's been there through the rough times; he's been there through the fabulous times. And he's always been there to support us in whatever decisions we had facing us. And he always reminds us that Jesus truly loves us and truly cares what happens to us.

Recently, I switched jobs and my father proved himself to me again. Over those agonizing weeks of deciding, my father would call me daily to affirm my abilities and me and to remind me that the Lord was in control.

"I'm praying that the Lord surrounds you with peace," he would often say to me. "Your mother and I are praying that the Lord reveals to you His plan." His words were a comfort to me.

And once again, I remembered who I was.

I am a person whose life is being guided by One who has only the best intentions for my future.

Mark and I were also reminded of who we were in our daily interactions with one another. Some days he was the pesky little brother who wouldn't give me my space. And sometimes he was my gopher who would do anything to please his big sister. But most of the time he was my friend who made me laugh. Our family is always laughing. Even today, laughter fills up most of our family time together.

We remember to take the serious things seriously, but to always look for the lighter side.

My father is probably the hardest–working man I know—in the office before dawn and working diligently until returning home for dinner. But even between administrative matters and sermon preparations, he knows how to live the abundant life. Whether it's watching a movie with his grandson or eating ribs and collard greens with me, he knows how to have fun.

I remember who I am.

I am a believer in Christ who knows what living the abundant life means.

I am proud to be a Gaither. Not because of some prideful family history, rather because being a Gaither means loving the Lord, loving your family and loving the sacred life you've been entrusted with.

Dad, today I can say to you without rolling my eyes, without quickly responding in that teenager–kind–of–way, but with a confidence that comes in knowing Christ, *"I remember who I am."*

And I owe much of that to you.

Michele Gaither Sparks
January 2006

The Journey

ISRAEL LEE GAITHER III

1944	October 27	Born in New Castle, PA
1961	August	Confirmation of God's call to officership
1962	September 4	Cadet, SFOT, Bronx, NY
1963	June 26	Cadet Summer Assignment—Brooklyn Citadel, NY Corps
1963	October 1	Return to SFOT for second year of training
1964	June 6	Commissioned Lieutenant; Assistant Officer at Pittsburgh (Northside), PA
1965	June 30	Appointed to Special Work; Pittsburgh, PA DHQ—Aliquippa, PA
1965	September 25	In Charge (under DHQ supervision); Aliquippa, PA (Outpost)
1966	June 1	Corps Officer, Aliquippa, PA (officially opened as a Corps)
1966	June 5	Promoted to Captain
1967	June 28	Corps Officer, Pittsburgh (Homewood), PA
1967	July 1	Marriage to Captain Eva D. Shue
1971	January 27	Corps Officer, Brooklyn (Bedford), NY
1975	September 10	Divisional Youth Secretary, Greater New York Division
1978	August 28	Divisional Secretary, Greater New York Division
1978	September 27	Men's Fellowship Secretary, Greater New York (added responsibility)
1981	July 1	General Secretary, Western Pennsylvania Division
1983	June 5	Promoted to Major
1986	November 1	Divisional Commander, Southern New England Division
1988	January 13	International College for Officers, London 1/13/88 to 3/7/88
1990	November 1	Divisional Commander, Western Pennsylvania Division
1991	January 22	Promoted to Lt. Colonel

1993	October 1	Lt. Colonel, Field Secretary for Personnel, USA Eastern THQ
1994	June 12	Promoted to Colonel
1994	July 1	Change in Nomenclature, Secretary for Personnel
1997	February 1	Chief Secretary, USA Eastern THQ
1999	January 1	Territorial Commander, Southern Africa Territory
2000	March 16	Promoted to Commissioner
2002	August 1	Territorial Commander, USA Eastern Territory
2002	November 13	Chief of the Staff, International Headquarters, London
2006	May 1	National Commander, USA

The Journey

EVA DOROTHY (SHUE) GAITHER

1943	September 9	Born in Sydney, Ohio
1962	September 4	Cadet, SFOT Bronx, NY
1963	June 26	Cadet, Summer Assignment, Hamilton, Ohio
1963	October 1	Return to SFOT for second year of training
1964	June 6	Commissioned Lieutenant, Assistant Officer, Pittsburgh (Homewood) Corps
1965	October 6	Assistant Officer, Erie (Central), PA Corps
1966	April 20	Assistant Officer (Pro–tem), Titusville, PA, Western PA
1966	June 5	Promoted to Captain
1966	June 29	Corps Officer, Erie (Central), Pa.
1966	November 16	Corps Officer, Pittsburgh (Homewood), PA
1967	July 1	Married to Captain Israel L. Gaither III
1967	July 1	Corps Officer, Pittsburgh (Homewood), PA
1971	January 27	Corps Officer, Brooklyn (Bedford), NY
1975	September 10	Divisional Guard & Sunbeam Director, Greater New York
1978	September 13	Director of Vol. & Women Aux & Camps Bureau Coordinator
1981	July 1	Divisional Home League Secretary, Western Pennsylvania
1983	June 5	Promoted to Major
1986	November 1	Divisional Director of Women's Services, Southern New England Division
1990	November 1	Divisional Director of Women's Services, Western Pennsylvania Division
1991	January 22	Promoted to Lt. Colonel
1992	March 1	Order of The Silver Star Secretary (added responsibility), Pittsburgh, PA
1993	October 1	Territorial League of Mercy Secretary, USA East, Deputy VAVS

1994	June 12	Promoted to Colonel
1996	July 1	Territorial Secretary for Order of Silver Star, (added responsibility)
1997	February 1	Territorial Secretary for Women's Organizations
1999	January 1	Territorial President of women's Organizations, Southern Africa
2000	March 16	Promoted to Commissioner
2002	August 1	Territorial President of Women's Organizations, USA East
2002	November 13	World Secretary for Women's Ministries, and World President of Salvation Army Scouts, Guides and Guards, International Headquarters
2006	May 1	National President of Women's Ministries, USA

Vita—Israel and Eva Gaither

[Adapted from Israel Gaither's official external biographical release, March 2006]

Commissioner Israel Gaither is one of five children and the only son born to the Rev. Israel L. Gaither, Sr., and Lillian Gaither. The Commissioner was born and raised in New Castle, Pa.

Commissioner Eva Gaither is a fifth generation Salvationist. She is also one of five children, born in Sidney, Ohio to Richard and Merle Shue.

On their graduation from the Army's School for Officers Training in June, 1964, Israel and Eva were ordained and commissioned as Salvation Army officers (clergy). For over 40 years their service in the Army has taken them around the world. In addition to the USA the Commissioners have lived in Africa and the United Kingdom.

They have served—individually and jointly—in numerous leadership positions, including as pastors of Salvation Army corps (congregations) in Aliquippa, Erie and Pittsburgh, Pa., as well as in Brooklyn, New York's Bedford–Stuyvesant.

Their four plus decades of ministry has impacted the Salvation Army's work in 111 countries and significantly so in Africa, England and the United States. Most of their visits to more than 50 countries and Army territories occurred during the time of leadership service at the Army's International Headquarters in London.

In November 2002, Commissioner Israel Gaither was appointed to serve as the Salvation Army's Chief of the Staff, the first African–American to hold the position since the founding of the organization in 1865. As the organizations chief executive officer, the Commissioner served as second–in–command of the worldwide organization. During that period Commissioner Eva Gaither served as the World Secretary for Women's Ministries—an executive responsibility for the advancing of women in developed and developing sectors of the world. These administrative positions were served at the Salvation Army's International Headquarters in London.

Described as an efficient administrator and gifted speaker, the Commissioner is a much sought after preacher having addressed thousands of Salvationists and Christians worldwide. Commissioner Eva has served as guest presenter and speaker for a variety of women's programs.

Among his varied leadership accomplishments, Commissioner Israel, as an African–American, in addition to serving as the Chief of the Staff, has obtained many "firsts" in Salvation Army history. He is the first to be conferred with the rank of commissioner, the highest that can be achieved in the organization.

The Commissioner is the first African–American to serve as a divisional commander; having served with Commissioner Eva as divisional leaders in Southern New England followed by a similar appointment in Western Pennsylvania. These assignments were followed by their appointments to several key territorial assignments for the Army's USA Eastern Territory encompassing 11 northeastern states, Puerto Rico and the Virgin Islands.

The Gaither's marriage in 1967—during the turbulence of the African–American civil rights era—marked the first racially integrated marriage of Salvation Army Officers in the USA.

Prior to being appointed to lead The Salvation Army in the USA Eastern Territory with headquarters in New York, the Gaithers served a similar capacity as the Territorial Leaders of the Army's work in Southern Africa. They received those appointments in January 1999, marking the first time for the appointing of an African–American Salvation Army Officer outside of the USA. In their respective roles as Territorial Commander and Territorial President of Women's Ministries, they gave oversight to the extensive work of the Army from its headquarters in Johannesburg, South Africa. The work under their charge included the countries of South Africa and Mozambique; the Kingdoms of Lesotho and Swaziland and the Army's ministry on the island of St. Helena.

The key administrative leadership appointments in New York and Johannesburg were historic as Commissioner Gaither was again the first African–American to serve in these top posts.

On May 1, 2006, the Gaithers assumed the key executive leadership assignments of National Commander and National President of Women's Ministries for the United States of America. Commissioner Gaither is the first African–American to serve in this top leadership position in the States.

The Army's USA Eastern Territory commissioned the writing of the biography of Commissioner Israel Gaither (to be published in October 2006). It is the story of the remarkable Christian leadership journey of the Commissioner and his wife, written by the extensively published author (Colonel) Henry Gariepy, author of 25 books.

In May 2005, the global leadership and ministry of Commissioner Israel was recognized by Asbury College in Wilmore, Ky., through the awarding of the honorary degree of Doctor of Humane Letters.

The Gaithers have two children. Daughter Michele Gaither Sparks holds a B.A. and M.A. from Asbury College and serves as the Director of Communications at the Gatton College of Business and Economics, the University of Kentucky. Their son Mark, a physical education teacher and varsity basketball coach at Ringgold High School in Monongahela, Pa., holds a B.S. degree from Asbury and a M.A. from Robert Morris College in Pittsburgh, Pa.

Three grandchildren are the joys of the Gaithers' life—Isaiah Highland Sparks (8), Matthew Israel Gaither (18 months), and Virginia Marie Gaither (born May 25, 2006).

The Author

Colonel Henry Gariepy is the author of 26 books, comprising the largest corpus of published works by a Salvation Army author. Most of his books have been on devotional and Bible topics. He crossed over into the genre of biography in writing the authorized biography of General Eva Burrows, followed by three other biographies, as well as the profiles of each of the 17 elected Generals for the Army's encyclopedic dictionary. A number of historical titles appear under his byline, including the commissioned Volume 8 of the *International History of The Salvation Army*,
the latter with a CD containing text, photos and video clips.

He has also contributed to more than 40 other books, including an essay in the Wesleyan *NIV Reflecting God Study Bible*, numerous writings in domestic and overseas publications, and several series for the Army's international radio program. Billy Graham selected two of Gariepy's books, sending out 150,000 copies of each to people on his mailing list. *Portraits of Christ* and other of Gariepy's works have been published in multiple editions and languages, including Chinese, Spanish and Finnish.

He earned his Master's and B.A. degrees, was honored by his alma mater with its 1994 Alumni Lifetime Leadership Award, and is listed in *Who's Who In U.S. Writers*. In 1966 he was appointed to the Army's International College for Officers in London, and was elected president of his session.

Following appointments as a corps officer, youth secretary, and in inner city work and administrative leadership, he served the last 15 years of his active service as National Editor in Chief and the first National Literary Secretary. During that tenure he organized the Army's first International Literary Conference and initiated its National Book Plan known as Crest Books.

In 1969 the Colonel pioneered and served for six years at the Army's first Multi–Purpose Center in the riot–scarred Hough ghetto of Cleveland. Its pacesetting program had more than 10,000 registered members and 1,000 different persons a day coming through its doors. Billy Graham visited the Center and said, "This is truly Christianity in action."

Since 1995, his "active retirement" has included teaching a corps Adult Bible Class that grew to include more than 80 members, serving as Corps Sergeant Major, conducting Bible study and writer's seminars, teaching for 12 years as an adjunct faculty at the Army's School for Officer Training, serving as a literary consultant, and as an instructor at annual officer institutes.

The colonel is currently engaged in writing a single volume history of the international Salvation Army, due for release by Eerdmans Publishers in 2009.

He is an outdoor enthusiast, including being a three–time 26–mile marathon finisher. He and his wife, Marjorie, take special delight in their four children and 12 grandchildren, and varied activity in their Lancaster, Pa., retirement home.

Index

CREST BOOKS

The Salvation Army National Publications

Shaw Clifton, *Never the Same Again: Encouragement for new and not–so–new Christians*, 1997

Compilation, *Christmas Through the Years: A War Cry Treasury*, 1997

William Francis, *Celebrate the Feasts of the Lord: The Christian Heritage of the Sacred Jewish Festivals*, 1998

Marlene Chase, *Pictures from the Word*, 1998

Joe Noland, *A Little Greatness*, 1998

Lyell M. Rader, *Romance & Dynamite: Essays on Science & the Nature of Faith*, 1998

Shaw Clifton, *Who Are These Salvationists? An Analysis for the 21ˢᵗ Century*, 1999

Compilation, *Easter Through the Years: A War Cry Treasury*, 1999

Terry Camsey, *Slightly Off Center! Growth Principles to Thaw Frozen Paradigms*, 2000

Philip Needham, *He Who Laughed First: Delighting in a Holy God*, (in collaboration with Beacon Hill Press, Kansas City), 2000

Henry Gariepy, ed., *A Salvationist Treasury: 365 Devotional Meditations from the Classics to the Contemporary*, 2000

Marlene Chase, *Our God Comes: And Will Not Be Silent*, 2001

A. Kenneth Wilson, *Fractured Parables: And Other Tales to Lighten the Heart and Quicken the Spirit*, 2001

Carroll Ferguson Hunt, *If Two Shall Agree*, (in collaboration with Beacon Hill Press, Kansas City), 2001

John C. Izzard, *Pen of Flame: The Life and Poetry of Catherine Baird*, 2002

Henry Gariepy, *Andy Miller: A Legend and a Legacy*, 2002

Compilation, *A Word in Season: A Collection of Short Stories*, 2002

R. David Rightmire, *Sanctified Sanity: The Life and Teaching of Samuel Logan Brengle*, 2003

Chick Yuill, *Leadership on the Axis of Change*, 2003

Compilation, *Living Portraits Speaking Still: A Collection of Bible Studies*, 2004

A. Kenneth Wilson, *The First Dysfunctional Family: A Modern Guide to the Book of Genesis*, 2004

Allen Satterlee, *Turning Points: How The Salvation Army Found a Different Path*, 2004

David Laeger, *Shadow and Substance: The Tabernacle of the Human Heart*, 2005

Check Yee, *Good Morning China*, 2005
Marlene Chase, *Beside Still Waters: Great Prayers of the Bible for Today*, 2005
Roger J. Green, *The Life & Ministry of William Booth*, (in collaboration with Abingdon Press, Nashville), 2006
Norman H. Murdoch, *Soldiers of the Cross: Pioneers of Social Change*, 2006
Henry Gariepy, *Israel L. Gaither: Man With a Mission*, 2006

All titles by Crest Books can be purchased through your
nearest Salvation Army Supplies and Purchasing Department

Atlanta, GA—(800) 786-7372
Des Plaines, IL—(847) 294-2012
Long Beach, CA—(800) 937-8896
West Nyack, NY—(888) 488-4882